VETERANS AND AMERICA

THE AMERICAN WAYS SERIES

General Editor: John David Smith
Charles H. Stone Distinguished Professor of American History
University of North Carolina at Charlotte

From the long arcs of America's history, to the short timeframes that convey larger stories, American Ways provides concise, accessible topical histories informed by the latest scholarship and written by scholars who are both leading experts in their fields and polished writers.

Books in the series provide general readers and students with compelling introductions to America's social, cultural, political, and economic history, underscoring questions of class, gender, racial, and sectional diversity and inclusivity. The titles suggest the multiple ways that the past informs the present and shapes the future in often unforeseen ways.

CURRENT TITLES IN THE SERIES

How America Eats: A Social History of U.S. Food and Culture, by Jennifer Jensen Wallach

Popular Justice: A History of Lynching in America, by Manfred Berg

Bounds of Their Habitation: Race and Religion in American History, by Paul Harvey

National Pastime: U.S. History through Baseball, by Martin C. Babicz and Thomas W. Zeiler

Wartime America: The World War II Home Front, Second Edition, by John W. Jeffries

Enemies of the State: The Radical Right in America from FDR to Trump, by D. J. Mulloy

Hard Times: Economic Depressions in America, by Richard Striner

We the People: The 500-Year Battle Over Who Is American, by Ben Railton

Litigation Nation: How Lawsuits Represent Changing Ideas of Self, Business

Practices, and Right and Wrong in American History,
by Peter Charles Hoffer

Years of Rage: From the Klan to the Alt-Right, by D. J. Mulloy

All American Rebels: The American Left from the Wobblies to Today,
by Robert C. Cottrell

Of Thee I Sing: The Contested History of American Patriotism, by Ben Railton

American Agriculture: From Farm Families to Agribusiness,
by Mark V. Wetherington

Germans in America: A Concise History, by Walter D. Kamphoefner

American Exceptionalism, by Volker Depkat

Making America's Public Lands: The Contested History of Conservation on Federal Lands, by Adam Sowards

Hoops: A Cultural History of Basketball in America, by Thomas Aiello

To Reach the Nation's Ear: A History of African American Public Speaking,
by Richard W. Leeman

How America Gets the News: A History of American Journalism,
by Ford Risley and Ashley Walter

Veterans and America: From the Revolution to Today, by Michael D. Gambone

VETERANS AND AMERICA

From the Revolution to Today

MICHAEL D. GAMBONE

BLOOMSBURY ACADEMIC
NEW YORK • LONDON • OXFORD • NEW DELHI • SYDNEY

BLOOMSBURY ACADEMIC

Bloomsbury Publishing Inc, 1359 Broadway, New York, NY 10018, USA
Bloomsbury Publishing Plc, 50 Bedford Square, London, WC1B 3DP, UK
Bloomsbury Publishing Ireland, 29 Earlsfort Terrace, Dublin 2, D02 AY28, Ireland

BLOOMSBURY, BLOOMSBURY ACADEMIC and the Diana logo
are trademarks of Bloomsbury Publishing Plc

First published in the United States of America 2026

Copyright © Bloomsbury Publishing, 2026

Cover images (top to bottom, left to right): Historic Collection / Alamy Stock Photo; iStock.com / History Skills; iStock.com / HelloBrianHogan; Bob Daemmrich / Alamy Stock Photo

All rights reserved. No part of this publication may be: i) reproduced or transmitted in any form, electronic or mechanical, including photocopying, recording or by means of any information storage or retrieval system without prior permission in writing from the publishers; or ii) used or reproduced in any way for the training, development or operation of artificial intelligence (AI) technologies, including generative AI technologies. The rights holders expressly reserve this publication from the text and data mining exception as per Article 4(3) of the Digital Single Market Directive (EU) 2019/790.

Bloomsbury Publishing Inc does not have any control over, or responsibility for, any third-party websites referred to or in this book. All internet addresses given in this book were correct at the time of going to press. The author and publisher regret any inconvenience caused if addresses have changed or sites have ceased to exist, but can accept no responsibility for any such changes.

Library of Congress Cataloging-in-Publication Data is available

ISBN:	HB:	978-1-5381-8663-3
	ePDF:	979-8-8818-6649-5
	eBook:	978-1-5381-8664-0

Typeset by Integra Software Services Pvt. Ltd.
Printed and bound in the United States of America

For product safety related questions contact productsafety@bloomsbury.com.

To find out more about our authors and books visit www.bloomsbury.com and sign up for our newsletters.

*This work is dedicated to
Dr. Michael P. Gabriel*

CONTENTS

Acknowledgments x
Preface xi

Introduction 1

  1 The Revolutionary War 9

  2 The Early Republic 27

  3 The Civil War 45

  4 American Empire 65

  5 The Great War 85

  6 The Interwar Period 103

  7 World War II 121

  8 The Early Cold War 143

  9 Vietnam 163

  10 The All-Volunteer Military 181

  11 After September 11th 207

Conclusions 231

Bibliographic Essay 242
Index 261
About the Author 271

ACKNOWLEDGMENTS

There are many people who deserve recognition for their help with this book. At the start of it all in graduate school, Dr. Jeffrey Clarke was an outstanding mentor and a constant source of advice and support as I worked my way through the basic elements of American military history. When I began researching veterans' history almost two decades ago, my colleague Mike Gabriel was instrumental in recommending essential reading, particularly William Henry Glasson's *History of Military Pension Legislation in the United States* (1900). Lastly, I greatly appreciate the support of my colleague, Dr. Stephen Ortiz at Binghamton University.

As always, I must recognize our staff at the Rohrbach Library, particularly Dawn Boody, who kept this project well supplied with primary and secondary source material.

My wife Rachel continues on as my first editor in a career of academic projects. Over many decades, this University of Chicago scholar has fostered ideas from the "madman" stage of brainstorming to their evolution into a coherent narrative. I would not be here without her.

PREFACE

When I first began studying military history, it was a reflection of a personal interest in my own service during the eighties. As an officer assigned to an airborne infantry battalion at then Fort Bragg, my mission was defined by being readily deployable around the world in eighteen hours. We prepared in particular for Central America and Sandinista Nicaragua and a war that never came.

In graduate school, I wanted to understand why we were interested in this region, a pursuit that led me to spend almost ten years researching America's role in Latin America and the Somoza dynasty in particular. Throughout, this was an academic exercise designed to satisfy my own personal curiosity but also bolster the classes that I would eventually teach as a college professor.

All that changed on September 11th, when the prospect of war became at once more immediate and personal. I deployed to Iraq as an army contractor in 2006 and got to witness firsthand American power in the new century. Homecoming was a reflection of the times. I lived in a country that celebrated veterans but had very little understanding about what made them tick.

Exploring the gap between recognizing veterans and understanding them became a new academic career of sorts. Four books and almost twenty years later, I have gathered some understanding of what defines our present-day civil-military relations. This book is intended to contribute to that understanding by examining the origin story of our country, its wars, and the men and women sent to fight them.

Introduction

People usually think that wars are a great cleansing; that, purified through sacrifice, they can start from scratch along their ideal paths after it is all over. Because of their innate wishfulness, people inevitably forget that every event is interrelated and one cannot go outside of history and "start over."

AN AMERICAN SAILOR WRITING HOME FROM THE PACIFIC, 1945

Shortly after Germany surrendered in May 1945, Norman Rockwell published *Homecoming G.I.* as the cover art for the *Saturday Evening Post* and applied his trademark sentimentality approach to the work. A soldier stands before his brightly rendered brick rowhome with all his worldly possessions packed into one small kit bag. His back is to the viewer. He is Rockwell's everyman, one of the millions in uniform during World War II. The soldier's family pours outside to greet him, their faces illuminated by expressions of joy and relief. Neighbors share in the celebration as part of a community coming together. On stage right, a young woman observes the unfolding scene, ready to move from the wings into her man's future. *Homecoming G.I.* reconstructed a scene endlessly repeated in the year following World War II. It is iconic in part because it captured an American experience not just in 1945, but at any point in America's past wars and homecomings.

Wars are great historical milestones for countries and people. The American Revolution, the Civil War, the world wars, the Cold War, and our recent global conflict against terrorism were definitive moments. Each war determined, in its own way, the evolving standards of national survival. Perhaps more importantly, the sacrifices made during our long history of warfare have also reconstructed many of the basic expectations that Americans have had about the definition of citizenship—rights, liberties, and obligations—for themselves and for later generations.

Time and again, our wars also continually redefined what it meant to be a veteran. In many cases, the veteran is celebrated as the ideal citizen, a person who took the ultimate risk for the sake of the greater public good. The status of veterans has been a political bona fide from George Washington to Tammy Duckworth. On the other hand, the veteran has often also been perceived as a threat. What might the "brutalizing" effect of war be on a person returning from it? Many academics and pundits predicted an easy postwar transition of combatants to crime. Before World War II had even concluded, Willard Waller described its veterans as "America's gravest social problem."

But overgeneralizing is an avoidable trap. Like any other social group, veterans are not a faceless monolith. Throughout American history, they have organized and been their own advocates for a long list of causes; pensions, medical care, employment, education, or simple recognition. Historian Michael Geyer has argued that group identity is a product of relations with the state. Considering the fact that veterans have engaged every level of government regarding benefits and pensions for hundreds of years, they may have one of the most developed ongoing group identities in American history. The long history of veterans' affairs in America is a chronicle of constant organizing and lobbying. Some groups—The Society of Cincinnatus (1783), the Grand Army of the Republic (1866), and the Veterans of Foreign Wars (1899)—are well known. Others, the Aztec Club of 1847, the Sons of Confederate Veterans (1896), or the United Spanish Veterans (1904), less so.

Perhaps more importantly, not all veterans are created equal. Each era has its own "good war"—the American Revolution, the Civil War, or World War II—that set the gold standard used to judge, fairly or not, the veterans who came next. Many World War II veterans, particularly members of Congress who controlled benefits legislation, never believed that Vietnam service equaled their own. Teddy Roosevelt, only a few years after his short campaign in Cuba, referred to veterans of his conflict as "my comrades of a lesser war."

A growing body of scholarship has begun to consider these developments in detail. Paul Fussell's outstanding *Wartime: Understanding and Behavior in the Second World War* (1989) was joined by Thomas Childers's equally excellent *Soldier From the War Returning: The Greatest Generation's Troubled Homecoming from World War II* (2009). Younger scholars such as Stephen R. Ortiz, Melinda L. Pash, and Mark Boulton, among many others, continue to contribute to this growing field of American social history.

As it approaches the veteran in American history, this book will construct a series of layers to the story. The foundation will be the context of the times surrounding each generation of veterans. When America was a colony, constant mobilization for the sake of survival required collective participation in military affairs. As the country matured, so did its interests, responsibilities, and capabilities. Secondly, as military affairs evolved, so too did the discussion about civil obligations to veterans. This dialogue included tangible public policy as well as public commemoration military service. Third, as American society debated the question of war, military service, and recognition, veterans naturally lent their voices to the narrative. For most of our history, they did so as individuals and a series of organizations that varied in terms of effectiveness and longevity. Lastly, this book will address the programs emerging from this lengthy discourse.

Chapter One focuses on the veterans in the colonial era. During the earliest stages of American settlement, a handful of weak outposts lived in a state of constant siege, by the elements, starvation, and Native Americans. Most men from sixteen to sixty joined in regular musters and local conflicts that constantly flared along the frontier. As the British empire matured, they reluctantly participated in expeditions that took them far from home. The costs of war were left to their friends and neighbors. As early as 1618, the Plymouth colony offered lifetime benefits to any disabled militiaman. Almost a century later, Rhode Island established medical care and an annual pension for its veterans.

Chapter Two looks at veterans of the American Revolution. Soldiers enjoyed a special agency in a country born from the conflict with England. Their sacrifice resulted in a break with one of the most powerful monarchies in the world and the start of a great democratic experiment. Veterans contributed to the earliest discussion of citizenship and American nationalism. Veterans' policies also revealed many critical weaknesses in the young republic. Lawmakers as early as the Confederation Congress promised lifetime disability payments to veterans, but almost always failed to properly fund these commitments. As the country entered the nineteenth century, it began its first long-term commitments to veterans and their dependents.

Chapter Three addresses the Civil War, America's first effort at industrial, mass mobilization. At its conclusion, approximately one in ten Americans were veterans, a proportion the country would not revisit until World War II. Veterans stood at the center of the early Gilded Age. They formed the Grand Army of the Republic, which turned out by the tens of thousands during Ulysses S. Grant's campaign for president in 1868 and helped shape both politics and federal social welfare policy for the remainder of the century.

Chapter Four introduces American military affairs and veterans' status as the country moved from frontier settlement to global empire. Veterans joined millions of homesteaders who spread throughout the continent after 1865. When the United States embarked upon war against Spain in 1898, they provided critical leadership ranging from "Fighting Joe" Wheeler in Cuba to George Dewey at the Battle of Manila Bay. As scandals over the treatment of soldiers soured the victory celebrations in the summer of 1898, veterans began organizing again on their own behalf. The United Spanish War Veterans and the Veterans of Foreign Wars formed local and state chapters that eventually coalesced into national institutions in the new twentieth century.

Chapter Five is dedicated to World War I. The so-called War to End All Wars added more than four million veterans to the nation's population, the largest cohort since the Civil War. Volunteers and draftees, representing both residents and newly arrived immigrants, enthusiastically entered the military, encouraged along by new wartime federal agencies like the Committee on Public Information. National accommodation for veterans was equally massive. Approximately 675,000 veterans took advantage of the War Risk Insurance Act (1918), which provided compensation and rehabilitation for war wounded. However, most returning doughboys garnered little more than a sixty-dollar separation bonus and a train ticket home. As veterans made their way back into normalcy, many joined the American Legion (est. 1919) to lobby for expanding benefits and public recognition at the state and federal levels.

In Chapter Six, we will follow veterans' affairs between the world wars. The interwar period is notable in that millions of freshly minted veterans made Armistice Day (est. 1919) and Memorial Day part of our annual routine. Veterans became key actors in policy debates about national defense and foreign policy, especially as the country edged toward intervention in World War II. The period between the world wars is also significant in that while military budgets bottomed out, veterans' benefits took up an impressive portion of the nation's annual outlays. In 1932, the year of the Bonus March when thousands of veterans demanded early payment of their benefits, approximately a quarter of the total federal budget was dedicated to veterans.

Chapter Seven examines veterans of World War II. The war saw the largest number of Americans in military service in the country's history. Although participation was not universal, it touched virtually every part of American society and formed an important part of the postwar consensus. Established groups like the American Legion and the VFW remained as powerful lobbies affecting public policy and an increasingly conservative national political discourse. Conversely, new organizations, like the American Veterans Committee (est. 1943) broke from the older organizations and provided a special agency to the next generation of civil rights activists in the forties and fifties. The Serviceman's Readjustment Act (1944) became a landmark piece of social welfare legislation, vastly expanding the scope of previous New Deal approaches as it established an extensive network of veterans' health care, housing, education, and work benefits. In many respects, their training, education, and leadership was the engine driving America's post-1945 boom.

Chapter Eight addresses service in the Cold War. Although World War II ended in 1945, the draft continued for the next twenty-eight years, sustaining a peacetime military establishment that was far larger than at any time in American history. Military service became a routine rite of passage for American men. Periodically, as was the case with the Korean War, service incurred substantial risks. For most, however, it represented only a periodic interruption in postwar life. The veterans' community grew and proliferated throughout America society. As Robert Timberg notes in *The Nightingale's Song*, their interpretation of service and patriotism collided with the emerging Baby Boom and presaged a fundamental generational split in the United States.

Within the Cold War narrative, Chapter Nine discusses Vietnam veterans. According to George Flynn in his landmark book *The Draft*, more volunteers served in the Vietnam War than World War II or Korea. Yet, service reflected the increasing divisiveness within the country over the conflict. By 1971, according to a Harris poll, most Americans characterized Vietnam veterans as "suckers, having to risk their lives in the wrong war, in the wrong place, at the wrong time." Despite their sacrifices, Vietnam veterans found themselves increasingly isolated from the public by virtue of the unpopular war they fought.

Chapter Ten reflects the significant impact of volunteer service on veterans after the Vietnam War. The last generation to fight the Cold War, one comprised with a rapidly increasing percentage of women and minorities, joined more often than not for the sake of service leavened with a desire for adventure and self-improvement. The Montgomery G.I. Bill (1984) proved to be a boon to these individuals. Although Cold War rhetoric became heated at points, particularly during the Reagan years, military service for the most part became a routine function for an increasingly smaller group of Americans. This trend grew more prominent when the Soviet Union collapsed, and Americans considered the possibilities of the "peace dividend" in the nineties. While the First Gulf War reinforced public acclaim for military service, it did not arrest the accelerating decline of people serving in uniform and the increasing distance between civilians and veterans.

Chapter Eleven addresses September 11 and men and women who served in overseas contingency operations. Twenty-first-century American wars are unique in that a tiny proportion of the country has borne their cost, while the remainder struggle with understanding their sacrifice even as they attempt to constructively acknowledge it. Millions deployed to fight in America's forever wars, a number that included the highest number of National Guard and reservists since 1950. In the meantime, the vast majority of the country could only imagine what Global War on Terror actually meant.

Veterans' policy in the twenty-first century possessed a scattershot quality. Multiple versions of the contemporary G.I. offered generous benefits to veterans and their families. Medical care was too often lacking, badly encumbered and mismanaged by the Department of Veterans Affairs bureaucracy. Growing numbers of women veterans suffered from institutional blind spots that prevented them from obtaining care for problems unique to their service (e.g., Military Sexual Trauma). Consequently, many of this new generation of veterans pursued their own advocacy outside official channels, creating organizations like the Student Veterans of America and the Service Women's Action Network.

1

The Revolutionary War

What has he in return for his services—When after a few Campaigns he must return with the loss of his fortune spent in the service, his Constitution destroy'd, & perhaps the loss of a limb, the World will say Honour; I Acknowledge if a Genteel provision was made to support a man after all this, Honour would be A Consolative recompence, but not else... I sincerely wish something of A Generous & manly provision was made for the Super[umerar]y Officers, & Something added that would Enable our officers to serve.

RICHARD BUTLER, 1778

In *Arms and Men*, military historian Walter Millis wrote that "The United States was born in an act of violence." In fact, that heritage was much older than the American republic. From the first landings on the Atlantic coast to the American Revolution, we developed a long military tradition of conquest, settlement, and social obligation reinforced by mutual sacrifice. As one historian put it, colonists' ongoing relationship with military service "defined their understanding of the nature of American republicanism and how they, as citizens and soldiers, were active participants in the republican experiment." This understanding would embody what Americans would later call the "Spirit of '76."

Military service was a constant necessity in tiny communities clinging to newly cleared patches of a dangerous continent. Able-bodied men formed small "trainbands," or companies who organized and regularly prepared for local defense. They maintained their own personal weapons and equipment. They built primitive log palisades and blockhouses. Women kept stores, tended to the wounded, and joined in combat when necessary. Communities lived and died as a whole.

There were no formal monuments to this enterprise. A successful fight meant more time to clear a few more acres for a better harvest and gather stores when winter came. It meant an opportunity to build a meeting house and a place to hold services. Periodic expeditions translated into more secure paths between communities growing together in a maturing colony. The prospect of a better future was its own reward.

The "common Defence," later articulated in the US Constitution, consequently was a powerful concept in American history. It was, according to Millis, part of a "living tradition" deeply embedded in how we mobilized for war, fought, and recognized military service. This tradition—with all its strengths and limitations—would shape a new country about to emerge. It would also establish the basic guardrails for the first generation of American veterans.

Colonial Legacies

Military service was a constant necessity on the bleeding edge of the American frontier. Conflict started with the first settlement at Jamestown. Within days of landfall, on May 26, 1607, approximately 2,500 Native Americans led by Powhatan attacked the English community. War in Virginia in 1622 between settlers and a confederation of Native Americans led by Opechancanough resulted in a quarter of colonists perishing. Not long afterward, in 1624, the Virginia Assembly created a standing militia. Further north, the Massachusetts Bay Colony raised its own militia regiments in 1636.

As the colonies grew, so did bloodshed. The Pequot War enveloped the Connecticut colony in 1637. In 1675, the Wampanoags, Nipmucks, and Narragansetts joined in attacks against colonial settlements in Massachusetts. King Philip's War, as it was eventually known, evolved into a full-scale conflict between area tribes and militia units drawn from Plymouth, Massachusetts and Connecticut, as well as their own native allies.

Given the time and distances involved, new colonies could not realistically rely upon timely help from the Royal Navy or the British Army. All males were obliged to meet the call to arms, although individual colonies set their own age limits. Connecticut initially mandated service until sixty, but eventually reduced it to forty-five. Individual militiamen had to maintain their own firearms and gear, something local officials were supposed to regularly monitor. Under the pressure of military necessity, some colonies resorted to drafting troops. Vagrants or, as the Virginia colony defined them, men "found loitering and neglecting to labor for reasonable wages," were particularly vulnerable. Individuals could file an appeal with the governor, hire a substitute, or pay a commutation fee, a practice that remained in place until the Civil War.

Local communities determined their own military standards. The quality and frequency of muster days was a patchwork that varied from town to town. Time might be spent on tactics and marksmanship or be used for family gatherings and drinking. Or both. For the most part, leaders, officers, and, in many cases, noncommissioned officers, were elected. Many town fathers served concurrently as military commanders. Officers were essentially self-taught from books they might come across in their personal study of war.

As the frontier shifted further and further west, the militia's role in maturing communities evolved beyond their original purpose. In much of the American South, it stayed on as a check against potential slave rebellion. In other increasingly secure and established eastern towns and cities, local militias "withered" without an imminent purpose, as historian Eleanor Hannah notes. Gaps between regular meetings grew, although the musters continued on as a means to network. In the meantime, officers and men pursued an "interest in military panoply and pageantry."

As they evolved, many local militias also became laboratories for American citizenship. The city of Philadelphia created the Pennsylvania Associators in 1747 as a democratic institution. Service was voluntary and self-governing. Many units wrote their own constitutions with the terms and conditions of service made clear for everyone involved, officers and enlisted men alike.

The American tendency for military organization based on consent had important consequences. Discipline was a constant problem in colonial era units. One Virginia officer, William Preston, complained to a subordinate that his men fired their weapons for no reason while on patrol. This "detestable practice... not only wastes Ammunition which is very scarce, but gives the Enemy notice where you are, so that they will either take the advantage of your Imprudence and surprise you, or Pass by the Company & ravage the Country." When on campaigns, Americans were prone to be sticklers about the terms of their service—its duration, geographical location, the quality of food—to the point where they would simply break camp and depart for home *en masse* if soldiers thought their officers had violated their rights. It was not uncommon for militia units to go on strike if they thought their compensation was unfair. In 1759, during the French and Indian War, a regiment of Massachusetts volunteers threatened mutiny when their British commander attempted to extend their service beyond the agreed-upon eight-month contract. Not surprisingly, these actions resulted in almost constant friction between British regulars and their colonial wards. According to F. W. Anderson, "As they [the British] saw matters, provincial troops were overpaid and undisciplined, a sickly, slack, faint-hearted rabble incapable of enduring even the mildest privations, officered by men unwilling to exercise authority for fear of losing favor with the mob."

During the American Revolution, this same spirit of rights and responsibilities informed both military service and the evolving concept of

US citizenship. In the minds of revolutionaries, serving in the militia, with all its concurrent commitments and risks, justified equally proportional rights and privileges. Expectations followed suit. At the start of the Revolution, the Philadelphia Committee of Privates demanded to be treated with dignity. The Committee chose their own officers, specifically "those who manifest the most sincere and warm attachment to the cause of liberty." If leadership observed the rank-and-file's basic expectations, units kept their good order. If officers broke their contract, rebellion was not only inevitable, but also just. A unit of Pennsylvania infantry mutinied in 1781 because, besides inadequate food and shelter, as Anthony Wayne wrote at the time, "they have not seen a single paper Dollar in the way of pay for near twelve months."

For more than 150 years, American military service was shaped by collective effort with the expectation that it would produce tangible benefits for colonial subjects of the crown or citizens of the new republic. In the beginning, the objective was simple. Well-defended communities would survive and perhaps prosper. Later, as militia units participated in the colonial wars that dotted the period, the militia was an exercise in sovereignty, an opportunity for Americans to define basic terms and conditions of colonial military service. This process grew more elaborate and abstract as the eighteenth century moved forward. Military participation became part of a citizen's compact that included "justice" and "equity," along with tangible needs like pay and adequate provisions. It established an important baseline for later policy discussions on veterans' benefits and pensions for the rest of American history.

Veterans of the American Revolution

We do not know exactly how many Americans served during the Revolution. Estimates vary according to the source. Contemporary Veterans Administration records have 217,000 men belonging to militia and regular units. The American Battlefield Trust lists 231,000 men in the Continental Army, though never more than 48,000 served at any one time, and never more than 13,000 in any one place. Colonial militias numbered upwards of 145,000 men. Historian C. Edward Skeen's numbers are much larger. His research found 395,858 Americans in uniform, a total that included 164,087 militia. This was in an estimated contemporary US population of 3.9 million or, one in ten Americans.

The Americans who fought were generally grouped into the militia and, as the war progressed, regular forces. Militia units were the primary source of manpower at the start of the Revolution. The call to arms was familiar, although the enemy in 1775 was not simply Native Americans or the French. As they had before, town fathers provided leadership in the mobilized militia companies. The enlisted ranks were drawn from yeomen farmers, laborers, artisans, the sons of clergymen, and town selectmen. One-third of Petersborough, New Hampshire served in the militia. The town "Alarm List" included the names of men from sixteen to sixty-five years old.

The quality of militia service varied throughout the war. At points, circumstances affected quality. Operating from cover or entrenchments, militia gave a good account of themselves. After they completed a costly retreat from Lexington and Concord back into Boston, a shaken British commander wrote to his superiors: "Whoever looks upon them as an irregular mob, will find himself very much mistaken. They have men amongst them who know very well what they are about." At Breed's Hill a few months later, entrenched militia took a heavy toll on attacking British infantry, which suffered 228 killed and 826 wounded, 42 percent of the total force engaged that day. At Cowpens in 1781, properly deployed militia proved effective in direct clashes with the British. However, their service at Germantown (1777), Camden (1780), and many other battles was much less distinguished.

Patriotism motivated many militia and regulars, although this waxed and waned throughout the war. Men flush with the novelty of fighting the British flocked to the colors in 1775 and 1776. The contingencies of the moment influenced their enthusiasm. When General Johnny Burgoyne marched through New England and New York, volunteers hurried to confront the invader. British abuses of local civilians provoked many men in the Pennsylvania to join up in search of retribution. Later, as the war shifted south, some Northerners remained in the Continental Line, but Northern service ebbed.

More than a few Americans needed more than patriotism to join. For the ongoing risk to life and limb on the battlefield and the prolonged hardships in garrison, soldiers sought what Lieutenant Colonel Richard Butler, a commander of the Pennsylvania continental line, called a "generous and manly provision." Recruiters offered enlistment bonuses, suffrage, or, in some cases, the prospect of freedom from enslavement. Both individual states and the national government used land bounties as an enticement. Starting in 1776, Congress offered colonels five hundred acres. Enlisted soldiers were promised one hundred acres, a substantial incentive for a commoner. Virginia offered land bounties for three continuous years of service in state or continental forces.

Militia units proved inadequate to sustain the American Revolution. As the war ground on, the US military evolved and took on a more regular form. Like their militia comrades, patriotism clearly motivated many citizens who joined Continental Line regiments that began to form after 1775, but it was not enough to meet the Army's needs. In many cases, recruiters invited Americans who came from what one historian called "dubious" circumstances. The local tavern was a gathering point for this process, where recruiters plied candidates with alcohol. Other recruiters simply lied, promising the glamor of the cavalry to men eventually assigned to infantry.

The Continental Line served well in the Revolution and eventually formed the backbone of the American war effort. However, tension between militia and regulars evident in earlier colonial wars emerged yet again for many of the same reasons. George Washington, in a moment of candor, described New England volunteers in the following terms when he took command of them in 1775: "I daresay the Men would fight very well (if properly Officered) although they are an exceedingly dirty & nasty people." However, as Fred W. Anderson has observed, in order to build a viable army, Washington "had no choice but to overturn the very military traditions that had summoned the army into existence." Despite what the Declaration of Independence might have stated at the start of the American Revolution, not all soldiers were created equal. This reality would affect the war effort and, importantly, how the new republic saw its first cohort of veterans.

African American Service and the Revolution

Prior to the American Revolution, local citizens and peers performed colonial military service. Generally, that meant eligible white male inhabitants, although a few colonies granted exceptions. Virginia prohibited African Americans from combat units in 1639 but permitted their participation as support troops. Connecticut allowed any type of service and African American soldiers fought in both Queen Anne's War (1702–1713) and the French and Indian War (1754–1763). In 1705, approximately one-third of Carolina muster rolls included Black militiamen, and many participated in the 1717 Yamasee War.

During the American Revolution, an estimated five thousand African Americans served in the military. They were drawn to serve for the same reasons as white citizens. Many African Americans were members of communities they wanted to defend. Others joined because military service offered perks for both slaves and free men. Military pay, when it came, was attractive. So was the prospect of manumission.

Resistance to arming African Americans in the South varied from state to state. Virginia allowed masters to use their slaves as substitutes for military service. In contrast, a South Carolina politician expressed the feelings of many whites in 1779: "We are much disgusted here at the Congress recommending us to arm our slaves, it was received with great resentment, as a various dangerous and impolitic step." More often than not, slave owners were reluctant to surrender slaves to service even with compensation from either state governments or the Confederation Congress. The hostility was quickly exploited by the British, who offered freedom in exchange for service in the British Army.

A number of important national leaders were equally antagonistic about the prospect of African American soldiers. Washington's July 10, 1775, guidance to recruiters in the Massachusetts Bay area was clear on the topic. The Revolutionary commander did not want "any deserter from the Ministerial Army, nor any stroller, negro, or vagabond, or person suspected of being an enemy to the liberty of America, nor any under eighteen years of age." Writing in Philadelphia three months later, John Addams concurred, writing that old men, boys, and Blacks in uniform at the time were "unsuitable for the military service."

Official obstruction of African Americans did not halt them from rallying to the colors. Free Black men enlisted in the militia and the continental line regardless. They served alongside white and Black members of their communities, many of whom accompanied them when they enlisted at local courthouses.

The fortunes of war eroded official resistance to African American service. As Thomas Paine wrote at the end of 1776: "These are the times that try men's souls: The summer soldier and the sunshine patriot will, in this crisis, shrink from the service of their country; but he that stands it now, deserves the love and the thanks of man and woman." Rising desertions and the horrible conditions of winter encampments in the bitter first winter of the war made many previously reluctant leaders change their tune. New England states like Connecticut, New Hampshire, and Rhode Island began to actively recruit

African Americans. Rhode Island and Connecticut offered freedom for service, although not all volunteers received that promise in writing. When it decided to form a Black regiment in February 1778, the Rhode Island General Assembly issued a proclamation that:

> every able-bodied negro, mulatto, or Indian man slave in this state may inlist [*sic*] into either of the said two battalions to serve during the continuance of the war with Great Britain; that every slave so inlisting [*sic*] shall be entitled to, and receive all the bounties, wages, and encouragements allowed by the Continental Congress.

In 1779, Alexander Hamilton proposed three or four battalions of Black troops in the South, offering freedom for service, although Congress did not act on his suggestion.

The changing fortunes of war also changed Southern attitudes. By 1780, as the British attempted to regain the initiative below the Mason-Dixon Line, Maryland and Virginia allowed African American enlistment. North Carolina freed slaves who served, but later passed a law that allowed them to be enslaved again if their service had not been "meritorious." In Virginia, the state assembly rebuffed efforts to do the same in 1783, noting that such actions by slave owners were "contrary to the principles of justice, and to their own solemn promise."

Virtually every state had racially integrated units during the Revolution. One Connecticut brigade of 1,065 included 117 African Americans. Close to the same proportion often appeared among Southern units. One North Carolina brigade claimed forty-two Black soldiers out of a total of 670 men present for duty. Within the Continental Line, a 1778 survey found 755 African American soldiers among fourteen brigades of regulars. Rather quickly, their service was part of the new norm. As one Massachusetts general, William Heath, reflected:

There are in the Massachusetts Regiments some Negroes. Such is also the case with the Regiments of the Other Colonies, Rhode Island has a number of negroes and Indians, Connecticut has fewer negroes and a number of Indians. The New Hampshire regiments have less of both.

A Hessian officer mentioned the presence of Black troops in the Continental Line in 1777: "You never see a regiment in which there are not negroes, and there are well-built, strong, husky fellows among them."

Although small in proportion to the Revolutionary War effort, African American service was a consistent feature of the struggle for freedom and highlighted the earned right of citizenship. Black men fought and suffered the consequences of war on the same terms as their white comrades. One of the many tragedies that followed with the creation of the United States was the country's failure to recognize the real gravity of this sacrifice.

Recognizing Revolutionary Veterans

When the British surrendered at Yorktown in October 1781 and American victory was assured, there was no national system to transition military men back into civilian life.

This was partly rooted in the contemporary assumption that Revolutionary veterans deserved no extra consideration for simply performing their duties as citizens. Their reward was a new country.

Tradition also affected postwar American veterans. In practical terms, compensation for service had always been the responsibility of the colonies and, later, individual states. Policy stretched back over a century and was consistent mostly when it came to wounds or disability suffered as a result of military service. After it formed its own militia units, Plymouth Colony granted disabled veterans lifetime support in 1636. Rhode Island provided medical care and pensions for wounded militiamen in 1718.

However, few states were up to the task of supporting their veterans in the new peace, many of whom needed immediate help. Thomas R. Saxton characterizes the common Revolutionary War soldier in the following terms:

> Historians investigating the socioeconomic origins of Continental recruits have found they were among the more marginal members of revolutionary society. The consensus has been that the Continental army was an integrated force, largely drawing its soldiery from the dispossessed, including sizable numbers of the landless, recent immigrants, blacks, strolling poor, indentured servants, and substitutes.

Muddying the issue further was the lack of agreement on what a "hero" might be. There was little agreement about who had properly earned a "heralded spot in the gallery of Revolutionary heroes," as historian Saxton put it. Despite the fact that militia service in the war had been inconsistent at best, many postwar discussions portrayed them as "hardy yeomen" who carried the weight of the Revolution. The regular army comprised of Continentals was often disparaged as containing the worst elements of society, a refuge for the illiterate, corrupt, and unwanted immigrants. It was a theme that would regularly resurface throughout American history.

As the country argued the relative merits of service, postwar American veterans grew increasingly restive. While they waited in encampments near Newburgh, New York, at the start of 1783, a group of Continental officers met to discuss their grievances, particularly regarding back pay owed them. Speaking on the topic with members of Congress, Brigadier General Alexander McDougall stated that lawmakers might expect "a convulsion of the most dreadful nature and fatal consequences." So began in the early months of 1783, the so-called Newburgh Conspiracy, a flurry of activity between a handful of officers and some members of Congress interested in constructing a more centralized national government. Their efforts, while worrisome, ultimately came to nothing. Lawmakers had no interest in any extralegal action. From his post in New York, George Washington met with his senior officers and famously quashed even the possibility of military action against civilian leadership.

Rather than engage in covert scheming, other officers led by Henry Knox, Washington's former commander of artillery, organized the Society of Cincinnati on May 13, 1783. The Society was formed to recognize Revolutionary service:

> To perpetuate therefore, as well the remembrance of this vast event, as the mutual friendships which have been formed under the pressure of common danger, and in many instances cemented by the blood of the parties, the Officers of the American Army do hereby, in the most solemn manner, associate, constitute, and combine themselves into one Society of Friends—to endure as long as they shall endure, or any of their eldest male posterity, and in failure thereof, the collateral branches, who may be judged worthy of becoming its supporters and members.

The Society's goals were commendable but limited. Its interests began and ended with the Revolutionary officer corps, not the vast majority of enlisted soldiers and sailors who served in the war. In its first year, more than two thousand officers joined the Society, a number that eventually included more than half the signers of the Constitution. For the most part, the Society of Cincinnati indulged itself in ceremony and ritual, honoring a variety of Revolutionary heroes, American, French, and Prussian. Overall, the focus on heraldry and honorifics was off-putting in a new egalitarian country. The Society's policy to allow firstborn male children to inherit membership recalled the traditions of Old World Europe and drew immediate criticism.

In the meantime, Massachusetts veterans became advocates in a much different way. The Revolutionary War had been hard on New England. Beyond the physical damage to the land and its infrastructure, the disruption of trade left farmers, shopkeepers, and state treasuries in desperate straits. Veterans were no exception. Many had sold federal promissory notes made in payment for military service at a fraction of their value out of simple desperation. Speculators like James Bowdoin, founder of the First Massachusetts Bank and the state governor, had earned a substantial profit at their expense.

When the Massachusetts legislature passed a new round of state taxes to pay off its war debts, an amount that ironically included £140,000 in debts to veterans, the state perched on the brink of open rebellion. Daniel Shays, a former officer who had served throughout the Revolution, joined hundreds of other veterans in the late summer of 1786 to protest their economic conditions and petition the state for relief. Not all were sympathetic. The *Massachusetts Sentinel* framed Shays' Rebellion with the following language: "How long will you permit your rights and authorities to be invaded, and your laws and constitution to be trampled on, by the most desperate bankrupts, plotting knaves and ignorant madmen?" The *Albany Gazette* described Shays as "A mere tool of a faction—a puppet which some political mountebank has played off upon the populace."

The state resolved the crisis by suppressing Shays' short-lived movement. The governor called out thousands of militia to halt former soldiers who proposed marching on Springfield, Massachusetts. After a brief confrontation in January 1787, which resulted in the deaths of four veterans, the campaign collapsed. Shay was pardoned for his involvement in the rebellion. However, the underlying economic problems that had motivated the clashes in Massachusetts continued to fester.

Compensating Revolutionary War Veterans

From the very start of the American Revolution, lawmakers understood military participation required concrete incentives. Only a month after the

Declaration of Independence was ratified, the Continental Congress approved half pay for the duration of any disability caused by military service. Individual states like New York and Pennsylvania also granted disability pensions for their own wounded veterans. In 1778, Congress went a step further and promised American (not foreign-born) officers who served for the whole war half pay for seven years. This provision was extended to their widows and orphans two years later. In 1780, Congress expanded the type of payment to include "specie, or other current money equivalent, and also grants of land at the close of the war." Lawmakers were not as generous with enlisted men "for their many dangers losses and hardships." For these, they were to receive a one-time lump sum of $80. At points, individuals also received special recognition. Three militiamen who captured British Major John André, potentially averting the capture of the American fortress at West Point, New York, were each awarded a $200 annual lifetime pension by Congress in 1780.

Unfortunately, good intentions quickly collided with fiscal reality. American finances were a disaster at the end of the Revolution. Virginia and Maryland tobacco planters owed British merchants approximately $10 million when the Revolution began. With the new peace, creditors descended upon them. Starting in 1785, seven states began printing paper money in an attempt to meet their debts. The national government, such as it was, took the same approach. The Continental Congress started printing money and issued $6 million in bills of credit in 1775. Between 1775 and 1777, this totaled an additional $32 million and, by 1779, the tally reached $200 million. National debt was a massive and chronic problem, particularly after the federal government took responsibility for state obligations, which included pensions, in 1790. At that moment, the United States was $75.4 million in arrears. There was little room on the balance sheet for veterans. Early estimates for officers' half pay for life pensions alone ran as high as $500,000 annually, far from what the new American government could afford. Burdened by the costs of war debt, lawmakers made some hard choices. On June 11, 1788, Congress resolved to limit invalid pension applications to a six-month window starting on that date. Four years later, when this limit expired, there were only 1,472 disabled veterans on federal rolls, a tiny fraction of the men who served during the Revolution.

The US veterans' system also suffered from poor administration. State and federal governments struggled with simple definitions of disabilities and who was in charge of administering policy. There was no common agreement regarding disabilities that were the result of battlefield wounds or sickness. States, unwilling or unable to afford payments to veterans or processing claims, wanted federal intervention. Congress, lacking any federal agency to oversee veterans' affairs, punted the problem to the judiciary. A 1792 pension law placing responsibility for disability pensions in the hands of US Circuit Courts was quickly overturned in one of the first legal battles over the separation of powers in US history.

By default, responsibility for veterans' policy fell to the War Department and its reluctant first secretary, Henry Knox. Presiding over a tiny military institution with expanding responsibilities on the western frontier and abroad, Knox had little time for veterans. He supported the 1788 six-month limit on disability applications and generally opposed special exceptions to men who failed to meet it. Consequently, as his term neared its end, there were 1,358 officers and enlisted on the general pension list and slightly more receiving invalid pensions.

Knox also did very little to establish the terms and conditions of veterans' disabilities or construct a clear administrative chain of command. A 1793 pension law required what one author described as a "decisive disability," but legislation lacked a clear definition of what that meant. Individual states were responsible to disburse pensions, but lacked the ability to do so, causing additional delays to veterans in need. The appeals process was equally cumbersome.

As the system struggled, so too did veterans. The financial problems that followed them through the Revolution worsened afterward. Officers and men alike suffered from hard times. Colonel Timothy Bigelow, a Massachusetts Minuteman who later served at Saratoga and was present to see General John

Burgoyne surrender, and weathered winter quarters at Valley Forge, died in a debtors' prison. Thousands more, officers and enlisted, white and black, shared the same hard existence. Years would pass before their country constructed a system adequate to meet their needs.

From first contact on the Atlantic coast to the Revolution, military service was firmly embedded in American life. Duty was based on contingency. At first, it was temporary, reflecting periodic conflicts with Native Americans or colonial rivals. During the Revolution, full-scale warfare defined the long-term obligation "to provide for the common defence and general welfare of the United States."

Military service allowed individuals and communities the opportunity to define the terms of citizenship long before it was codified in US law. Militiamen engaged in constant debates over the practical definition of service within their towns, but especially when called to arms against a foreign enemy. American militia were fractious because it was often a matter life and death when they were far from home. Principle mattered as well. In a larger sense, American military service was one of the earliest practical examples of John Locke's contract theory of government.

American veterans occupied a place of honor after the Revolution. The men who served and suffered evoked the true spirit of the young country. A 1799 monument in Lexington, Massachusetts commemorates the militia who fought as "the first Victims to the Sword of British Tyranny & Oppression."

But when the time came to follow these words with actual support, the United States failed its veterans. The young republic—states and federal governments alike—simply lacked the means to keep the many promises made during the American Revolution and afterward. Even when meager aid found its way to Revolutionary veterans, it was often stymied by a bureaucracy unprepared to aid the former militiamen and regulars who came home. It was a situation made worse by a tendency to favor former officers over their comrades in the enlisted ranks. Left to fend for themselves, too many struggled to find their footing in their new country.

2

The Early Republic

Now these men have tasted the idleness, the intemperance, the debauchery of a camp—tasted of its riot, tasted of its blood! They will come home before long, hirelings of murder; what will their influence be as fathers, husbands?

MINISTER THEODORE PARKER, 1848

Much like the citizens who served in the Civil War and World War II, veterans of the American Revolution left a stamp on their country for more than a generation. Their service became an exemplar of American citizenship. In 1807, Republican Congressman Ezekiel Bacon described veterans as "[T]hose aged citizens, whose venerable countenances, and locks silvered with lapse of years, bespeak them to have been Patriots of the days sacred to Liberty, and Heroes of the Battles of our Independence." They were part of a growing mythology about reluctant rebels who fought against British oppression as a last resort. Veterans' successful prosecution of war against the empire became one of the first expressions of American exceptionalism.

And there were many examples of American exceptionalism in practice. The time between the American Revolution and the Civil War was filled with ongoing conflicts. The United States weathered an undeclared war in the 1790s, continuous fighting along the western frontier, a second war with England, and a war with Mexico. Not a few Revolutionary War veterans answered the call to serve in these conflicts. As they did, these old patriots were joined by new generations of American veterans.

The country struggled with how it might recognize this growing cohort of veterans and compensate the consequences of their service. Flowery rhetoric offered little consolation to the sick, the wounded, or their families. Prior to the Civil War, there was no national veterans' organization to represent their needs. However, the ongoing privations of aging Revolutionary War veterans made the problem impossible to avoid. In the new nineteenth century, momentum built towards a landmark and problematic 1818 law dedicated to the men who served the country.

The Continuing Reliance on the Militia

Two legacies of the British colonial era continued into the early years of the American Republic: a fear of standing armies and an ongoing reliance on the citizen soldier. State and federal governments shared authority over the militia as part of the constitution. However, questions emerged over how to "provide for the common defence."

Federalists and Republicans disagreed on the matter. Alexander Hamilton wrote in *Federalist* No. 25, "Here I expect we shall be told that the militia of the country is its natural bulwark, and would be at all times equal to the national defense. This doctrine, in substance, had like to have lost us our independence. It cost millions to the United States that might have been saved." Thomas Jefferson took a different tack, arguing for "a well-disciplined militia, our best reliance in peace and for the first moments of war, till regulars may relieve them."

There was no consensus in post-Revolutionary America on the matter. The regular military was often portrayed as either a haven for mercenaries or a dumping ground for unwanted immigrants. The latter was partially true. New arrivals to America were prominent in the US military in the late eighteenth century and would continue to be so. A survey of the 1st American Regiment (1786–1789) indicated that immigrants, primarily Irish and German arrivals, accounted for more than half of its personnel. That said, the militia was also not free from criticism. Despite all the accolades for the citizen soldier after the Revolution, many were not pleased with the prospect of national defense resting on volunteers. Charles Nisbet, who served as president of Dickinson College, wrote to a friend in 1792, "Our Leaders flatter the People by declaiming against standing Armies, and pretending to believe that the Militia is the best Security of a Nation."

Regardless, local militia became the backbone of American national security policy for more than a century, a role codified by the Uniform Militia Act of 1792. The law followed established tradition by requiring states to maintain rosters of able-bodied white men between eighteen and forty-five, each responsible for providing their own arms and equipment. The president could call the militia into national service, but with strict limits; a judge had to certify that there were no nonmilitary options available. Service was limited to three months. It contained no sanctions for noncompliance with the law. On paper, the law could count on an enormous force: 1,033 regiments containing 647,827 troops and commanded by 306 generals. Essentially, American defense was based upon wishful thinking. Yet, the Uniform Militia Act remained as the basic policy for military mobilization until the passage of the Dick Act in 1903.

This tiny regular military was tasked with the day-to-day defense of the nation. Regulars represented a cross-section of a young but maturing country. At the start of the nineteenth century, they increasingly were a mix of rural and urban recruits. Approximately 80 percent were native born. Although records are incomplete at best, the number of recruits of color was much smaller than the Revolution, perhaps as low as 2 percent. Artisans (39.7 percent), farmers (28.7 percent), and laborers (21.6 percent) were the most common enlistees. Their overall numbers, particularly in contrast to the massive armies of the

Napoleonic era, were embarrassingly small. In 1802, Congress saw fit to cut the Army from 4,051 to just 2,873 officers and men.

American regulars and militia were hard pressed to defend the frontier after the Revolution. A series of military disasters in Ohio prompted the government to re-create the Army as the Legion of the United States in 1791 under the command of Anthony Wayne. Wayne spent two years preparing his 5,280 officers and men before embarking on successful campaigns against Native Americans who were contesting American settlement in the Old Northwest. While Wayne was victorious, the entire process highlighted a military system inadequate to preserve security against western tribes much less the major European powers that dominated the world at the time.

The New Orleans "Battalion of Color"

As discussed in the previous chapter, race had a significant impact on American military service. Regardless of their type, American militia and regular forces were predominantly white during the colonial era and the Revolution. African Americans, both free and slave, served, although the terms of that service were often poorly defined and inconsistent. Shortly after the Revolution broke out, the Virginia General Assembly followed Connecticut and Rhode Island when it allowed slaves who had served as substitutes to earn their freedom. Sadly, Virginia proved to be an exception in the American South. After the Revolution, many Southern states increased restrictions on free Black residents, veterans and civilians alike.

African American militia service in the Louisiana Territory followed an interesting path after the Revolution. France originally formed a three-hundred-man unit for defense of the region and the Spanish maintained it largely because the *milicias de color* was the only well-trained, led, and armed unit near the strategic port of New Orleans. Free men of color fought in actions against the Chickasaw tribe as early as 1735 and served in campaigns against the British during the American Revolution. At the start of the nineteenth century, the battalion served as a check against encroaching European interests, Native Americans like the Choctaw, and, ironically, slave rebellion.

Military service came not only with regular pay, but also a number of benefits not normally enjoyed by the population of Spanish America. First among these was the *fuero militar,* the code that dictated that military officials would preside over crimes committed by soldiers. Officers of color had the same rights as their Spanish counterparts, while enlisted soldiers not on active duty enjoyed military jurisdiction in criminal cases and full military protection when they were deployed on campaigns. In practice, the *fuero militar* placed soldiers above their civilian peers in the law and insulated the Spanish-American military from civilian accountability.

When the United States purchased the Louisiana Territory in 1803, the *milicias de color* wanted to keep this system under the new American dominion. The unit's leadership submitted multiple appeals to American officials, but were stymied by white elites, caught in lingering fears of the Haitian slave revolt, who opposed arming African Americans. The New Orleans city council officially disbanded the unit in 1805.

Necessity caused American leaders to backtrack. The unit deployed in January 1811 against the German Coast Slave Rebellion. A year later, it was reconstituted under white officers. When the War of 1812 reached Louisiana, Andrew Jackson enjoyed the participation of at least four hundred freedmen during the defense of New Orleans.

The African Americans who had served the French and Spanish never regained the status they enjoyed under those old empires. Andrew Jackson applauded their contributions as part of the polyglot defense of New Orleans. In recognition of their service, the Louisiana legislature enacted a resolution in 1815 that allowed African Americans wounded in the battle to receive monthly pensions of five to eight dollars a month. It was a small concession in a country where slavery defined the daily course of life for millions.

The War of 1812 and the Myth of the Citizen Soldier

The US Army was barely recovered from its post-Revolutionary trough before the second American war with England. When hostilities broke out in 1812, the country could count on approximately 12,000 regulars to guard its eighteen states and sprawling western territories. The US Navy was less fortunate. It was comprised of just sixteen ships, what the London *Times* characterized as a "few fir-built frigates with strips of bunting, manned by sons of bitches and outlaws."

American ambitions were far greater than her capabilities for war. As H. R. Brands notes, the emerging group of American "War Hawks" saw the approaching conflict with England as their historical moment, where the baton passed from the Revolutionary War generation to them. They were confident in the outcome. Henry Clay claimed of his fellow citizen-soldiers that "The militia of Kentucky are alone competent to place Montreal and Upper Canada at your feet."

He was wrong. Although a combined force of regulars, militia, and Native Americans successfully defeated British forces and their allies at the Battle of the Thames in October 1813 and Perry triumphed over British ships on Lake Erie a month earlier, much of the war was an unmitigated disaster. The US invasion of Canada was undercut by incompetent commanders, impossible logistics, and not unexpected trouble with the militia, a point highlighted when Ohio and New York state volunteers refused to enter Canada in 1812. A series of British raids on the eastern US seaboard, and an embarrassingly inept defense of Washington, resulted in British troops burning the nation's capital in August 1814.

As American fortunes suffered, so did interest in military service. At the end of 1814, the Madison administration introduced a bill to begin wartime conscription. The measure passed in the Senate but was thwarted in the House of Representatives. Daniel Webster condemned the concept of "forcing the free men of this country into the ranks of an army for the general purpose of war" as an affront to democracy.

Few Americans living at the time would forget this record. But what shaped the country's evolving perception of the War of 1812 was Andrew Jackson's successful defense of New Orleans on January 8, 1815, just a few weeks after the war had officially ended. On that day, two US infantry regiments were joined by a collection of sailors, privateers, marines, free Blacks, and militia and withstood a series of mass British assaults against the city's hasty fortifications. British forces under Major General Edward Packenham suffered approximately 2,000 casualties as a result. The American toll was thirteen dead, thirteen wounded, and nineteen missing.

For contemporary Americans, it was a triumph of arms. The Catholic church in New Orleans recognized Jackson's victory with a celebratory *Te Deum* in the city cathedral. The battle, reflecting the success of natural-born American citizen-soldiers against European professionals, quickly became woven into popular culture. Such was the message of the 1815 song "Kentucky Rifles":

> But Jackson he was wide awake,
> And was not scar'd at trifles,
> For well he knew what aim we take,
> With our Kentucky rifles:
> So he led us down by Cypress swamp,
> The ground was low and mucky;
> There stood John Bull in martial pomp,
> And here was old Kentucky.

New Orleans became part of annual national commemorations after the war. On July 4, 1818, John Mason burnished Jackson's victory as did many speakers each year:

Gentlemen of the Army, the events of the late war in which you were engaged has shown that you have not studied the deeds of your fathers in vain. You have proved that their blood has not denigrated in your veins ... You have repeatedly vanquished the veterans of Europe, the conquerors of the Peninsula. You have raised the National Character, for valor, to the high ground on which it stood at the close of the Revolution. You could not hope to do more.

In the flush of victory, veterans of the War of 1812 joined their Revolutionary brothers as paragons of civic virtue.

For whatever purpose, the mythology of the War of 1812 took on a life of its own as Americans began curating history, often at the expense of the facts on hand. This was clear with respect to what had happened at New Orleans. Some of the militia there, particularly John Coffee's Tennessee brigade, which contained veterans of conflict against the Creek tribe, performed very well under fire. Other units were far less reliable. Kentucky militia arrived late and barely a third were armed "& those very indifferently," according to Andrew Jackson. Part of this 2,500-man contingent were deployed on the far right of Jackson's line. After the battle, he assessed their poor performance: "The want of Discipline, the want of Order, a total disregard of Obedience, and a Spirit of insubordination, not less destructive than Cowardise [sic] itself, this appears to be the cause which led to the disaster."

Yet the myth persisted for a number of important reasons. The war was a common symbol of the young, resilient United States against the power of the Old World. For ambitious politicians contemplating increasing numbers of men with the new franchise of voting, war and military service was a common thread between them and the electorate. For military reformers, the War of 1812 was a cautionary tale, a potential springboard to rehabilitate perceptions of a standing army. In July 1815, Gouverneur Morris spoke on the need for regulars as a matter of military practicality: "We had often been told that standing armies are dangerous to republics ... no people however brave can prudently rely for defense on militia alone." In all, the war was a call to action on many fronts.

Commemorating Veterans in the Early Republic

The second war against the British embellished a sense of American nationalism that was passing into younger hands as time took its toll on the old generation of Revolutionary War heroes. Anthony Wayne died in 1796, followed by George Washington (1799), Daniel Morgan (1802), Henry Knox (1806), Benjamin Lincoln (1810), and Henry Lee (1816). The same was true of enlisted men and noncommissioned officers who departed with each new year.

Each death fostered a sense of obligation to recognize these old heroes. Some tributes came in the form of published works that addressed the history and experience of the Revolutionary War generation. Chief Justice of the Supreme Court John Marshall contributed a five-volume biography of George Washington after his death in 1799. Many veterans wrote their own personal accounts of the war. When Israel Potter published his memoir in 1824, it was largely to obtain a pension. It went on to inspire Herman Melville's 1855 fictional adaptation *Israel Potter: His Fifty Years of Exile*.

Annual patriotic ceremonies for the Revolutionary War and its veterans also increased in frequency as the century moved forward. Independence Day celebrations on July 4 displaced the annual observance of the Boston Tea Party and other Revolutionary milestones. In Boston, the city government wanted Independence Day to reflect the gravitas of American nationhood and help citizens "more sensibly feel and understand the occasion of this yearly festival."

The Revolutionary generation also received their just due in stone. In 1825, the Marquis de Lafayette set the first cornerstone for the Bunker Hill memorial in a ceremony attended by two hundred veterans of the battle. Daniel Webster would describe it as "an eloquent symbol of American exceptionalism." When it was completed, the Bunker Hill obelisk remained the tallest national monument in the country until the Washington Monument almost forty years later. Not to be outdone, the town fathers of Cambridge, Massachusetts began organizing a memorial for their own twelve veterans "who fell martyrs to the cause of liberty and independence… in the Battle of Bunker Hill."

As this recognition gathered momentum and became part of regular public affairs, it placed new pressure on lawmakers to adequately compensate veterans. When the government raised troops for the War of 1812, it borrowed from 1802 pension legislation for the regular army. Disabled enlisted men qualified for $5 each month. Eligible widows and orphans could receive half pay for up to five years. Congress did not grant a regular pension for all veterans of the war until 1871. The number of War of 1812 pensions rose to 18,266 by 1873, while the number of widows receiving benefits peaked at 26,029 in 1881.

More importantly, the War of 1812 refocused attention on Revolutionary veterans. Advocates of pension reform contrasted the ongoing separation between honorable service, the poverty suffered by many old soldiers, and the small number receiving assistance. In 1816, there were 185 Revolutionary officers and only 1,572 enlisted on the general pension list. One contemporary publication noted:

> He has dearly earned the privilege to beg. Come then—it is yours, it is mine, it is the business of us all, to make the countenance of this man's smile with our blessings; And chase away, if it be but for a moment, the lines of sorrow from the face of misfortune!

A body of law was already on the books to speed this remedy along. An 1806 statute made all types of forces—regulars, militia fighting for the federal government, and state troops—eligible for pensions. An 1808 law reaffirmed federal responsibility for Revolutionary War veterans still on state rolls.

With peace at hand in 1815, lawmakers moved forward with new policy. Many saw an opportunity to not only recognize veterans but also repair some of the regional divisions that had appeared as the United States struggled through the second conflict with England. An 1816 pension law increased disability payments to enlisted soldiers from $5 to $8 a month. Junior officers of the rank of captain or below received $20 a month. Individual states took their own initiatives. Pennsylvania approved legislation that increased annual payments to disabled veterans from $40 to $80 a year.

James Monroe aspired to make his own personal mark on veterans' policy after his 1816 election. The new president traveled the country on a national tour and spent part of it meeting with state chapters of the Society of Cincinnati. In an Independence Day speech before the Society, Monroe paid tribute to veterans' defense of freedom:

> You fought to obtain it in times when men's hearts & principles were severely tried, and your public sacrifices and honoarable [sic] actions are the best pledges of your sincere and devoted attachment to our excellent constitution. May your children never forget the sacred duties devolved on them to preserve the inheritance so gallantly acquired by their fathers—May they cultivate the same manly patriotism, the same disinterested friendship and the same political integrity, which has distinguished you, and thus unite in perpetuating that social concord and public virtue on which the future prosperity of our country must so essentially depend.

Monroe was confident that the fiscal state of the union allowed for the possibility of real generosity for veterans' service. He revisited the topic of veterans' benefits in December 1817:

> It is believed that among the survivors there are some not provided for by existing laws, who are reduced to indigence and even to real distress. These

men have a claim on the gratitude of their country, and it will do honor to their country to provide for them.

On December 2, 1817, Monroe informed Congress that the country had retired $18 million in debt and enjoyed a $2.7 million surplus. The time seemed ripe for action.

Congress quickly took up the challenge. In the next few weeks, lawmakers hotly debated as yet unprecedented terms and conditions in federal social welfare policy. First among these was qualifying veterans' pensions on economic need rather than disability. If a veteran could provide proof of at least nine months of Revolutionary War service and swore an oath regarding his poverty, he received a pension. The terms were generous for their time. The law offered lifetime pensions of $20 a month for officers and $8 a month for enlisted men.

In contrast, Congress was much more precise when it came to what type of military service qualified a veteran to merit federal assistance. The final version of the 1818 law applied only to Continental regulars and not the militia. Southerners loudly protested the measure, which overwhelmingly favored Northerners, who dominated the regular ranks. As much as the country celebrated the prowess of the citizen-soldiers after the Battle of New Orleans, Congress moved in a much different direction.

Few officials believed that the new pension would overly burden the treasury. Senator Robert Goldsborough of Maryland estimated that only 1,614 Revolutionary War veterans were alive at the time Congress debated the 1818 law. However, the facts did not support his assessment. In 1818, the government paid out $104,900 to veterans. The following year, the amount increased almost twentyfold to $1.8 million. By 1820, veterans' pensions were 16 percent of the total federal budget. The *Niles' Weekly Register* commented in 1820:

The amount paid on account of these pensions—more than three millions of dollars *per annum*, has justly caused considerable enquiry and surprise;

and the reports have gone abroad that many persons are receiving the bounty of government, who are not entitled to it.

Amendments to the law also expanded eligibility. After 1836, for example, Revolutionary War widows qualified for benefits. Between 1818 and 1869, regular and disability pensions paid to about 60,000 Revolutionary veterans amounted to approximately $49 million.

Other controversies accumulated along with expenses. Southern concerns about bias in the new pension law turned out to be true. Two-thirds of benefits went to veterans from New York, Connecticut, and Massachusetts. Corruption also became a significant problem. The unexpected number of applications overwhelmed the War Department. Federal officials had little time to oversee the application process that was often rife with corruption. Many pension agents and judges responsible for processing claims were accused of receiving kickbacks from applicants.

There were some attempts to rein in costs. In 1820, federal legislators amended the pension law and introduced means testing as a requirement for military pensions. It would be one of the first federal definitions of poverty in US history. New applicants had to provide a statement regarding their health and an inventory of all their assets. Local courts would determine the assessed value of property.

Although the 1818 law was technically race blind, African American veterans faced many distinct obstacles to receiving their pensions. Many free Blacks and slaves who served under "civil contract" as support for the military did not qualify for a pension. Others who were actually members of Continental units could not read or write and struggled with the application process. This was further complicated when Black veterans shed the slave names that appeared on Revolutionary muster rolls. Although many of their white comrades attested to their service, the courts and many federal officials proved skeptical. Consequently, African American pension recipients consistently lagged behind white veterans in the years before the Civil War.

Antebellum Veterans

The national consensus on veterans proved fickle and vulnerable to hard times in America. Monroe's "Era of Good Feelings" was followed by a succession of economic collapses, or "Panics," in 1819, 1837, and 1857. These calamities sharpened the burden of escalating pension costs in the public mind and the halls of Congress. They also resurrected popular biases against regular service. Many laborers and immigrants, lacking prospects in the factory or on the farm, turned to the active-duty military as a vocation of last resort. Once again, the Army and Navy appeared to be a refuge for the untalented, unemployable, and undesirable. Colonel Enos Custer, who was responsible for recruiting in eastern states, noted many recent immigrants of "turbulent character and intemperate habits." A British visitor to the United States in the 1830s was less charitable, describing soldiers as "The scum of the population of the older states, or ... the worthless German, English, or Irish emigrants." This ridicule famously affected a future Civil War hero and president. When Ulysses S. Grant visited Cincinnati in 1843, a little boy mocked the newly commissioned officer: "Soldier! will you work? No, sir-ee; I'll sell my shirt first!!"

In the meantime, military service carried forward in a form familiar a century earlier. Antebellum militia units waxed or waned according to their location. As the frontier moved west, the absence of imminent danger caused some muster rolls to shrink. Regular meetings reverted to social occasions as they had on much of the East Coast before the Revolution. Even without a mission, many volunteer militia devoted time and effort to form specialty units of light infantry, grenadiers, and cavalry. Their membership reflected the changing makeup of communities in a growing nation. Two-thirds of volunteer militia members in New York City were foreign born in 1853. Many units composed of immigrants often found themselves in the awkward position of maintaining order when friction between nativists and new arrivals exploded into violence. Philadelphia was forced to call out the militia in 1844 to quell rioting between city residents and Irish immigrants.

In the Antebellum South, the militia became a means for states to assert their sovereignty over the federal government, a practice that became increasingly pointed in the time leading up to the Civil War. Starting in 1832, South Carolina required its militia to take the Militia Test Oath, which required members to pledge "faithful and true allegiance" to the state. Meantime, Southern states maintained the colonial practice of using the militia to preserve slavery. South Carolina established patrols that regularly roamed the countryside in search of escaped slaves as early as 1690. More than a hundred years later, in 1819, all males over the age of eighteen were liable for the same duty. In the early nineteenth century, Virginia passed an "Act for Making Provision Against Invasion and Insurrection," making the militia responsible for "peace and order." Their concerns were real. Although Nat Turner's 1831 revolt is well known, there were hundreds of slave rebellions in the South before the Civil War. The North did not escape the same violence. Local government called out the militia to combat race riots in Providence (1831), New York (1834), Boston (1843), and Philadelphia (1849) before the Civil War.

The regular military also kept much of its eighteenth-century character. Compared to Europe's professional armies and navies, it was a tiny, sequestered force. The Army stood at approximately 16,000 when the Civil War began. The Navy was even smaller at roughly 9,000 officers and men. Most soldiers served on the frontier scattered amongst isolated posts and far from family where the tempo of life was generally monotonous. Food, housing, and medical care were appalling as a rule.

American forces were not idle. Warfare against Native Americans from Florida to Texas and the Illinois Territory and points west characterized much of the era. In Mexico, the United States embarked upon a war of invasion that included mostly regulars bolstered by hastily assembled volunteer militia. National mobilization again pierced the fiction that 1.5 million men on militia rosters were available for service. When hostilities concluded in 1848, approximately 115,000 Americans served in the Mexican American War.

The war did little to improve perceptions of militia service. One regular artillery officer described Louisiana volunteers as a "lawless drunken rabble." Writing of his experience in Mexico, Brigadier General George Meade said of the militia that its "men are good material, and with good officers might readily be molded into *soldiers*, but the officers, as a rule with but very few exceptions are *ignorant, inefficient, and worthless*."

Regardless of the contempt many held for volunteers, the myth of the citizen-soldier was reborn after the war. Again, victory, in this case the massive addition of more than a half million square miles to US territory, was balm enough for many Americans. Aspiring politicians who served in the war understood this. When Nathaniel Hawthorne composed an election biography for Brigadier General Franklin Pierce, he appealed to the average voter: "The valor that wins our battles is not the trained hardihood of veterans, but a native and spontaneous fire; and there is surely a chivalrous beauty in the devotion of the citizen soldier in his country's cause."

The benefits program for Mexican War veterans was essentially identical to what was provided for the War of 1812. Wounded volunteers received the same disability payments as regulars. Benefits included five years' half pay to widows and orphans, a provision extended to lifetime for widows and the age of sixteen for young children.

One important addition regarded long-term veterans' care. A small number of facilities were built at the start of the century for the sick and injured who lacked the means or family support to help. The Naval Home in Philadelphia started in 1811 for "disabled and decrepit navy officers, seamen, and marines." The War Department recommended an "Army Asylum" in 1827, although progress toward it was very slow. Robert Anderson, the future commander of Fort Sumter, wrote in 1840 that "The soldier now knows that, when he is worn out in service, destroyed in constitution, and unfitted, by his habits, for embarking in a new pursuit, he must be discharged, and thrown, and outcast, upon society." Congress officially authorized the Soldiers' Home in 1851 but did not fund it. Instead, private donations, among them $100,000 that Winfield Scott "collected" in Mexico City, managed to start four asylums for men too old, sick, or injured to continue service. Only one of the institutions, located in Washington, DC, was still active at the beginning of the Civil War.

While America grew and expanded into the nineteenth century, so did its military responsibilities, conflicts, and population of veterans. Much like the colonial era, these veterans came from a variety of sources. As it had in the past, America relied heavily upon the militia along a violent western frontier and in larger conflicts with foreign powers, in this case England and Mexico. Volunteers consistently bolstered a regular military that was minuscule by Napoleonic standards. With equal consistency, traditional frictions between militia and regulars continued as the rule. American professionals ridiculed the volunteer, much like their British predecessors. However, for a public manifestly hostile to a standing armies, the citizen-soldier was held in high regard.

Veterans were at the center of a discussion of what citizenship meant in a new nation. As the United States moved forward and groped its way toward understanding service and nationalism, its veterans were an important yardstick to measure these qualities. The men who sacrificed life and limb were exemplars of what an American could be. Their dedication was a living example of democracy in action.

In contrast, the actual post-Revolutionary lives of too many veterans was a cautionary tale for their countrymen. Too many struggled during the hard economic times that followed the war. Although Daniel Shays illustrated that a few were willing to take up arms in defense of their interests, most veterans suffered without serious advocacy in the Congress or the War Department. Men disabled by their service could receive some assistance, but their ranks were small compared to overall need.

That began to change after the War of 1812. Flush with national pride and a federal surplus, James Monroe broke with forty years of precedent regarding veterans' policy. During his first term, Monroe established policy precedents—economic assistance for indigents, a national definition of poverty, means testing—that were far ahead of their time. Ironically, it was the regulars, vilified by so many people, who were the chief beneficiaries. Even so, such recognition was an expensive proposition. When Fort Sumter was fired upon in April 1861, approximately ten thousand veterans and widows were receiving federal benefits at an annual cost of $1 million. However, these formidable numbers would be dwarfed once the states joined in battle.

3

The Civil War

Stranger, when the fight was fiercest,
When my comrades round me fell,
I was sounded in the trenches,
By the bursting of a shell.
Hundreds died—all crushed and mangled;
Some in agony of pain,
Bit the very dust beneath them,
Soaked with life blood of the slain.
It was not my fate to perish
In the storm of iron hail
But, a mutilated soldier,
I have come to tell the tale.

"CRIPPLED SOLDIER'S SONG" (ca. 1861–1865)

The American Civil War was a massive conflict involving millions of combatants who were mobilized, armed, and transported by the might of the early Industrial Revolution. The scale recalled the Napoleonic era, augmented by modern innovations like the Minié ball and rifled weaponry. Yet, even as war became significantly more deadly, modern medicine was unable to keep pace. When it was over, approximately 206,500 Americans had died in combat and an estimated 417,500 perished as a result of disease. Nearly half a million men were wounded. Only World War II had a larger number of total casualties.

Americans on both sides flocked to their respective banners for a number of reasons.

Southerners joined to protect states' rights, which included the right to own slaves. Northerners enlisted to protect the Union. Not all were dedicated abolitionists, but many were. More than a few young men were bored and seeking what they perceived as a glorious adventure, at least in the early stages of the war. Many native-born citizens and immigrants were patriots. Friedrich Berstch noted in 1861 that

> For us German citizens, the hour has come to pay a sacred obligation to our adopted fatherland and show the wretched nativists, that we knew well, what we did when we took the citizen's oath, and that we with full citizens [sic] rights are at least just as worthy as the so-called native born are, because we hasten in the hour of danger to do our duty, regardless of what may be.

While volunteers' decisions were defined by the present moment, the future clearly played an important part. Of all the different constituents making up veterans of the Civil War, African Americans knew this perhaps the best. Corporal Thomas Long commented in 1864, "If we hadn't become sojers, [sic] all might have gone back as it was before …But tings [sic] can never go back, because we have showed our energy & our courage & our naturally manhood."

The massive commitment of manpower and the equally terrible casualties suffered contributed to a consensus that the United States owed a debt to its Civil War veterans. Among the flags and banners on display at the great 1865 victory parade down Pennsylvania Avenue, one expressed the sentiments of many Americans at the time: "The Only National Debt We Can Never Pay, Is The Debt We Owe To The Victorious Soldiers." The Civil War marked a rare instance when the country did not wait to act.

Wartime federal pension legislation proved to be a landmark in veterans' affairs and social welfare policy in general. Benefits represented a significant financial commitment to hundreds of thousands of recipients. Yet, how this might be effectively administered, and by whom, was an open question. The process did prompt lawmakers to revisit topics left over from the time of James Monroe. Did the veterans' benefits stop at individual social assistance for their wartime disabilities? Or would the United States enter the ranks of modern industrialized nations with a permanent commitment to social insurance for housing, income assistance, and other needs?

Serving in the American Civil War

When the war began, the United States maintained a tiny active-duty military, comprised of approximately 25,000 officers and men in the Army and Navy. Both sides heavily relied upon state militias out of necessity, although many formations had declined, particularly in states far removed from the western frontier.

From this humble start, truly immense forces grew. Overall, about 2.2 million Union soldiers served during the Civil War, 37 percent of Northern men from 15 to 44 in 1860. As noted above, the casualty rate was high, with a death rate higher than both world wars. Many injuries resulted from modern weapons that consistently overwhelmed tactics still rooted in the Napoleonic era. Many more fatalities came from diseases, like pneumonia, typhoid, and dysentery, that ravaged Northern encampments. Military surgeons had practically no understanding of communicable diseases, sterilization, or effective preventative medicine. Soldiers rarely practiced basic hygiene.

In the South approximately three-quarters of a million men served out of a total of 5.5 million non-slave population. Southern casualties included 261,000 dead, one-fifth of the region's adult white male population, and 194,000 wounded. Confederates were just as likely to fall victim to disease during the war as Northerners.

When the war ended, these formidable armies went home. Approximately 800,000 of the one million men in blue left the service within the first six months of peace. In short order, the regular Army settled down to approximately 25,000 soldiers and stayed at that level until the war with Spain. The Army and Marine Corps basically became a small expeditionary force occupied in wars scattered across the continent and some parts of the world. It was a small fraction of a country that numbered 62.9 million people by 1890. Many remaining officers accepted demotions to remain in uniform. George Armstrong Custer finished the war as a brevet major general in charge of a division of volunteers but reverted back to lieutenant colonel in the new peacetime.

Soldiers, Veterans, and the Meaning of the Civil War

Many historians have commented on just how much the works of Walt Whitman are a window to the Civil War. His poetry is one way to track the course of the conflict, from a patriotic call to arms, to the shock at the carnage of the first battles, to efforts at grappling with the war's aftermath. Whitman's 1867 poem "Reconciliation" explained the war's immediate legacy:

Word over all, beautiful as the sky!
Beautiful that war, and all its deeds of carnage, must in
      time be utterly lost;
That the hands of the sisters Death and Night, incessantly
      softly wash again, and ever again, this soil'd world:
… For my enemy is dead—a man divine as myself is dead;
I look where he lies, white-faced and still, in the coffin—I
      draw near;
I bend down and touch lightly with my lips the white face
      in the coffin.

The end of the war had a profound meaning that contemporary Americans expressed in many ways. Peaceful demobilization marked the survival of democracy. Watching thousands of citizen-soldiers marching in the Union's massive victory celebration in May 1865, the editor of the *Philadelphia North American* asked, "Is it not as great a tribute to free governments as was ever paid?" The idea became woven into popular memory about the war. A speaker in 1882 said of the reconstructed United States, "the authority of its government undisputed and absolute ... the results of the war accepted everywhere, its primal cause forever ended!"

Giving a concrete definition to these words involved tasks that were both simple and profound. The massive death toll resulting from the Civil War required a commitment by the country and the soldiers' survivors to find facilities appropriate to permanently lay the dead to rest. Postwar America saw a rapid expansion of military cemeteries. By 1871, there were seventy-four public grounds around the country, containing the remains of 300,000 veterans.

As they had after previous wars, veterans sought out their old comrades and organized around their former military lives. The company of old, familiar faces offered a counterpoint to peacetime routine. In the years following the war, regimental societies appeared in both the North and the South. National bodies like the US Soldiers and Sailors Protective Society and the Military Order of the Loyal Legion of the United States emerged as early as 1865.

Among these, the most important organization was the Grand Army of the Republic (GAR) founded in 1866 in Illinois. Beyond being a place for veterans to congregate, the GAR promised "fraternity, charity, and loyalty." At its core, the Grand Army of the Republic promoted honoring the Union cause of a restored nation and the abolition of slavery. In short order, chapters spread throughout the Midwest and the East Coast.

The early days of the GAR were not easy by any stretch of the imagination. Although it was a national organization, it was difficult for the headquarters to obtain reports from local posts or even verify their existence. In the meantime, the GAR experienced something of an identity crisis. It drew upon a huge body of recent veterans and potential members, but lacked a clear idea as to its purpose. The GAR was at once a place for old comrades to meet, part of the private social safety net for those in need that was common in the late nineteenth century, and an embryonic political organization. After an initial flush of enthusiasm, organizational drift set in and membership dwindled to just 26,899 by 1876.

Luckily for the GAR, changing circumstances helped it back into relevancy. As was the case in Antebellum America, the country suffered a series of devastating economic "Panics" in the late nineteenth century that overwhelmed both private charities and government policy. When official sources buckled under the weight of widespread poverty, the Grand Army of the Republic became part of a social and economic safety net for veterans. Historian Stuart McConnell notes, "The cardinal principle of 'charity' was expressed in a variety of quite personal ways—provision of food, coal, a loan, a job, free medical care, or a funeral service; payment of rent or a modest stipend to a widow, schooling or work for an orphan." In these areas, the Grand Army of the Republic did its part, offering $253,934.43 (approximately $8.4 million in modern currency) for public relief in 1887 alone. Thousands of veterans benefited from food and medicine distributed by the GAR. Many posts also approved stipends to veterans' widows and intervened on their behalf to secure employment for them.

Meanwhile, the GAR advocated for veterans at the state and federal levels. In 1873, it lobbied Pennsylvania lawmakers to help orphaned children of veterans. In 1887, the GAR convinced New York legislators to allow it to directly participate with local governments in veterans' welfare programs. At the federal level, the GAR was a permanent, powerful fixture, shaping a pension system that became continually more generous as the century wore on. Its national leadership worked with a cottage industry of claims agents, lawyers, and lobbyists that eventually grew up and around the millions of dollars flowing from Washington.

While it pressed forward, the GAR had to address contemporary ambivalence about the value of charity. As Benjamin Stephens wrote in 1868,

"Thousands of our poor, helpless, crippled comrades have been placed in positions where they could not earn their own bread, who, but for our instrumentality, would be left to seek their support from the cold hand of charity, and the Union soldier disdains to beg." The debate recalled the same concerns voiced after the American Revolution. Veterans had fought for the cause of union, democracy, and freedom. In the minds of many contemporaries, their preservation should have been reward enough. The risk of an elaborate social safety net was to make the veteran a ward of the state, nullifying his own freedom. Henry W. Bellows, who led the US Sanitary Commission during the Civil War, wrote in 1862 that veterans had the potential to be men who believed they had a "right to be idle, or to beg, or to claim exemption from the ordinary rules of life."

As it navigated this discussion, the Grand Army of the Republic offered veterans an honorable choice. It equated patriotism with military service and promoted the basic idea that veterans' programs were not handouts but a concrete recognition of service for the greater good of the nation. In some respects, it was the same argument that New Dealers would make with programs like the Civilian Conservation Corps in 1933.

This approach worked well. In the last two decades of the nineteenth century, the GAR recovered its membership as a social and patriotic organization and become a potent political force in American politics. When Ambrose Burnside eulogized Indiana senator Oliver P. Morton in 1877, acknowledging his "great care and love for soldiers, not only when they were in the field but after their return to their homes," the old general paid a compliment that Gilded Age American politicians coveted and sought out. For obvious reasons, Ulysses S. Grant was the first presidential candidate to enjoy an endorsement by the

GAR. So too did a generation of Civil War officers—Rutherford B. Hayes, James Garfield, Benjamin Harrison, and William McKinley—who dominated national politics until the new century. By 1890, the GAR stood at 409,000 members, representing almost half of surviving Union veterans.

The General Pension Act of 1862

When the Civil War began, the federal government had spent $90 million for military pensions and granted 65.5 million acres of bounty land for its veterans. In terms of people, its responsibility was fairly small. The 1861 pension list consisted of 10,700 veterans, of whom sixty-three were Revolutionary War survivors. The federal government was also aiding 2,728 widows.

Precedent initially guided Civil War era veterans' policy. When Lincoln called up troops in 1861, the United States reverted back to old standards applied to disability benefits for all troops, whether regular or volunteer. However, the early catastrophic human cost of the war soon shifted attitudes away from past practice. The Battle of Shiloh (April 6–7, 1862) resulted in 23,746 killed, wounded, captured, and missing, close to the cost of the entire Mexican War. It established a bloody precedent that became the norm as the war ground on.

The accumulating toll of the war mandated changes to federal policy for veterans. When the Congress considered the first drafts of the 1862 pension bill, they revisited old legislation that went back to the beginning of the century. As before, the immediate qualification for government benefits was disability and not poverty, specifically wounds or injuries "incurred as a direct consequence of ... military duty." The same benefits also applied to dependents of soldiers who succumbed to injuries caused by their wartime service.

Congressional Democrats opposed the legislation. William Steele Holman of Indiana described the proposed pension as "a mere bounty or gratuity from the Government—just and reasonable, but still a bounty." Republicans countered that the pension was not intended as the only income veterans would subsist on. For disability payments, a key question was whether or not a veteran could perform manual labor.

Another debate was over rates paid to veterans for their wounds and injuries. There was "a feeling, shared by several members of Congress, that in an army made up of citizen soldiers rather than mercenaries, it would be unjust discrimination to pension an officer at a higher rate than a private." Advocates of equity lost that argument. As it applied to officers and enlisted men, the 1862 pension law was segregated by rank much in the same way as Revolutionary War legislation.

With debate concluded, the new law made an easy passage through Congress and was signed by Abraham Lincoln on July 14, 1862. It provided disability pensions for wounds and injuries suffered after March 4, 1861. Monthly payments were a function of both rank, ranging from $30 for a lieutenant colonel to $8 for enlisted soldiers and sailors. As noted earlier, surviving widows, children, and dependent mothers or orphan sisters were eligible for the pension if the service member succumbed to wounds or disease.

The 1862 Pension Act also included one very important caveat that impacted millions of Americans. Reflecting the federal government's basic approach to the war, which counted Confederate rebels as lawbreaking US citizens, the Pension Act created a loyalty requirement for recipients. The Bureau of Pensions suspended payments to veterans who refused to take an oath after September 4, 1861, a policy that immediately disqualified all Southerners, eventually almost three quarters of a million Confederate veterans. In practice, more than three and a half years before Lee's surrender at Appomattox, US veterans' policy was setting the foundation for national reconstruction.

As the war evolved, so too did the Pension Act. Amendments to the original law, made on July 4, 1864, added a complex series of provisions for veterans' disabilities. For example, the loss of both hands or eyes entitled a veteran to

$25 a month. Separate rates applied to different types of amputation and their locations. However, there was no system for the era's version of post-traumatic stress, addiction, or other diseases related to military service. Problems attributed to "rheumatism" or "dyspepsia" had no real place on the increasingly elaborate federal tables.

When the war ended, the number of pensioners predictably grew from 126,722 in 1866 to 244,201 by 1885. Due to a series of amendments to the law (discussed in the next chapter), the pension law became increasingly inclusive. The total number of veterans receiving federal benefits peaked at 741,259 (74 percent of living Union veterans) in 1900.

Veterans and Reconstruction

Most Union veterans treated their military service like past generations in American history, as a necessary evil. They were justifiably proud of their accomplishments. They had saved the Union and righted some of the country's worst wrongs. Once the guns were silent and peace had thankfully arrived, it was time to go home, and the overwhelming majority did just that.

The future held a great deal of potential for Northern veterans. Tens of millions of dollars in new federal spending for the war had been a boon for what would become the smokestack belt, an industrial region stretching from Maine to Illinois. Manufacturing concerns and industry offered generous prospects for veterans either rejoining rank and file workers or becoming entrepreneurs in their own right. If life in the rapidly growing cities did not appeal, the western frontier offered its own prospects, bolstered by land grants under the Homestead Act (1862).

Northern communities welcomed their veterans as they returned home. Families joyously reunited with long-absent fathers, sons, and brothers. Local parades, which combined displays of both patriotism and individual recognition, mirrored the gigantic 1865 celebration in Washington. For some veterans, and their loved ones, the transition back to normalcy was difficult. Communities often struggled with veterans' post-traumatic stress, or what contemporaries called the "soldier's disease," as well as alcoholism and addiction. Despite the substantial support offered to individual veterans by 1862 Pension Act, local communities were left to fill in gaps in federal programs, especially with respect to physical accommodations for the disabled and mental health care.

The experience of Confederate veterans was drastically different. When her brother returned to Louisiana, Kate Stone wrote, "We are so glad to have Jimmy safe at home, but oh, what a different homecoming from what we anticipated when he enlisted. No feasting. No rejoicing. Only sadness and tears." These men return to a ruined South. Constant warfare between Union and Confederate forces had ravaged the countryside and its people. Union communities in Missouri and Kansas suffered brutal raids at the hands of William Quantrill and responded in kind. Throughout the South, the modern practice of total war had wreaked havoc. When he arrived in Atlanta, William Tecumseh Sherman bluntly informed the mayor and city council of this fact in no uncertain terms: "You cannot qualify war in harsher terms than I will. War is cruelty and you cannot refine it; and those who brought war into our country deserve all the curses and maledictions a people can pour out." The governor of Arkansas wrote of his state:

> The desolations of war are beyond description… Besides the utter desolation that marked the tracks of war and battle, guerrilla bands and scouting parties have pillaged almost every neighborhood… It would be safe to say that two thirds of the counties in this state are in destitute circumstances.

The consequences of total war set the stage for Confederate veterans. In this bitter peace and without federal assistance, they were essentially left to their own devices. Mutual aid groups, such as Confederate Survivors' Association of

South Carolina, appeared throughout the region. Other Confederate veterans formed unit organizations like the Society of the Army of Northern Virginia.

As they progressed, Southern veterans' activities closely mirrored those in the North. Civic organizations like the Ladies Memorial Association oversaw Southern military cemeteries immediately after the war. Veterans lobbied for their own Confederate Memorial Day. Some states established theirs on Jefferson Davis's birthday (June 3).

In time, much larger organizations would emerge. The United Confederate Veterans (UCV), founded in 1889, became the Southern counterpart to the Grand Army of the Republic, although much smaller in size. It grew to approximately 80,000 members and organized into 1,555 local posts, or "camps," by the turn of the twentieth century. Like Northern organizations, the UCV performed a social function, sponsoring both regular local meetings and national reunions. Its members attended funerals for their comrades and followed a set "Confederate Veteran's Burial Ritual," which focused on honoring the departed: "He fought a good fight and has left a record of which we, his surviving comrades, are proud, and which is a heritage of glory to his family and their descendants for all time to come." The UCV assisted widows of veterans who fell through the safety net of the reconstructed South.

The UCV and its allies, United Daughters of the Confederacy (est. 1894) and the Sons of Confederate Veterans (est. 1896), also lobbied state governments for veterans' pensions. Following the war, Southern states passed a series of laws that addressed disabled veterans and war widows. In 1879, North Carolina paid $60 a year for a veteran suffering from blindness or loss of both hands or feet. Georgia paid $5 per year for a missing finger or toe. A veteran could receive $150 annually for the loss of two or more limbs or blindness in both eyes. Georgia pensions were generous, but far less so than the wealthier North, where a blind Union veteran received $1,200 a year.

A few states did not wait for the veterans' lobby. Florida was a relatively new (1845) entry to the United States, yet it passed its own emergency relief for soldiers' families in December 1861. By 1864, support amounted to $291,443, more than half the total state budget. In 1885, the Florida legislature approved a pension act for veterans. It included means testing and applied only to Confederate regulars, not the state militia.

As time went on and Southern states slowly recovered from the war, their pension systems became somewhat more generous. By the 1890s, some states provided benefits for veterans suffering from poverty. Support eventually extended to veterans' wives and widows. In 1888, Mississippi included former slaves who had served with their owners in the war.

Confederate veterans were at the center of the postwar "Lost Cause" mythology. Participating in what historians have called a "civil religion," they reconstructed the past by burnishing Southern heroism during the war and their honorable struggle against Northern aggression. The Lost Cause made constant references to veterans as heroic martyrs. They argued that failure on the battlefield did not negate the principles Southerners fought to preserve. Brigadier General Thomas Neville Waul, speaking at a reunion of John Bell Hood's Texas Brigade in 1881, spoke to the issue in simple terms: "We cannot forget the war; we do not want to forget it and he who was a soldier, and pretends to forget it, is a hypocrite and a traitor."

This discussion persisted well into the new century. A 1904 ceremony recorded by the Confederate Memorial Association invoked a theme heard throughout the South:

> the poor Confederate soldier ... came wandering o'er desolated fields and blackened heaths, to find his home dismantled, his family in want, himself proscribed, and an alien upon the soil which gave him birth.

Long after most of his comrades were gone, G. B. Harris reflected in a November 1916 edition of the *Confederate Veteran*, "Defeat is not the test of righteousness of a cause. Right is right."

To deny Southern veterans' sacrifice was an affront to their service.

Confederate veterans wanted to have a hand in their own history. The United Confederate Veterans created a "Historical Committee" for this purpose at its third annual reunion in 1892. On their face, the reasons for such a committee seemed good. The UCV wanted to

> direct the ambition of our Southern youth to explore the mines of historical wealth, which now lie hidden in legends in scattered records, in unpublished manuscripts, and in the memories of a few old pioneers, who still linger amid the institutions that they helped to create.

Taking the matter further, the 1895 UCV Grand Reunion set down goals regarding teaching Southern history, specifically "unbiased" required textbooks. The organization appealed to local and state boards of education in South Carolina and Virginia to consider topics such as state sovereignty, slavery, and secession, and the conduct of the war.

Not satisfied with simply shaping the public narrative, more than a few Confederate veterans crossed over into violence. Former soldiers joined the Ku Klux Klan by the thousands and wreaked havoc throughout the South. Many followed the same officers who commanded them during the war. Nathan Bedford Forrest became the Klan's first Grand Wizard in 1867. George W. Gordon, a former Confederate general and lawyer, was an early member. Edmund Pettus, an infantry officer in the Army of the Tennessee, assumed leadership of the Alabama Klan. James Rufus Bratton, who started the war as a military surgeon in a volunteer regiment and later commanded the Winder Hospital in Richmond, led South Carolina's Klan.

John B. Gordon's status is a more interesting story. The Georgia native, who served in Lee's Army of Northern Virginia throughout the war and was wounded in multiple battles, dedicated his postwar energies to assisting his Southern comrades-in-arms by becoming the first commander of the United Confederate Veterans. Gordon consistently denied any affiliation with the Klan. During a five-hour session before a Congressional committee in 1871, he acknowledged being part of a secret organization made up of a "brotherhood of property holders, the peaceable, law-abiding citizens of the State, for self-protection." It existed because Northern "carpetbaggers" were manipulating free African Americans in Georgia and inciting them to violence against the white population. Gordon described the organization, which he never named, as "a peace police—a law abiding concern."

After the Civil War, former Confederates shared the South with an old type of veteran given a new agency. During the conflict, approximately 200,000 African Americans served in the Union Army. Although there was ample precedent for their service, it took years of intensive lobbying for the federal government to accept it. Frederick Douglass argued in February 1863 that "Whoever sees fifty thousand well drilled colored soldiers in the United States, will see slavery abolished and the union of these States secured from rebel violence."

During the Civil War, African Americans were represented in nearly every state of the Union as volunteers and "United States Colored Troops." Many regiments served in combat and fought well at places like Fort Wagner and Petersburg. Service gathered a sense of worth based on substantive accomplishment. As one Black veteran recalled, he "felt like a man with a uniform on and a gun in my hand." Military training fostered self-discipline, as well as organizing actions within a larger group. The military institution, with its rules, requirements, and punishments, also facilitated a much more sophisticated understanding of how the law worked. This was especially so among men who served as NCOs and the small handful who were officers.

After the war, African American veterans acted as their own advocates. Before the Fifteenth Amendment was ratified, they demanded the right to vote in North Carolina and Louisiana. They formed military clubs and community organizations in places as far apart at Maryland and South Carolina. African American veterans served in the Bureau of Refugees, Freedmen, and Abandoned Lands (otherwise known as the Freedmen's Bureau). They were among the first federal officials active in the South after the Confederate surrender. One of these was Major Martin R. Delany, who followed service as an officer in the US 52nd Colored Infantry Regiment as a Freedmen's Bureau agent in South Carolina. Delany believed that economic development was the primary goal for freed slaves. He saw capital, land, and labor as part of "a domestic triple alliance" for progress.

Unfortunately, neither economic nor political reconstruction existed in a vacuum. Spreading racial violence in the postwar South, committed by the Klan and other paramilitary groups, required direct military action and it would come from an interesting source. The initial version of the 1867 Reconstruction Act banned provisional white militias, which left free African Americans in their place as protectors of communities. In the first decade and a half after the Civil War, nineteen states, including the entire former Confederacy (except Arkansas), raised local units comprised of free Blacks. Many of them derived their names from historical figures. In Richmond, for example, the Attucks Guard took its name from Crispus Attucks, who died during the 1770 Boston Massacre.

African American militia membership was groundbreaking in many respects. Before the Fifteenth Amendment created universal male suffrage, it allowed free Black citizens to be active participants in the administration of the law, an incredible opportunity in the former Confederacy. A soldier's uniform also carried with it social prestige. A number of these men joined to establish their new freedom and status. Historian Otis A. Singletary argues that Black women were effective at pressuring men to join for the same reason.

The old Southern establishment fought against free Black militias from the start. Many states simply starved units of basic funding. Robert K. Scott, a Republican and South Carolina's first postwar governor, diverted $50,000 appropriated for the militia and used the money to bribe three state legislators during his own impeachment proceedings. As a result, African American volunteers suffered from chronic problems of pay, shoddy uniforms and equipment, obsolete or unserviceable weapons, and poor morale.

African American military service produced considerable friction with a white population vested in an Antebellum social hierarchy. According to one historian, "The very fact that the Negro wore a uniform and thereby enjoyed certain rights was an affront to most Southern whites." White opposition proved a significant barrier to Black militia units performing their duties. African American volunteers were rarely called out for riot duty and routinely prevented from deployment after public lynchings. In Missouri, the National Guard Inspector General made his opinion clear in 1885: "I regard colored troops as an injury rather than a benefit to the service, as in case of trouble they could not only not be used, but would have to be housed and guarded by white troops."

It was not uncommon for whites to actively harass African American militia members.

At some points verbal physical harassment sometimes escalated to murder. Such was the case of Captain Jim Williams, a former slave, who was killed in South Carolina in March 1871.

Race also affected African American veterans' benefits. Despite the fact that the 1862 Pension Law was race blind, racism was a determining factor affecting African American veterans. Whether they had suffered as a result of their Civil War service was not the point. Policymakers and citizens, reflecting the conventional wisdom of the era, questioned if African Americans (and some immigrant groups) had the ability of "self-government," that is, were capable of managing their own personal affairs, to include veterans' benefits. The Social Darwinists of the time believed that the Black veteran was more likely to become a victim of fraud. A War Department pension official wrote in 1878 that he was troubled about "the general credulity with which the race is apt to listen to the proposals of a sharper." Some of these concerns were based upon actual evidence of abuse. One claims agent reportedly cashed benefits checks destined for African American veterans, deducting amounts that ranged from $15 to as much as $2,000, the latter taken from lump sums granted by the Arears Act.

Many African American veterans suffered these abuses because they lacked advocates. They did not enjoy consistent support from the Grand Army of the Republic, the US Sanitary Commission, or the War Department when navigating the complex and lengthy process of pension application. According to a survey by the University of Chicago Center for Population Economic, far fewer Black veterans applied (19.7 percent) for pensions under the 1862 law than white veterans (43.9 percent). Before 1890, white Civil War veterans were almost twice as likely to have pension applications accepted, 77.9 percent to 39.4 percent.

By 1910, half a million American men were receiving federal pensions by virtue of their Civil War service, 28 percent of all men sixty-five or older. Recipients also included more than 300,000 widows and other dependents. America had not yet moved to a full-scale, social insurance system, like England or Germany, but the war had pushed the federal government far past poorly defined individual social assistance. The 1862 Pension Act expanded eligibility and transformed what constituted a disability.

Civil War veterans were intricately involved in the process of recognition and support. While the Grand Army of the Republic took time to get on its feet and establish a consistent identity, the organization became a powerful force in American politics and veterans' affairs. It helped shape what historians Larry M. Logue and Peter Blanck describe as the "honorable scars" of Civil War service.

In the South, the national divide carried forward into the lives of veterans. Federal policy deliberately treated Confederates as paroled criminals rather than citizens deserving of assistance or recognition. Confederate veterans responded in kind, creating their own sequestered tribute in the Lost Cause narrative and a series poorly funded, state-managed veterans' programs. These cleavages awaited African Americans fresh from their Civil War service and as they prepared to enjoy active citizenship in the South. Old scars inflicted before the war and during it ran deep and outlasted the rest of the century.

4

American Empire

We have not finished our fighting. Our whole life is a fight, but one thing I want to warn you against. Don't go back home and attempt to lie on your laurels. Laurels wither in time. Don't go back and pose as heroes who have fulfilled their life duty and have nothing more to do.

THEODORE ROOSEVELT SPEAKING TO HIS REGIMENT
BEFORE IT DEMOBILIZED, SEPTEMBER 1898

As American empire grew, it produced a new generation of veterans. Some late-nineteenth-century military service told a very old story. Tiny contingents of regulars, bolstered by local volunteers, fought an endless series of skirmishes and campaigns against Native Americans, in this case in the western Great Plains, the Rocky Mountains, and beyond. Yet, even as western conquest continued, new missions more akin to a modern nation demanded military attention. The militia, reconstituted in state National Guard units, fought bloody battles against workers in the cycles of economic disaster that plagued the country in the last part of the century. Foreign deployments, reflecting America's multiplying international interests, required greater military muscle. By 1900, veterans of Cuba, the Philippines, and many other faraway places accompanied the graying Civil War generation.

Despite these rapidly changing times, the Civil War kept a firm grip on how Americans perceived veterans and crafted policy for them. Civil War veterans, like the men who fought the American Revolution, were paragons of virtue in their time. The generation that wore blue and gray set the boundaries of honorable service and public recognition. Later generations who fought in smaller wars traveled in their wake. At the time when the new century began, a generational divide between the Grand Army of the Republic and its successors was clearly evident. In practical terms, public acclaim translated into increasingly generous revisions and additions to the 1862 General Pension Law that expanded compensation for both veterans and their surviving families. As the law evolved, the cost and impact of veterans' policy grew accordingly, often at the expense of younger veterans who demanded the same generosity.

Veterans became embroiled in new controversies as the century wore on. Civil War pensions crossed paths with a new cohort of Progressive reformers who challenged a system that was not only increasingly expensive, but also fundamentally corrupt in many of its practices. The crusade for efficiency and public accountability begged for change. At the same time, nineteenth-century Social Darwinists contested the need for a social safety net, arguing that veterans' benefits interfered with the natural order of human evolution. As the United States matured into a modern nation, its veterans were at the forefront of a host of social and political debates that expressed both the problems and possibilities of a still-young country.

Soldiers of a New Nation

The years following the American Civil War were a period of almost constant bloodletting on the western frontier. Military historian Warren W. Hassler counts thirteen campaigns and 1,067 engagements between the American military and Native Americans from 1865 to 1891. Frontier warfare was peppered with brutal clashes that ranged from the Fetterman Massacre (1866) to the Battle of Wounded Knee (1890). As he did during the Civil War, Walt Whitman wrote about frontier fighting. He published "Far From Dakota's Cañons" in June 1876:

The battle bulletin,

The Indian ambuscade, the craft, the fatal environment,

The cavalry companies fighting to the last in sternest heroism,

In the midst of their little circle, with their slaughter'd horses for breast works,

The fall of Custer and all his officers and men.

Army life for the frontier military was anything but poetic, with the conditions of service were nearly identical to the Antebellum era. As before, regular forces atrophied in peacetime. Congress reduced the regular Army to just 25,000 men in 1874, where it remained until the Spanish-American War. Once again, immigrants dominated the enlisted ranks. Their desertion rates were high and fluctuated around economic hard times. In the Army Division of the Atlantic, 33.5 percent of soldiers fled military service on the eve of the Panic of 1873. Once national economic depression really showed its teeth, the rate dropped to 5.1 percent as more soldiers kept their army pay and relative economic security. A soldier's day-to-day routine reverted to its pre–Civil War form for the most part, although health conditions improved as the military establishment tried to address the quality of food and shelter. Regardless, daily life was dominated by isolation and civilian indifference to service.

A handful of reformers did try to help their institution. Emory Upton addressed basic tactics and the overall organization of the Army. His mentor and the commander of the Army, William Tecumseh Sherman, initiated a professional school system to improve military aptitude. Alfred Thayer Mahan attended to naval strategy. His scholarship, which focused on fleet actions and global commerce, had a special appeal to a young Theodore Roosevelt, who wrote about naval affairs during his time as a student at Harvard University.

Modern times also mandated significant changes for the militia. In America's growing industrial belt, local volunteers found a new mission as they transitioned to the state National Guard, which included 100,000 members organized into fifty-four brigades by 1893. Deployments in the decades after the Civil War were punctuated by significant labor unrest that often turned violent. The clash between six hundred soldiers from the Philadelphia "First Division" and workers in Pittsburgh during the 1877 railroad strike was typical of the time. Almost as soon as they arrived to quell angry workers, the national guardsmen came under attack. The paving brick was the weapon of choice, although any thrown projectile would do. The unit opened fire, resulting in dozens killed, including a woman and three children. This scenario played out many times as the country was roiled by economic disruptions from the Great Railroad Strike of 1877 to the Pullman Strike in 1894. Between 1877 and 1903, state National Guard units were called out more than seven hundred times in response to urban unrest.

Late-nineteenth-century National Guard culture kept many of its old militia characteristics. As the frontier shifted west, local volunteer units in regions left behind stagnated and lost their purpose. In the place of imminent threats, military routine became an excuse for socializing and networking. Historian Eleanor Hannah notes that service was also a place to openly assert citizenship. The guard attracted older, established communities but also units comprised of newer immigrants intent on marking their assimilation into mainstream American society.

For the most part, a small but active expeditionary corps of men provided military muscle for America's growing empire. Soldiers manned isolated frontier outposts. Sailors and Marines, transported by a growing fleet of steel warships, protected and advanced American interests around the world. The mass mobilization of the Civil War seemed like a thing of the past.

As the United States grew and gathered itself, the growing tempo of American foreign affairs demanded additional military attention. In his excellent *The Savage Wars of Peace*, Max Boot notes that the US Marine Corps alone landed forces abroad 180 times between 1800 and 1934. American forces intervened in China (as early as 1854), Korea (1871), and

Samoa (1899). Latin America also saw frequent American military action. US Marines and sailors landed in Colombia in 1885 to crush a rebellion in its Panama territory. In 1894, the United States intervened in Brazil to support pro-American president Floriano Peixoto. American military forces were a regular feature in Latin American and Caribbean affairs, particularly in Honduras (1903, 1907, 1911), Nicaragua (1912), Mexico (1914), Haiti (1915), and the Dominican Republic (1916).

By the turn of the twentieth century, the United States also joined the other major powers in Asia. After ousting Spain from its Pacific colonies, America quickly became embroiled in the Philippine Insurrection (1899–1902) and subsequent sporadic violence, such as the Moro Rebellion (1902–1913), for years afterward. US military units joined other European powers when they intervened in China during the Boxer Rebellion in 1900.

The Spanish-American War

At the end of the nineteenth century, Spain's sick, old empire in the Western Hemisphere was on its last legs. Cubans, motivated by the desire to shed their foreign monarch, initially embarked on a series of rebellions against the Spanish colonial occupation in 1868. Within a generation, Spanish dominion was under a full-fledged siege.

American sympathies and interests were with Cubans almost from the start. US businesses had millions in investments on the island, mostly in sugar. The public identified with with rebels, fighting as Americans had against the worst excesses of an Old World European empire. In this atmosphere, the rebel leader José Martí become a celebrity as he advocated *Cuba Libre* in the United States. The emerging national media industry, particularly publications owned by William Randolph Hearst, helped promote Martí's cause and shape opinion against Spain and the atrocities reported in American newspapers.

The Grand Army of the Republic was part of that national audience. It lobbied for American intervention and war years before the *Maine* was destroyed in Havana Harbor. The GAR commander of Indiana spoke at its 1896 encampment, denouncing "the inhuman cruelties recently inaugurated by the Spanish Government in its attempts to still popular liberty in Cuba and to restore its further misrule, has filled the civilized world with horror and has aroused, on behalf of that struggling people, the sympathy of the friends of popular government everywhere."

The sinking of the USS *Maine* was a final straw for veterans and citizens alike. When the US warship exploded in Havana Harbor on February 15, 1898, with the loss of 260 lives, demands for action against Spain reached a crescendo. After weeks of delay, President McKinley asked Congress for a resolution authorizing the use of force against Spain. It overwhelmingly gave him that power on April 19, 1898.

From the start, victory was anything but assured. Army regulars, including just 28,000 soldiers scattered across the continent when the *Maine* exploded in Havana Harbor, were not close to what the country needed for full-fledged global deployment. President McKinley called up state National Guard units for federal service and filled in the remaining gaps with additional volunteers. Eventually, 274,717 officers and men saw service in the short conflict with Spain. For the first time since the war against Mexico, a truly national force—comingling regiments from the North and South, from places as far apart as Pennsylvania and Georgia—served American interests abroad.

African Americans joined this effort as part of a segregated military. After the *Maine* was destroyed, only four states allowed Black regiments to participate in the first call for volunteers. As African American units were raised during the summer mobilization of 1898, many did so with the provision that white officers command them. Governor John M. Tanner of Illinois, however, demanded that the 8th Illinois US Volunteer Regiment keep their African American officers. The 8th USV Regiment eventually deployed to Cuba in August 1898 and served with distinction.

For all its formidable size, US forces suffered relatively few casualties during the war against Spain. Of an estimated 3,000 fatalities, approximately 385 were caused by combat. In contrast, disease and sickness ravaged American ranks, particularly in the opening weeks of the Cuba campaign. In August, not long after American forces landed, Theodore Roosevelt joined other officers in a letter to the Associated Press lamenting "That the army is disabled by malarial fever to the extent that its efficiency is destroyed, and that it is in a condition to be practically entirely destroyed by an epidemic of yellow fever which is sure to come in the near future." Fortunately for the American expedition to Cuba, Spanish resistance collapsed before US casualties overwhelmed the invasion.

Commemorations from the Centennial to the First World War

The Civil War dominated American celebrations of its veterans and helped shaped a national definition of patriotism before World War I. Individual states set aside time to recognize the war as early as 1866. For its own part, the Grand Army of the Republic created national Decoration Day in 1868, which would eventually evolve into Memorial Day. The GAR was a regular feature of annual patriotic events. During the official Philadelphia Centennial Exhibition in 1876, five thousand Union veterans led a march that included "workingmen, political clubs, civic societies" and other citizens celebrating the nation's birthday. Beyond being simple, ritual demonstrations, the celebrations held a larger meaning. In 1890, at its annual encampment, one GAR member noted that "Every patriotic act, every gathering where patriotic sentiments are expressed help to build a wealth that can not be represented in figures, because every such act breathes the life that will perpetuate our love for the nation." In the decades following the Civil War, the Grand Army of the Republic reconstructed itself as an essential instrument of Americanism. After the war, a GAR chaplain spoke about the mission of a "religion of patriotism" that taught "love of country" as a bedrock principle. The organization saw a duty to cultivate these ideas. Every GAR post had the potential to be "a school of patriotism."

Public celebrations of America's frontier wars were much less deliberate. Custer's horse Comanche became a minor national celebrity after having survived the Battle of Little Big Horn when the country reached its centennial. Other men who served in the West, pursued different types of recognition. One of these was William Frederick "Buffalo Bill" Cody. Cody was a Civil War veteran who spent his time with the 7th Kansas Cavalry as a teamster. His service was honorable if not glorious, but what made him famous was author Ned Buntline, who wrote a series of popular dime novels that captured and embellished Cody's exploits. Part of Buffalo Bill Cody's genius was his ability to market frontier conflict as part of his Wild West show, which included reenactments of frontier battles. Veterans on both sides were plentiful. Cody hired paroled Lakota survivors of the 1890 Wounded Knee Massacre from federal prison in Illinois so that they could appear in a European tour of his show.

Commemorations of the Spanish-American War took on a more traditional form at the end of the century. In fact, they began even as the war unfolded in Cuba and the Philippines. Americans rejoiced when news of Rear Admiral William T. Sampson's victory at Santiago reached the country right before the Fourth of July. Later that summer, thousands turned out in Boston when nine warships, led by the battleship USS *Massachusetts*, returned from the Cuban campaign.

When they returned home, Army veterans also received their due. The 71st New York Volunteer Infantry left for Cuba with over 1,000 men. When it returned for its own parade in August 1898, where "Flags and war emblems abounded in luxurious profusion," there were 348 almost fit to march. Spectators commented on their state, one woman saying that the marching soldiers looked "half-starved." Many soldiers fainted in the street as the parade proceeded through New York City in the hot August sun.

Although his Rough Riders, officially the 1st US Volunteer Cavalry, mustered out before they could parade, the war made Teddy Roosevelt a national hero. Roosevelt began campaigning for governor of New York even before his regiment was demobilized from its final posting at Camp Wikoff, Long Island. His newly won credential as a veteran and legitimate hero was a significant asset for the next step in Roosevelt's political career.

The war against Spain transformed the National Peace Jubilee, originally begun in 1869 to celebrate the end of the Civil War. The 1898 Philadelphia celebration of the Jubilee was attended by 10,500 troops, including four Pennsylvania regiments as well as units from Connecticut, Maryland, Massachusetts, Michigan, Missouri, New York, Ohio, and Tennessee. The Jubilee gathering in Chicago that same year featured a number of themes. President McKinley spoke to the war's just cause and America's growing greatness:

> The war with Spain was undertaken, not that the United States should increase its territory, but that the oppression at our very doors should be stopped. This noble sentiment must continue to animate us and we must give to the world the full demonstration of our purpose. Duty determines destiny. Destiny which results from duty performed may bring anxiety and perils, but never failure and dishonor.

Following the president was Clark Howell, editor of the *Atlanta Constitution*, who framed the war as proof of national reconciliation:

> Drawing alike from all sections of the Union for her heroes and her martyrs, depending alike upon North, South, East, and West for her glorious victories, and weeping with sympathy with the widows and the stricken mothers wherever they may be, America, incarnated spirit of liberty, stands again to-day the holy emblem of a household in which the children abide in unity, equality, love, and peace.

Howell's point was important to his contemporaries. With the passage of time and distance from the Civil War, veterans increasingly became a symbol of reconciliation and the common cause of national unity. "Blue-Gray" reunions were a regular feature of veterans affairs by the 1880s. Both Union and Confederate officers served as pallbearers during Ulysses S. Grant's funeral in 1885. William Tecumseh Sherman and Phil Sheridan joined Joseph Johnston and Simon Bolivar Buckner in honoring their fellow West Point graduate. William McKinley, who served as an Ohio volunteer during the Civil War, made a point of meeting with Confederate veterans during his run for president in 1896. McKinley later supported Confederate burials at Arlington National Cemetery in 1898 with the spirit of healing in mind:

> Sectional lines no longer mar the map of the United States. Sectional feeling no longer holds back the love we bear each other. Fraternity is the national anthem, sung by a chorus of forty-five States and our Territories at home and beyond the seas. The Union is once more the common altar of our love and loyalty, our devotion and sacrifice.

At the close of the century, Americans also used the land itself as a memorial of military service. For years, Gettysburg attracted veterans from both sides to relive their part in one of the greatest battles of the Civil War. Old soldiers gathered annually and celebrated the milestone twenty-fifth and fiftieth anniversaries in significant numbers. In 1913, as many as 54,000 former Union and Confederates soldiers attended the event to exchange stories and pose for still and motion pictures. Between 1890 and 1925, Congress recognized the meaning and popularity of these reunions by designating ten national battlefield sites or parks, a list that included Gettysburg, Antietam, Shiloh, Vicksburg, Chickamauga, and Kennesaw Mountain.

Individual Civil War monuments populated the countryside by the thousands. Veterans' organizations on both sides placed markers on battlefields recognizing both individual commanders and units. Towns and cities did the same, taking advantage of a blossoming monuments industry. Mass-produced statues could be found in town squares throughout America. Most were cast in zinc rather than bronze because they were cheap (starting at $150). The greatest surge in monument construction came between 1890 and 1930, peaking right before World War I.

As the nation continued the process of healing the old wounds left from the Civil War, a new divide appeared at the end of the century that was generational rather than regional. Like the men who fought in the Revolution, Civil War veterans saw their military service simply as more valuable and more deserving than the generation succeeding them. A number of factors contributed to this belief. One was the scale of the past conflict. As desperate as the fighting had been at places like El Caney or Santiago, they were dwarfed by Shiloh, Gettysburg, and a dozen other battles. The respective lengths of the two conflicts prompted additional dismissal. Civil War veterans scoffed at a campaign in Cuba that had lasted a few short months. As a coming-of-age milestone for a generation, the two wars simply did not compare. Even Teddy Roosevelt, arguably one of the most famous heroes of the Cuban campaign, referred to his compatriots in 1902 as "my comrades of a lesser war."

For obvious reasons, veterans of the Spanish-American War took offense at such derision. For them, the measurement of a conflict was not its duration, but the deadly risks involved. John F. Kendrick wrote a memoir of his service in Cuba, where he suffered through yellow fever, noting "those who don't understand that a short campaign in a short war can be deadly."

These claims carried little weight, particularly among established veterans' organization. The Grand Army of the Republic was clear about the status of veterans of Cuba and the Philippines: it did not want them. Not surprisingly, Union veterans saw the Spanish-American War as an inferior product, undeserving of equal recognition. When the commander of the Grand Army of the Republic referred to the 1898 conflict as a "very little war," he was expressing the accepted wisdom of his generation.

Closed out of mainstream organizations, veterans of the Spanish-American War formed their own. The Veterans of Foreign Wars appeared just a year after hostilities ended. Five years later, a separate group of veterans in Illinois created the United Spanish War Veterans (USWV). It peaked at 126,000 in the early thirties, representing almost half of the 345,000 Americans who served in Cuba and the Philippines. Like mainstream veterans' groups in the North, the USWV emphasized making amends with old enemies. In 1920, its national commander noted, "The son of Johnny Reb and Yankee Doodle locked arms in comradeship, broke bread in the same mess, and stood grimly shoulder to shoulder in the same embattled trench."

Reconciling veterans according to race was a different and difficult story. The Grand Army of the Republic did not officially endorse segregation and left the decision to individual posts, resulting in effective if not official separation of its members by race in most of the country. The United Spanish War Veterans was not willing to pay even lip service to equality, segregating its membership from the start. In the end, while many Northern veterans might embrace legal and social emancipation in principle, they followed the standards of *Plessy v. Ferguson* (1896). It was clear that, in practice, not all veterans were created equal.

The Evolution of Gilded Age Veterans' Policies

In the years following the Civil War, lawmakers repeatedly reopened the debate about wartime service and compensation, inviting a growing body of veterans, widows, and dependents into federal programs. Long before the Progressive movement began to explore obligations to the poor and disadvantaged, veterans were pioneers in the earliest forms of modern social welfare in America. The process invoked a debate about the significant costs involved, even for a growing world industrial power, but also what dependency might mean for Social Darwinists concerned with the literal evolution of the American people.

The Gilded Age saw the long overdue business of past wars and their veterans finally addressed in official policy. In 1871, the small number of surviving veterans of the War of 1812 finally obtained pensions regardless of their finances or health. Veterans of the Mexican War also received some attention, although they had nothing as effective as the Grand Army of the Republic to promote their needs. Instead, the Aztec Club, founded in 1847, primarily sponsored reunion dinners. It was not until long after the war, in January 1874, that veterans from thirty-two states established the National Association of Veterans of the Mexican War. Led by Alexander M. Kenaday, a member of a dragoon regiment raised to fight in Mexico, the Association claimed 5,095 members by 1879. As was the case with the Grand Army of the Republic, it took the familiar path from social organization sponsoring reunions around the country to a dedicated lobby for veterans' benefits. In 1874, the Association asked Congress for an $8 monthly pension for all who served for at least sixty days. Unfortunately, successful passage proved to be a legislative slog. Remaining Mexican War veterans with at least two months of service, as well as unmarried widows, eventually received their $8 monthly amount at the start of 1887. During the first year of the pension, 7,503 veterans received benefits, with the number peaking at 17,158 in 1890.

The treatment of veterans of Mexican campaigns offered an interesting window on the issue of national reconciliation after the Civil War. Advocates of the pension plan argued that Mexican veterans could "better settle those differences" that bedeviled the North and South in the 1870s. However, in doing this, legislators had to reconsider a problem left over from the original 1862 General Pension Act: the ongoing ban on granting federal benefits to former Confederates, many of whom served in both Mexico and the Civil War. This stumbling block proved unbreachable until 1885 when the Grand Army of the Republic decided to support the Mexican veterans' pension bill. Grover Cleveland finally signed it into law in February 1887.

The Grand Army of the Republic's support of the Mexican War pension plan was just one measure of how much political power the organization enjoyed during the Gilded Age. With a membership peaking at a formidable 425,000 men in 1890, the GAR represented a disciplined national constituency within the Republican party. It both populated and shaped the composition of state legislatures as well as the US Congress. More than a hundred and fifty Union and Confederate veterans served in the Senate alone, the last being Francis E. Warren, Wyoming Republican who died in office in 1929. In an era when Civil War veterans provided a majority of presidents—Grant, Hayes, Garfield, Harrison, and McKinley—its influence was self-evident.

That power translated into consistent legislative action. One of the first major revisions of post–Civil War veterans' policy was the Arears of Pension Act (1879). The law essentially allowed veterans and dependents receiving pension benefits to backdate them to their discharge from the military or death caused by service in the Civil War. Applications for pensions skyrocketed from an average of 1,600 a month before passage of the Arrears Act to over 10,000 a month afterward. By 1881, the average payment for a veteran was $953.62. For widows and children, it was $1,021.51. These were substantial amounts at a time when the average monthly salary for a coal miner in 1879 was $39.64.

Problems almost immediately began to emerge from this generosity. The Commissioner of Pensions reported that claims were coming to his agency at "an unprecedented rate" and that the volume had resulted in "many and very serious complaints at the delays in answering the inquiries relative to pending claims." Overwhelmed federal officials often failed to separate legitimate claims from fraud. And, as they struggled, the costs of the Arrears Act grew. In 1877, the government was paying $3.2 million for pensions. The new law added $24.8 million to the US Treasury's obligations. Pension payments for the Civil

War, to include both the initial 1862 law and subsequent amendments, peaked in 1893 at $158.1 million.

Despite the incredible generosity of the Arrears Act, it did not eliminate veterans' troubles. According to an 1890 the *Iowa State Register* editorial, "It has not been so difficult for those who bore commissions, drew larger pay, and had more privileges and comforts than privates throughout the war to prove up their claims!" Enlisted men, in contrast, had been "shamefully neglected," a problem highlighted by the ongoing economic troubles affecting the country at the time.

Additional help was on the way. Following a period of federal surpluses in which public debt declined from $2.4 billion in 1870 to $961 million in 1893, Congress was in a generous mood. It passed the Dependent Pension Act in 1890, which allowed support for Union veterans with only ninety days wartime service, waived documentation of service disabilities and, in the case of dependents, proof of death in the war. The Invalid Pensions Act appeared the same year. It allowed for federal support for Union veterans unable to do manual labor.

It did not take long for veterans' programs to become entangled in Gilded Age patronage politics. Conflicts of interest and corruption were evident at all levels. Commissioner of Pensions W. W. Dudley, a Union veteran who lost a leg at Gettysburg, was appointed in 1881 and worked directly with the GAR when the time came to draw up pension lists. "Corporal" James Tanner, a member of the GAR Pension Committee, briefly took charge of federal veterans' programs in 1891 and famously was reported to have said when discussing veterans' pensions: "God Help the [budget] Surplus."

In practice, veterans' pensions proved to be important Gilded Age political tools. Republican office holders saw them as part of a rewards system that provided incentives for loyalty. In contrast, Democrats lumped abuses of the veterans' pension system into their campaign for civil service reform. Grover

Cleveland, who broke a twenty-year Republican grip on the White House, made a point of vetoing the 1887 version of the Dependent Pension Bill. All told, Cleveland vetoed 228 pension bills in his first term alone. His obstinance became a campaign issue that Benjamin Harrison used in his own run for the presidency in 1888:

> Let Grover talk against the tariff tariff tariff
> And pensions too.
> We'll give the workingman his due
> And pension the boys who wore the blue.

In the meantime, between 1885 and 1887, 40 percent of House legislation and 55 percent of Senate legislation was devoted to special individual pension bills that moved around the chief executive. With a substantial push by the Grand Army of the Republic, Benjamin Harrison signed the Dependent Pension Act in 1890, reversing one of Cleveland's earlier vetoes.

Veterans clearly were an influential part of the Gilded Age. Through organizations like the Grand Army of the Republic, they were highly effective political actors, shaping the careers of a generation of nineteenth- and early-twentieth-century lawmakers. In doing so, they facilitated the normalization of public social welfare and helped overcome the stigma associated with it. Through their relationship with state and federal politicians, they were instrumental in assigning priorities and budgets. Numbers tell the story. By 1893, almost a million people receiving aid through veterans' legislation and pensions consumed 40 percent of the federal budget.

Interestingly, as benefits grew and became more elaborate, they highlighted veterans' remaining needs. The Dodge Report (1899) defined military medicine during the Spanish-American War in terms of "criminal neglect." Veterans' medical care was equally poor. As noted earlier, the Spanish-American War also served as a crossroads in the pension debate. With only 385 killed in combat and another 3,000 deaths as a result of disease, did the next generation of veterans merit the same attention lavished on the Civil War forbears? There was little agreement on the topic.

The Attack on Veterans' Pensions

Hiram Cronk, allegedly the last surviving veteran of the War of 1812, died in 1905. After lying in state at City Hall, guarded by 150 New York City police, his body was taken to Brooklyn's Cyprus Hills Cemetery by a procession made up of the 14th Regiment of the New York National Guard, relatives, city officials, and a variety of veterans' groups that included the US Grant Post of the Grand Army of the Republic. Approximately fifty thousand people attended the event. For all intents, it was an important moment in American history. But what was the purpose of such a large, solemn event? Was it a celebration of honorable service in the second war against England that city fathers voted to commemorate? Or was it a cynical device designed to deflect criticism of Tammany Hall corruption?

As the United States entered the twentieth century, veterans were at the center of a series of controversies about politics, public policy, and the proper direction of American society. Although veterans' benefits dramatically expanded in the years before World War I, not everyone supported social welfare in principle or practice. One of these influential voices was William Graham Sumner, a clergyman who preached the gospel of Social Darwinism. In his opinion, poverty was beneficial: "Certain ills belong to the hardships of human life. They are natural. They are part of the struggle with Nature for existence. We cannot blame our fellow men for our share of these." In an 1891 article for *The Century Illustrated Monthly Magazine*, William M. Sloan was equally blunt:

> Various trains of argument have been used to justify the indiscriminate and lavish distribution of pensions in which the national government has lately been indulging. Every intelligent man who is not blinded by partisanship apprehends the true cause—a determination to be rid of the Treasury surplus in any way productive of political results, and therefore under the guise of patriotic gratitude to secure the vote of the soldiers in the late war with it.

In a call back to the time following the American Revolution, he argued that men joined the military and accepted the risks of service. According to Sloan, a veteran, "is neither legally nor morally right in demanding a pension for disability, much less for service." Consequently, he considered veterans' pensions to be "socialism of an extreme and dangerous type."

For many Progressives and other critics, the post–Civil War pension system was also one of best examples of Gilded Age patronage and corruption. Such an immense, expensive system was ripe for abuse by an army of lobbyists. The Pension Bureau in particular became a magnet for late-nineteenth-century reformers interested in honesty, efficiency, and transparency. Federal officials tried to protect policy through "justice, and justice alone," but found their agency under constant siege from pension attorneys and claims houses bent on "perjury, forgery, bribery, and every species of available fraud." As a stream of scandals unfolded, many painted veterans and their advocates with the same brush. In this context, the Civil War soldier was "no better than [a] deserter, a straggler ... a coward." However, even the substantial weight of proof did not stop additions to veterans' benefits. As much as he believed in Progressivism, Theodore Roosevelt extended pensions to all veterans over the age of sixty-two by executive order in 1904.

The Civil War left a deep mark on the American idea of military service, patriotism, and manly behavior. William James captured these ideas in 1910 when he wrote, "Those ancestors, those efforts, those memories and legends, are the most ideal part of what we now own together, a sacred spiritual possession worth more than all the blood poured out." A few even reflected on how the absence of war might hurt the country's ability to withstand future threats to its survival. Oliver Wendell Holmes spoke in 1895 to the intrinsic value of war that was more personal in terms of what it defined:

> That the joy of life is living, is to put out all one's powers as far as they will go; that the measure of power is obstacles overcome; to ride boldly at what is in front of you, be it fence or enemy; to pray, not for comfort but for combat; to keep the soldier's faith against the doubts of civil life, more besetting and harder to overcome than all the misgivings of the battle-field, and to remember that duty is not to be proved in the evil day, but then to be obeyed unquestioningly; to love glory more than temptations of wallowing ease, but to know one's final judge and only rival is oneself.

Regardless of its impact, Americans recognized a clear hierarchy of its many nineteenth-century veterans. At the top of the pyramid stood the men who fought the Civil War. Frontier service might have provided plenty of grist for dime novels, but it did not gain much in the way of public acclaim or special benefits. Americans celebrated their entry into global power after the twin victories in Cuba and Manila, but very few counted that service on par with the aging generation of Union veterans. Region and race determined the lower reaches of the veterans' hierarchy. Washington did not count the hundreds of thousands of surviving Confederate veterans who were left to husband their resentments and subsist on the anemic support of their reconstructed states. African American veterans enjoyed a brief glimpse at their own agency before many old, racist practices snapped that door shut.

As American wars accumulated, so did veterans' organizations. After initially taking a few uncertain steps in its early years, the Grand Army of the Republic developed into a powerful and influential organization that set the pace for nineteenth-century veterans' groups. Other newer groups, such as the Veterans of Foreign Wars, joined the field, each intent on repeating the same success as the GAR.

Federal policy largely moved in sync with the country's growing population of veterans. With the 1862 Pension Law serving as both a precedent and foundation, the United States devoted enormous resources to this population, establishing its first dedicated national social welfare program. At the same time, veterans from older conflicts going as far back as 1812 finally received attention.

Yet, for all its growth and commitments, veterans' policy did not reflect a national consensus on benefits or service. Despite their honored status, veterans did not escape concerns that benefits impeded their personal autonomy. Reformers rightly contested the significant corruption that followed the millions of dollars dispensed through veterans' programs. Both of these debates would linger as Europe prepared for war in the new century.

5

The Great War

Out there, we walked quite friendly up to Death,
Sat down and ate beside him, cool and bland,
Pardoned his spilling mess-tins in our hand.
We've sniffed the green thick odour of his breath,
Our eyes wept but our courage didn't writhe.
He's spat at us with bullets, and he coughed
Shrapnel. We chorused if he sang aloft,
We whistled while he shaved us with his scythe.

WILFRED OWEN, "THE NEXT WAR," 1917

In 1917, the United States learned some of the important consequences of being a world power. When it joined England, France, Italy, and the other Entente nations, America committed the largest expeditionary force assembled in its history. Approximately four and a half million Americans served in the world war, with almost half deploying to France.

When the war began, many Americans entered it singing and cheering. Few living citizens, with the exception of the Civil War generation, could remember the costs involved in mass mobilization. For many young men, war offered the prospect a short-term adventure, as it had in Cuba. One of the most influential Americans at the time believed the stakes were larger. Theodore Roosevelt wrote at the start of 1917 that "For the sake of our own souls, for the sake of the memories of the great Americans of the past, we must show that we do not intend to make this merely a dollar war. Let us pay with our bodies for our soul's desire."

Much of this enthusiasm was encouraged by deliberate propaganda. George Creel, who led the Committee on Public Information, applauded the all-encompassing value of military service in 1917: "It makes better citizens, even while turning out fit defenders, invigorating and strengthening American manhood, and at the same time safeguarding American institutions. Service would have an invigorating effect on American men. Chests will deepen and shoulders broaden and eyes brighten." For many of these citizens, World War I was a conflict fought because, according to President Woodrow Wilson: "The world must be made safe for democracy."

Millions of Americans had a more personal interest in joining the fight. Military service was, as it had been for most of the country's history, a pathway to social legitimacy. In May 1918, Congress made enlistment a legal prerequisite for naturalization and citizenship. It was an important consideration in a country where 16 percent of the almost twenty-four million men eligible for the draft were immigrants. Between 1918 and 1920, 244,300 veterans became citizens this way.

World War I had a significant influence on both America's standing in the world and expectations regarding postwar domestic affairs. The Wilson administration invested billions of dollars into training, armaments, transportation, and communications for the military force that won the war. It mobilized millions of its citizens—farmers, factory workers, and many others—who had contributed, often at great personal sacrifice, to this victory. Overall, the unprecedented collective achievements of World War I established basic expectations for what the United States might achieve in the future.

Veterans' policy was a product of these times. After 1918, the intent was to build veterans' programs beyond compensation for service or wounds suffered during the war. Many Americans were influenced by the belief that appropriately designed and implemented social policies could not just rehabilitate the wounded and injured, but also improve an individual's standing and, by extension, society and a whole. While the war had ripped away some of the high-minded faith in human nature, it refocused reformers on practical, pragmatic, grassroots reform. In the human disaster that was World War I, many Americans saw an opportunity to shape and improve the peace. Veterans were to be an important part of this plan.

The Nature of Industrial War

Military historian J. F. C. Fuller captured the paradox that confronted all the nations engaged in World War I:

> Their carefully planned war was ... smashed to pieces by firepower ... so devastating that ... there was no choice but to go under the surface ... like foxes. Then ... to secure these trenches from surprise ... each side ... spun hundreds of thousands of miles of steel web around its entrenchments ... Armies, through their own lack of foresight, were reduced to the position of human cattle. They browsed behind their fences and occasionally snorted and bellowed at each other.

The Great War saw many existing tools repurposed for the sake of conflict. Accompanying the "steel web" of barbed wire was an extensive network of telephone land lines to coordinate artillery fire and infantry assaults. The industrial age made its own contributions to the weapons of war. The machine-gun, rapidfire artillery, and poison gas magnified the lethality of combat on an order of magnitude from past conflicts.

Neither the generals nor their soldiers were prepared for modern war. Existing training and doctrine, basically an artifact from the previous century, failed to comprehend existing reality. In his excellent *Eye Deep in Hell*, John Ellis explains what came next:

For the officers of 1914—still the commanders of 1918—their conception of war was based upon the memories of Waterloo or before. They pictured, above all, a warfare in which man himself, *en masse*, was the decisive element. They yearned for the glorious charge, particularly by the cavalry, in which the courage and impetus of man and beast was sufficient to bring victory. They revered the bayonet and the *arme blanche* as a more than adequate response to anything produced by the technological revolution.

Meantime, life in the trenches was constant struggle to survive and adapt. Soldiers wrestled with the burden of personal equipment, which could easily equal half as much as their weight. They tried to avoid random death from artillery bombardments and shrapnel, or gas attacks. During the intervals between bombardments, men in the trenches worked to keep nature at bay. They fought water in the low-lying areas of Flanders or the endless parade of rats, lice, and vermin that challenged a soldier's daily existence. Life in "No Man's Land" was alternately wet, dirty, boring, and terrifying.

The resulting human toll was massive. Although estimates vary, the military forces involved in World War I suffered as many as 37.5 million casualties, which may have included approximately 10 million dead. For American forces, the carnage came as a shock. The Second Battle of the Marne (1918), which resulted in almost 40,000 American casualties, was on par with Gettysburg half a century earlier. Overall, a total of 204,002 Americans were wounded during the war, along with 116,516 who died of combat, disease, or illness.

These significant amounts represented a minority of the US forces mobilized for the war. Fewer than half of the 4.7 million Americans mobilized actually deployed to France and, of these, 1.2 million saw action.

The types of wounds and injuries varied among the hundreds of thousands returning home. Approximately 5,000 men were amputees. Disease plagued American forces and, much like the Civil War and the Spanish-American War, caused more fatalities than combat. Tuberculosis was a major source of illness and disability, accounting for 15 percent of American casualties. Although the final statistics may never be clear, as many as 70,000 Americans were affected by post-traumatic stress, "shell shock" to use the contemporary term.

Homecoming: 1919

The America awaiting its returning veterans was a much changed place from what they left behind. As it ramped down wartime production, mass layoffs followed, and the country descended in to a recession. Inflation was a daily and serious reality. In Seattle, rapidly rising housing and food prices triggered a general strike, which Mayor Ole Hanson denounced as a Bolshevik plot. According to Robert Murray, the cost of living for an American family was 99 percent higher in 1919 than it was when the war began. In the first year of peace, the country was engulfed by 3,600 strikes involving four million workers.

Social conflict also roiled the American landscape. Race riots flared in St. Louis (July 1917), Chicago (July–August 1919), and Washington (July 1919), resulting in hundreds of dead and injured. Overall, according to Jennifer Keene, there were twenty-five such bloody clashes around the country in the second half of 1919 alone. African American veterans were often caught up in the violence. Mobs lynched at least seventy-seven African Americans, of whom eleven were veterans. Bud Johnson, a Florida veteran, was actually burned at the stake in his Army uniform in 1919. Harry Haywood, a member of the Illinois 370th Infantry Regiment, recently returned from France, commented at the time, "the war and the riots of the 'Red Summer' of 1919 left me bitter and frustrated. I felt that I could never again adjust to the situation of black inequality."

Capping this moment of historic upheaval was the Red Scare and a pandemic. In the spring of 1919, the US postal service discovered and confiscated dozens of letter bombs addressed public officials, judges, and business leaders. John

D. Rockefeller and J. P. Morgan were among the potential recipients. Each package was seven inches long and three inches wide and marked with the return address "Gimbel Brothers." Inside was a wooden tube filled with high explosives. The bomb scare, which continued into the summer, accelerated an atmosphere of paranoia about loyalty and subversion present throughout the war. Meanwhile, the Spanish Flu arrived in America. Influenza wreaked havoc throughout the country, accounting for at least 675,000 deaths.

Millions of returning World War I veterans demobilized into this maelstrom without a coherent plan. When the war ended, almost 600,000 troops were immediately sent home. Within a year, most of the massive army built to fight in France had vanished back into society. The rapid process may have satisfied impatient families and veterans, but it also invoked significant and personal consequences. The War Department estimated that 41 percent of veterans were unemployed by April 1919.

Just how vulnerable a restive veterans' population without good economic prospects might be to radicalism was a question of great concern. Assistant Secretary of War, Colonel Arthur Woods, wrote that "the soldier is unsteady … he is wayward and impatient and unsettled … We cannot let them alone to wander about the streets and listen to the Bolsheviki." How might policy avoid this outcome?

It was a critical question at an equally critical moment. As Scott Gelber has argued, wartime mobilization and combat forged a "mutually binding covenant" between the soldier and the state. The scope and scale of the sacrifices made in the trenches of the Western Front established the baseline for expectations in peacetime. One veteran put it this way: "All we seek is justice and justice likewise demands that some of these [war] profits be now conscripted to pay this debt to the returned soldier." The next step involved finding a way to implement this contract, return former soldiers back into the civilian fold, and avoid the potential problems of social, economic, and political instability.

Veterans' Advocates and the Great War

Most American soldiers returning home from Europe or domestic military duties mustered out from one of thirty-three camps scattered around the country. Each man received a new uniform, shoes, a coat, and a $60 bonus. From that point, the newly minted veteran was usually a train ride away from home.

A number of existing and newly formed veterans' organizations saw a unique opportunity in this moment. The sheer volume of discharged men presented both new constituents in need of real help as well as an incredible recruiting opportunity for thousands of new dues-paying members. The Veterans of Foreign Wars jumped at the opportunity to expand beyond its original contingent of Spanish-American War soldiers, sailors, and marines. In January 1919, the VFW began a campaign to increase its membership to two million, recognizing the chance to become the "new Grand Army of the Republic."

While it moved forward, the VFW shared the stage with rivals both small and large. The Private Soldiers and Sailors' Legion appeared shortly after the armistice and grew to almost 100,000 members. It recruited veterans specifically aligned with unions such the American Federation of Labor and the Amalgamated Metal Workers of America.

In the spring of 1919, the American Legion joined the fray. Its founders included Medal of Honor winner Alvin York, Theodore Roosevelt, Jr., fresh from his service with the 1st Division on the Western Front, Henry Stimson (Secretary of State under Herbert Hoover and Secretary of War for Franklin Roosevelt), and William J. Donovan (later head of the O.S.S.). Roosevelt described the Legion's initial purpose in a *New York Times* article. It was

> an association which should keep alive the principles of justice, freedom and democracy for which these veterans fought; to preserve to future generations the history and incidents of their participation in the war; and to cement and perpetuate the ties of comradeship formed in service.

The intent was for the Legion to be a nonpartisan advocate. Its first national commander, Franklin D'Olier, spoke to veterans' status and its relationship with American society in December 1919:

> The American Legion represents nearly 5,000,000 citizens who have demonstrated their loyalty and patriotism. We realize, however, that there are 100,000,000 other Americans just as patriotic and loyal. We represented the spear point, keen and true, and back of us was the power of the whole nation at war. Our effectiveness against the enemy was in proportion to the strength of the country back of us.
>
> And now we must realize that the strength of the legion and our influence and service to the nation will be measured only by our ability to co-operate effectively with the 100,000,000 other loyal and patriotic American citizens in the promotion of 100 per cent. Americanism and the maintenance of law and order.

The Legion also offered itself as a big tent to other older veterans and their organizations. It welcomed both the Grand Army of the Republic (GAR) and former Confederates to its first annual convention in Minneapolis in 1919. To drum up new recruits, the junior Roosevelt visited thirty states to spread the word and recruit new additions to the Legion. Along the way, he gained an important public endorsement from *Chicago Tribune* owner Robert McCormick.

By September 1919, the Legion claimed some 600,000 members. Shortly afterward, New York delegate George Brokaw Compton told newspapers that his organization "has firmly taken root in every county in every State, and soon every local community will have at least one local post."

The American Legion was more than ready to flex its organizational muscle after World War I. Rhetorically, its leadership promised to apply the experience of war for the betterment of American society. The social, economic, and political tumult evident around the country presented a unique, self-declared mission: preventing radicalism. Like the Veterans of Foreign Wars, the Legion promised to be a bastion of stability. At its first national conference, Legion national commander Franklin D'Olier asserted that his veterans were "ready for action at any time... against these extremists who are seeking to overturn a government... for which thousands of brave young Americans laid down their lives." Many Legion chapters took it upon themselves to act as a counterbalance against unionists and radical unions like the International Workers of the World (IWW), otherwise known as the "Wobblies." In November 1919, police in Spokane, Washington went so far as to start deputizing members of the Legion to serve with the National Guard against rumors of an impending IWW "invasion" of the city. A number of unions retaliated against Legion assistance with strikebreaking and anti-labor actions in New York, Kansas, Massachusetts, Oregon, and Washington state. Detroit Local 127 of the Automobile, Aircraft and Vehicle Workers of America assessed a $100 fine for all members who refused to resign their membership from the veterans' organization.

As it developed its role as a protector of American democracy, the Legion also wove itself into the nation's social safety net. Local Legion posts served as places where unemployed veterans could network and find jobs. When federal assistance fell short, they served as advocates. A Legion report published in late 1919 leveled particular criticism at the War Risk Insurance Bureau:

> The strongest indictment against the bureau lies in the distress its delinquency has brought upon crippled veterans, through sluggish action on disability claims. The situation dates back to the period of the partnership, dictated by a ridiculous law, between the bureau and the Federal Board for Vocational Education, by which two mutually inefficient organizations share the responsibility for the disabled man's welfare.

However, the Legion was not always critical. The same report noted some progress in processing veterans' claims with the government. To help out, the Legion maintained staff in each state to assist veterans when filing paperwork with the bureau. In the meantime, the Legion began what would be a continuous lobbying campaign for better benefits. A month after its first national convention, Legion representatives met with members of the House and Senate about the need for action regarding disabled veterans, specifically "compensation, hospitalization, medical care, and vocational training on an adequate and liberal basis."

Beyond the immediate needs of national stability and veterans' compensation, the Grand Army of the Republic, the VFW, and the American Legion also took an active role in the national discussion about military service and patriotism. Every major veterans' organization participated in the inauguration of the Tomb of the Unknown Soldier in 1921.

The Legion took its campaign into classrooms, pledging its desire to "eradicate illiteracy" and teach "American history and civil government in all schools." Their interest was not altogether neutral. At its second annual convention, delegates passed a resolution that "the English language be the controlling medium of instruction in all schools of elementary and high school grade, both public and private." More pointedly, its Committee on Anti-American Propaganda encouraged a "continuous, constructive educational system" and curriculum to "Foster and Perpetuate a 100% Americanism."

African American Veterans, Service, and the American Legion

For African American veterans, the meaning of World War I recalled their contributions and subsequent expectations in earlier conflicts. Willis Goodwin, who served in the Illinois 370th Infantry Regiment, echoed a sentiment heard often after the Civil War: "after the fighting, and my return to this country [the] U.S., it made me wonder why can't all men be treated equally. What did we fight for? Democracy. Are we living it?" Writing in May 1919, W. E. B. Du Bois grasped the moment in his "Returning Soldiers":

We return,

We return from fighting.

We return fighting.

William M. Colson was another Black veteran who had the rare opportunity to serve as an officer in the 92nd Division. As a writer for A. Philip Randolph's journal *The Messenger*, he saw many opportunities coming from the wartime experience. Peace offered a chance to secure earned rewards, particularly compensation for wounds and injuries. More to the point, Colson believed that African American veterans could obtain a meaningful voice in public affairs. The Black veteran could "cut a wedge into the American Legion if he joins in sufficient numbers." As citizens, they might begin "a new law and order in the South." Colson believed that "the returned black veteran, by virtue of his service and experience, has a certain special function which he cannot afford to fail to press to the limit."

Sadly, too much of the country rejected Colson's optimism. Segregation remained firmly entrenched in the South and more than a few other places in America. Black veterans found federal officials actively resisting their attempts to obtain job training in order to improve their prospects. African Americans wounded in combat or sick as a result of their service were rewarded with substandard medical treatment in segregated hospital wards. One veteran in Hampton, Virginia complained that "we are invariabl[y] received and treated as a colored man and not a disabled soldier."

Thousands of African Americans joined the American Legion for the sake of their own advocacy but discovered that the new, rapidly expanding organization was unprepared to welcome them as equals. The original Legion constitution did not mention race in its membership criteria:

> Any person shall be eligible for membership in the American Legion who was regularly enlisted, drafted, inducted or commissioned, and who served on active duty in the Army, Navy or Marine Corps of the United States at some time during the period between April 6th 1917, and November 11th 1918 ...

However, the national leadership temporized by leaving membership standards to individual states. Southern states either required segregated posts or, like Louisiana, refused to allow African American posts at all.

Faced with these obstacles, African American veterans sought out their own alternatives, in some cases following the same affirmative logic as the American Legion. At the end of the war while awaiting transport home, African American officers and men often met in secret to discuss racism in the military and at home. One group of Black veterans in Harlem founded the League for Democracy in March 1919. The short-lived organization, according to historian Chad L. Brown, "appealed directly to black veterans' sense of martial collectivity and sought to harness their political energy." When traditional action failed, small numbers of African American veterans joined radical organizations. A few gravitated to the National Colored Soldiers and Citizens Council, the paramilitary African Black Brotherhood, and the Communist Party.

When the American Legion rebuffed them and smaller alternatives proved inadequate, many African American veterans gravitated to the National Association for the Advancement of Colored People (NAACP). Founded in 1909, its membership swelled from 9,200 in 1918 to more than 62,000 a year later, bolstered in part by men fresh from the Great War. It investigated cases of violence and promoted anti-lynching legislation to protect members of the armed forces. In the twenties, the NAACP directly intervened in many cases where African Americans filed complaints about medical care in the new federal Veterans Bureau.

Like their Civil War predecessors who came into peacetime two generations earlier, African Americans of the Great War had many hopes that curdled in the face of the social, economic, and political realities of their time. Federal veterans' programs kept the standard of being separate and unequal from the mainstream of the millions who served. The same rule applied to private organizations—the American Legion foremost—created to serve their needs. Unfortunately, these same obstacles would linger and await the next generation of African American veterans during and after World War II.

The Evolution of World War I Veterans' Policies and Programs

Like in the Civil War, the federal government did not wait for peace to begin constructing veterans' policies. Lawmakers approached it as a practical duty. Mobilization for the sake of veterans was part of the overall national effort to sustain American involvement in World War I. National action was also essential because the conflict dwarfed the scale of private charity. The American Red Cross started the Institute for Crippled Men in 1917 during the first deployment of the American Expeditionary Force, but soon found itself overwhelmed by the sheer number of casualties. Ongoing rivalries and turf battles did not help private charities. It was not uncommon for local chambers of commerce to refuse to work with the US Employment Service because they associated the agency with unionism.

Even as the federal government devoted increasing resources to the growing influx of veterans, national policy, such as it was, did not belong to a single office. Instead, a constellation of separate agencies, including the War, Treasury, Interior, and Labor departments, as well as the US Public Health Service, tried to address a host of needs, from health care to vocational rehabilitation and employment.

For many veterans, military medicine was the first contact with this system. Wounded taken from the front line received trauma care and basic stabilization from hospital units deployed along with American forces in France. From that point, long-term treatment was a more problematic exercise. When it was founded in 1909, Walter Reed was intended to apply the hard-won medical lessons of the Spanish-American War, what the Dodge Report called the "criminal neglect" of the sick and wounded, by incorporating the modern practices of twentieth-century medicine. It would be a pioneer for permanent facilities that both treated individuals and trained a new generation of physicians. Still, its first version had only eighty beds.

Rapid adaptation followed American entry into the war. Even before the first units of the American Expeditionary Force deployed to Europe, teams of American doctors visited England to observe British treatment practices. Their wartime experiences returned home where they were incorporated into medical curriculum.

The United States was unique among the Allied nations in that it made rehabilitation mandatory for its injured soldiers. The Army Medical Department created the Division of Special Hospitals and Physical Reconstruction in 1917. Walter Reed augmented its own facilities with an artificial limb lab in 1918 intended to improve existing prostheses. Over the next two years, 120,000 soldiers received treatment through physical and occupational therapy, "curative workshops" in the terminology of the time, and other programs dedicated to recouping some degree of normalcy. The American military took it as an article of faith that medical treatment could return war wounded back to a productive civilian life.

American doctors, like their European counterparts, struggled with "shell shock," a term that broadly covered the mental trauma caused by the incessant trench warfare of World War I. The malady, which one British soldier described his as a "mental internment camp," affected thousands of returning veterans.

Treatment reflected both modern science and contemporary ignorance about post-traumatic disorders. For example, progressives within the medical community acknowledged the need to refashion "mental hygiene" within the field of psychiatry. Doctors examining World War I veterans, much like those treating PTSD casualties after September 11, recognized the correlation between shell shock and preexisting conditions carried from civilian life into military service.

A number of factors worked against these fairly advanced and nuanced approaches. The conventional medical wisdom of 1918 held that wartime neurosis was a temporary and treatable medical problem. A second obstacle was administrative. Mental health care was routinely subject to staff shortages and a lack of trained staff. At Camp Grant, Illinois, one physician kept pace by conducting intake exams of men in groups of fifteen. Perhaps the most formidable barrier to WWI veterans was cultural. Even when appropriate treatment was possible, veterans returned to an American society vested in preserving "masculine dignity," a standard that placed a premium of stoic self-sufficiency at the expense of therapeutic candor.

Once they left uniformed service, veterans' care fell to a number of federal, state, and private programs. Wounded men entered the US Public Health Service, which maintained partnerships with hundreds of civilian hospitals for the treatment of physical and mental illness after the war. A far more elaborate veterans' safety net appeared through the 1917 version of the War Risk Insurance Act, what historian Beth Linker has described as "a piece of Progressive Era legislation par excellence." Approved by Congress without a single "no" vote, the law contained three main components. It mandated allotments of $15 or at least half pay each month to a soldier's family while he was deployed on active duty. It provided voluntary disability insurance paid for by individual soldiers. The law also revisited the old Civil War era law by allowing for disability compensation based on a published standard of types and degree. At the end of World War I, the act was budgeted at a formidable $450 million.

In general, World War I programs were far more ambitious than Civil War era legislation. The Vocational Rehabilitation Act (1918), which followed the War Risk Insurance Act, for example, created mechanisms to either help veterans return to their prewar occupations or train them in new ones if they were unable to do so. The law gave federal job counselors significant discretion to determine career possibilities for handicapped men.

A growing array of federal agencies shepherded these new programs. The War Department established an Emergency Employment Committee for Soldiers, Sailors, and Marines of the Council of National Defense in March 1919. Its job was to coordinate with federal agencies that included the Departments of Agriculture, Labor, Interior, and the US Post Office. In its first year of operation, the committee sent press releases to thousands of newspapers and contacted additional thousands of private businesses, offering incentives for cooperation. In a move that no doubt created some confusion for veterans, the Bureau of War Risk Insurance, as part of the Treasury Department, shared responsibility for death and disability payments with the Bureau of Pensions in the Interior Department.

Job training and placement was a major enterprise of new federal programs. At the end of the war, the US Employment Service added a special branch for veterans, the Bureau for Returning Soldiers, Sailors, and Marines. It joined the Federal Board of Vocational Education (FBVE), created in 1917 and comprised of representatives from commerce, labor, agriculture, and education to address the significant need for skills in the industrial workplace. Both acted as important venues for veterans' rehabilitation.

The home front was well prepared for job training, especially for injured and crippled men. Despite years of labor reforms, the American workplace was an extremely dangerous place in the early twentieth century. The year the FBVE was created, American workers suffered 875,000 job accidents that left 74,530 permanently disabled. In comparison, during the first year of American combat in World War I, 24,541 soldiers were discharged for disability from wounds.

Like their crippled civilian counterparts, disabled veterans might go back to their old jobs or learn a new vocation. Training had multiple purposes. As historian Michael J. Lansing notes, engineers such as Frank Gilbreth saw technology—in the form of artificial limbs—as a solution for both the worker and the workplace to become more efficient. Beyond simple functional economic skills, rehabilitation was an opportunity to make veterans' lives better. It could transform him and make the veteran a contributing, productive member of society. With help, the returned veteran might regain his status as a breadwinner able to support a family.

However, the path to a restored life was anything but easy. Veterans' communications skills, in a military where recruits spoke dozens of languages and dialects, proved to be a severe obstacle to vocational training. Worse still was the common practice among federal counselors to deny requests for training as "non-feasible," that might move an individual into white-collar work. Faced with this resistance to self-improvement, many disabled veterans simply dropped out of federal programs or did not enroll.

World War I had an impact on lives that was unimaginable before 1914. Millions marched off to war and millions suffered the consequences, both on the battlefield and on home fronts around the world. Whole dynasties collapsed and revolutions, chronic instability, and prolonged suffering became the rule in many places. The influenza pandemic was a final, devastating blow to an already reeling globe. Although the United States entered the war late, it did not escape its own reckoning.

New veterans' organizations benefited from the scale of wartime mobilization. The Grand Army of the Republic was passing from the stage by 1918, displaced in numbers and influence by younger, much larger organizations. The American Legion and the Veterans of Foreign Wars entered the postwar era with an ambitious social agenda and the political clout to match. They would embrace much of the old GAR platform regarding patriotism, education, and advocacy of veterans' causes.

The breadth of American veterans' needs—from compensation for service-related disability to vocational training—mandated assistance through federal agencies. Although a broad variety of private charities existed for the sake of assistance, only the US government had the financial resources and reach appropriate to the task. Consequently, the federal welfare state grew ever more elaborate by virtue of veterans' programs. In the years after the war, for example, approximately 1.3 million veterans registered with the Bureau for Returning Soldiers, Sailors, and Marines. The agency eventually placed 949,901 in jobs.

It was clear that, although America rallied to "make the world safe for democracy," the country lacked a consensus when it came to helping its veterans. Race and class were among the most obvious points of division. Other concerns emerged over costs, to society, good governance, and the treasury. Writing in August 1918, Teddy Roosevelt worried that "mere sentimental pampering would be ruinous to the men and to the commonwealth." Given the proposed expense of government programs, Progressive skepticism about corruption was redoubled in the new twentieth century. The overall cost also caused many lawmakers to pause. Total federal payments for Civil War veterans actually peaked in 1916 at $5 billion, an amount, according to historian Beth Linker, that exceeded the actual cost of the war. Overall, in 1914, federal payments to all veterans were $172.4 million of $689.8 million in total federal expenditures (24.9 percent), a proportion that would remain consistent for most of the decade following the war.

As the United States entered the twenties, its veterans presented an interesting dilemma. Americans craved a return to peace, something veterans also wanted but, in many cases, needed time to achieve. The country made a commitment to this process in the form of substantial budgets for a plethora of federal agencies. A cultural shift was more difficult. To help them along the way, civilian society needed to recognize this trauma, a pursuit many deemed "unfashionable" in the words of historian Eric Leed.

6

The Interwar Period

> *A nation without heroes is a nation without a history and a nation without a history is a nation without patriotism, and must fall. The heroes of the world have opened the way for the triumphant march of civilization, and the nation whose people are proud of their heroic ancestry will always produce heroes.*

ALVIN OWSLEY, AMERICAN LEGION, ARMISTICE DAY, GREENVILLE, TEXAS, 1920

At the start of the twenties, Americans craved distance from the Great War. When he ran for president in 1920, Warren Harding captured the mood of the country perfectly and built his platform on the idea of "normalcy."

> America's present need is not heroics, but healing; not nostrums, but normalcy; not revolution, but restoration; not agitation, but adjustment; not surgery, but serenity; not the dramatic, but the dispassionate; not experiment, but equipoise; not submergence in internationality, but sustainment in triumphant nationality.

Veterans wanted normalcy just as much as anyone else, a goal motivated by the price they paid during the First World War. Millions returned home to restart their lives, build families, and take advantage of the new opportunities presented during the Roaring Twenties. Many did so with the help of vocational training, job placement, and rehabilitation courtesy of the federal government. These programs redefined the meaning of social security and set basic expectations for veterans between the world wars.

It was not always an easy path. Successive Republican administrations focused on deregulation and reducing the federal government's role in daily life and were very reluctant to expand programs created during World War I. The Great Depression tested the relationship between veterans and conservatives in government further, ultimately resulting in a disastrous confrontation with the Hoover administration during the tragic Bonus March of 1932. For all intents, Franklin Roosevelt's incoming New Deal offered veterans the prospect of relief. In practice, however, their place in the new Roosevelt coalition was problematic from the start.

Commemoration and the Lost Generation

As they had in the past, veterans of World War I saw peacetime as an opportunity to celebrate the country and consolidate their strength. The Grand Army of the Republic, the Veterans of Foreign Wars, the American Legion, and other veterans' organizations were fixtures in annual celebrations of service and American patriotism. The opportunities to do so multiplied after the Great War. Veterans marched in ranks, by post, in honor guards, and as individuals on Memorial Day, Fourth of July, and Armistice Day (November 11). As late as September 1932, eight hundred aged members of the GAR showed up to parade in Springfield, Illinois and took it as a point of pride that only five of their number did not complete the one-mile procession.

Both the American Legion and the VFW commonly used historical themes to celebrate the country and the value of democratic ideals. One Legion post from Racine, Wisconsin built a float in which veterans posed as bronze statues of American Revolutionary War heroes. A Minnesota post took its re-creation in a different direction, with a display that depicted the Battle of Belleau

Wood: "Helmeted fighting men and bandaged wounded added to the thrill which the float gave to those who watched it in a parade." Other veterans took this approach a few steps further. It was not uncommon for various groups to conduct "sham battles" for onlookers. Other posts sponsored marksmanship contests. Sports, which included baseball and the highly popular game of football, rounded out these events.

American Legion baseball became an ongoing project to pass along patriotic values and the principle of teamwork to American youth. When it began in 1926, American Legion youth baseball was intended as a civilizing experience for both veterans and their young charges. Veterans, whose military experience embodied what one historian called the "essence of good citizenship" became mentors on the playing field. Legion-sponsored leagues across the country embraced the idea that good character could be taught. The effort was informed by two articles of faith common to the time. The first was the old Progressive ideal that an individual could learn something by doing it. Secondly, Legion leaders believed that well-disciplined training, incorporating the simplicity and practicality that defined their own military experience, could lead to a defined outcome. In essence, by joining a Legion team, a young boy could improve both his athleticism and social virtues.

The twenties, like the Gilded Age, also saw a boom in war art. Memorial depictions of the Doughboy as a "common man" recalled the Union soldier of the Civil War. The heroic figure represented a combination of the "self-reliance of manhood" and American exceptionalism. While generally popular among the lay public, the trend irritated many artistic luminaries, like Charles Moore, head of the National Commission of Fine Arts, who complained about the "plague of war memorials."

Not every American, veteran or otherwise, wanted the celebrate the Great War. Ernest Hemingway, who served as an ambulance driver in Italy, spoke for many of his comrades in "The Age Demanded" (1925):

> The age demanded that we sing
> and cut away our tongue
> The age demanded that we flow
> and hammered in the bung.
> The age demanded that we dance
> and jammed us into iron pants.
> And in the end the age was handed
> the sort of shit that it demanded.

Erich Maria Remarque's widely read *All Quiet on the Western Front* expanded on this theme as it related the wartime experiences of a German soldier, Paul Bäumer. The book was intended, the author noted, "Neither as an accusation nor as a confession, but simply as an attempt to give an account of a generation that was destroyed by the war—even those of it who survived the shelling." World War I memoirs and literature testified to a crisis of faith, in science, industry, rationalism, and progress in general. They challenged, as one historian put it, "this reassuring sense of temporal continuity between past, present, and future."

Popular fiction associated future war with the apocalypse. H. G. Wells's *The Shape of Things to Come* (1933) saw a final conflict as almost inevitable: "War was manifestly drawing nearer, in Eastern Asia, in Eastern Europe; it loitered, it advanced, it halted, and no one displayed the vigour or capacity needed to avert its intermittent, unhurrying approach."

In the end, these approaches to war and military service produced an ambivalence among Americans between the world wars. Many celebrated their pride in the developing sense of modern American patriotism. For others, as Paul Fussell notes in *Wartime: Understanding and Behavior in the Second World War*, particularly veterans of World War I, service was a cautionary tale, something to warn the next generation of young men against. These contradictory stances help explain why so few sang and celebrated when the final battle lines were drawn in 1939.

Growth and Expansion of the Veterans' Lobby

In the two decades between the world wars, the American Legion, the Veterans of Foreign Wars, and other smaller veterans' advocacies broadened and deepened their role in the public sphere. A November 1923 edition of the *American Legion Weekly* listed just a portion of an ambitious agenda. Setting a position regarding military readiness, the Legion supported "an adequate national defense on land, sea, and air." At home, it desired "a nationwide program of community welfare." The Legion stood against child labor and any organization that promoted "racial, religious, or class strife," which included, at the time, the Ku Klux Klan.

The Legion devoted particular energy to the meaning of American citizenship. As noted in the previous chapter, its civic displays of "Americanism" were common in school curriculum, park statuary, and patriotic music played during municipal concerts. The Legion sponsored Boy Scout troops and youth rifle clubs.

The immigration question was a favorite Legion topic. The organization unsuccessfully lobbied for mandatory civics classes for immigrants in twelve states. It also wanted English language instruction for new arrivals, which Legion national commander Alvin M. Owsley characterized as "the language of Lincoln ... the first step in Americanization." The Legion supported citizenship for some veterans who were new or recent immigrants, but not immigration as a whole. At its 1921 national meeting, leadership noted that "we declare ourselves in favor of the exclusion of all aliens for a period of five years; provided, however, that the father, mother, sister, wife or husband of an American citizen be allowed admission."

The Legion's underlying philosophy on immigration appeared in an August 1923 *American Legion Weekly* article by a "noted biologist," Dr. Edwin Grant Conklin. He described the risks of "humanitarian idealism as applied to immigration," describing new arrivals to America as "social parasites" who placed an unsupportable burden on "prisons, reformatories, and almshouses." Stripped of his academic veneer, Conklin was a Social Darwinist, arguing that immigration had "debased" the country's "human stock" rather than improve it.

He was not on the fringe of American thought, specifically regarding veterans who were not citizens when they joined the military. The conventional wisdom of the moment, including contemporary racial beliefs, shaped just how the federal government applied naturalization and citizenship to veterans. According to lawmakers, this meant veterans who were considered "white" or of African origin. Historian Nancy Gentile Ford notes this meant most of the 18 percent of the military during World War I (approximately 500,000 total) who were born in forty-six different countries. However, naturalization rights did not apply to veterans of Asian birth, an issue that was finally resolved by the Nye-Lea Act in 1935.

Beyond education and immigration, veterans' groups focused their efforts on expanding federal benefits. The Legion was a key force behind a 1919 proposal that all veterans receive a "bonus" of cash for their services. Political momentum favored them. Between 1918 and 1921, thirty-eight states passed some form of veterans' compensation legislation. Programs ranged between a one-time payment—Maine, Massachusetts, and Rhode Island set the amount at $100—to monthly allotments based upon total time spent in uniform during the Great War. The fact that the Legion claimed that it could muster as many as five million votes in 1920 made aspiring politicians take note.

Federal action proved more difficult, however. The House of Representatives approved a $2 billion bill for additional veterans' benefits in the summer of 1920. When word of the vote came to him, Warren Harding balked at the prospect of spending more money on top of the billions already allocated by the government for veterans. As a candidate during his 1920 campaign, Harding promised improvements to federal policy and, during his nomination acceptance speech, he singled out veterans: "they command our pride, they have our gratitude, which must have genuine expression. It is not only a duty, it is a privilege to see that the sacrifices made shall be requited, and that those still suffering from casualties and disability shall be abundantly aided and restore to the highest capabilities of citizenship and its enjoyment."

Gratitude had its limits. The president concurred with Treasury Secretary Andrew Mellon that tax cuts—both reductions in excess profits taxes and corporate taxes—were necessary to help the economy out of its postwar recession. A more pressing concern was the national debt, which had expanded from $1.2 billion in 1914 to $24 billion by 1920. Consequently, when the House bill on a veterans' bonus went to the Senate, Harding took the rare step of speaking directly to the body in order to quash the measure, arguing that it would break the federal budget. Harding pointed out that the federal government had already spent significant sums on its veterans. Claims from 813,442 veterans were on record with approximately $500 million in benefits already paid. The president noted that 107,824 veterans had already enrolled in vocational and rehabilitation programs. As far as Harding was concerned, Washington was doing its job. He eventually vetoed the veterans' bill in September 1922.

His decision had significant political consequences. The Republican Party experienced crushing losses in the midterm elections that year. Eight senators and seventy-five representatives lost their seats.

In the end, Congress passed a form of the bonus legislation shortly after Harding's death. The World War Adjusted Compensation Act of 1924 promised payment—in what was called Adjusted Service Certificates—for wages lost by veterans who served in World War I. It provided $1.25 a day up to $625 for overseas time and as much as $500 for those who did not deploy to Europe. However, because federal lawmakers were unwilling to address the immediate costs of the act, they deferred payment for most veterans until 1945.

The Veterans Bureau

When World War I ended and America settled back into the rhythms of peacetime, there was time to think about how the country could improve its approach to veterans. During the war, Washington had committed hundreds of millions of dollars to both compensate veterans for their service and ease their path back into civilian life. A potpourri of federal agencies both old and new oversaw these efforts, sometimes at cross-purposes. It was a well-meaning system, but one filled with too many well-publicized redundancies and inefficiencies. To remedy these problems and provide direction for a growing body of former military men and women, Congress created the Veterans Bureau in 1921.

Leadership fell to Charles R. Forbes, who served as the first director of the Bureau. Forbes was an interesting character in an administration filled with them. As a young man of just fifteen, he joined the Marine Corps as an apprentice musician. In 1896, after a freak accident, Forbes developed pneumonia and received a medical discharge, which qualified him for a disability pension. Later service in the Army Signal Corps exposed him to some of the era's most advanced communication technology. As a civilian, Forbes worked for the Hurley-Mason Company in the Pacific Northwest and was later directly involved in the construction of the Pearl Harbor naval base. Both experiences provided valuable experience and future temptation. During World War I, Forbes rejoined the Signal Corps and served in the 41st and 33rd divisions, earning the Distinguished Service Medal as well as the French Croix de Guerre while in France. At the time of his appointment to lead the Veterans Bureau, he seemed to be a good fit for an organization with a $450 million budget and 30,000 employees.

At the start of his tenure, Forbes pursued reasonable reforms. The Bureau consolidated some existing programs, taking over the functions of the Federal Board for Vocational Education and the Bureau of War Risk Insurance. At the same time, Forbes launched a "clean-up" campaign that addressed the tens of thousands of veterans who had not applied for benefits because they were uninformed or ignorant of existing programs. In its first year, the campaign reached 179,868 veterans and processed 48,958 new claims. In the meantime, the Bureau made improvements to rehabilitation programs, job training, and placement.

Federal officials devoted significant attention to veterans' medical treatment. The Bureau transferred fifty-seven hospitals from the US Public Health Service to its direct control. It additionally coordinated care with hundreds of private hospitals throughout the country for the physical and mental casualties of the war, the latter including as many as 70,000 veterans suffering from "shell shock." As the decade progressed, Bureau officials estimated a need for at least 10,000 additional hospital beds to meet ongoing veterans' care.

Unfortunately, not all the news was good, particularly with respect to the Bureau's director. In an administration infamous for scandal, he somehow found a way to stand out among his peers. Forbes used his short time in office as a for-profit enterprise. He received a loan of $5,000 in exchange for granting preference to the Thomas-Black Company for Veterans' Bureau hospital construction contracts. Forbes made similar deals with his old employer, the Hurley-Mason Company. He was directly involved in a land speculation scheme whereby the government paid $105,000 for a plot valued at less than $20,000. Later investigation revealed plans that include selling warehouses in Perryville, Maryland, containing hospital supplies for the Public Health Service. The Senate began its own inquiry of Forbes in October 1923, just three months after Harding's death. Forbes was eventually convicted in 1926 of stealing almost $2 million in federal funds and served twenty months in prison at Ft. Leavenworth.

A new round of reforms followed the scandal. The Hoover administration created the Veterans Administration (VA) by executive order in July 1930 with some of the same old reforms in mind. The VA took three agencies, the Veterans

Bureau, the Bureau of Pensions within the Department of the Interior, and the National Home for Disabled Volunteer Soldiers and consolidated them under one agency for the sake of efficiency. However, with the country in the teeth of the Great Depression, additional money was impossible. In fact, given its $800 million budget—one quarter of the federal spending at the time—the Veterans Administration was a target for retrenchment. In the press conference announcing the change, President Hoover promised "to make important economies in administration of hospitalization and domiciliary questions and in the better handling of fiscal relations with veterans throughout the entire organization."

The Bonus March

The Great Depression was a devastating blow to the American economy and the public's faith in the country as a whole. Its causes are a well-documented combination of factors: speculation on an overinflated stock market, bad debt extended to foreign borrowers (especially Germany), and the impact of the Dust Bowl all contributed to the hard times enveloping America. With thousands of businesses shuttered, joblessness skyrocketed in just a few short years. By 1933 the official unemployment rate was 25 percent, a figure that included nearly thirteen million men and women. Some sectors were completely crippled. Outlays for industrial construction dropped from $949 million in 1929 to $74 million in 1932. The periodical *The Iron Age* reported in July 1932 raw steel production at 12 percent capacity, the lowest on record. Millions roamed the country in search of work and a place to live. In 1932 alone, the Southern Pacific railroad trespassed 683,000 people from its property.

Jennifer Keene's research indicates that the Great Depression disproportionately affected veterans. During these years, veterans made up 21 percent of men ages thirty to fifty-four, yet they comprised 32.9 percent of the unemployed. Additional federal relief was grudging at best. In 1931, Congress passed a measure, over Hoover's veto, allowing veterans to borrow against 50 percent of the face value their expected bonus from the old 1924 World War Adjusted Compensation Act at a 4.5 percent interest rate.

Early payment of the remaining 50 percent of the outstanding bonus was a hot topic in the veterans' community. The American Legion debated the issue at its national convention in September 1931. The rank-and-file generally supported the idea. In North Carolina, 119 of 124 American Legion posts voted in favor of early payment. However, national leadership dragged their feet, drawing immediate criticism. One member said of national commander Henry L. Stevens, "I'm a little afraid that $10,000 a year [his salary] and hobnobbing with presidents has distorted his judgement."

The subsequent Bonus March was a spontaneous, nonviolent protest of veterans' conditions and one remedy. It was made up of overwhelmingly working-class and destitute veterans, starting with a few hundred unemployed workers from Oregon who caravanned east by car, truck, and train. Hundreds more from around the country joined the procession as it converged on the nation's capital. The *New York Times* described three hundred and thirty veterans when they arrived in Washington from the West coast as "Weather-beaten, travel-stained, and dog-tired."

Eventually, twenty veterans' encampments grew in and around the capital to contain approximately 20,000 men. The largest was at Anacostia Field, on the southern bank of Potomac River in the southeastern part of the city. Both white and Black veterans congregated in the makeshift tent cities. Estimates are that African Africans may have constituted one-fifth of the veterans who assembled in the nation's capital, although the protest was not integrated in general.

Public responses to the Bonus March varied across the spectrum of political and social sympathies. Some, to include Army Chief of Staff Douglas MacArthur, believed the protest was inspired by communists. The leftist Workers' Ex-Servicemen's League was in fact present, although its meetings attracted a relatively small following. Some communities saw the marchers as a "poor man's lobby" and contributed tons of food and supplies for the encampment. Washington, DC, police chief Pelham Glassford, a WWI veteran, was among the people assisting with housing, meals, and medical supplies.

As the summer wore on, the official policy of tolerance promoted by Chief Glassford slowly began to fade. At the end of July, local police began clearing veterans from the encampments. They were met with hurled bricks, one of which struck Edward G. Scott, a World War I Medal of Honor winner, in the head. Police opened fire in response, wounding a number of veterans and killing one. Regular Army units, to include 1,500 infantry, cavalry, and armor, then moved in to clear the encampments of veterans. MacArthur's orders from Secretary of War Patrick J. Hurley were blunt:

> You will have United States troops proceed immediately to the scene of disorder. Cooperate fully with the District of Columbia police force which is now in charge. Surround the affected area and clear it without delay.
>
> Turn over all prisoners to the civil authorities.

The Army Chief of Staff applauded the restraint demonstrated by his troops. One account noted veterans "being prodded, though gently, by bayonets." In actuality, the soldiers were anything but gentle with their older comrades. Scenes of battered, bleeding, tear-gassed veterans were common. A number of the tent cities burned out of control.

Disturbances between the assembled veterans, police, and the Army were blamed on a "radical element among the bonus-seekers," according to the *New York Times*. President Hoover specifically referred to "Communists and persons with criminal records" at the heart of violence. Older veterans' organizations believed the marchers were at fault for the disaster. From its annual encampment, the Grand Army of the Republic blamed violence on the protestors' "insistence and excessive demands."

The Bonus March was a terrible moment for the country, veterans, and Herbert Hoover, who lost his reelection bid in a massive landslide. During the winter of 1932–33, the newly minted lame-duck president considered federal budget reductions to address mounting deficits. When the Congressional Joint Veterans Affairs Committee met at that moment, on the table were $400 million in cuts, approximately 50 percent of total veterans' spending. The open question at the start of 1933 was whether or not the New Deal, with all of its vague optimism, might apply to millions of American veterans.

Veterans and the New Deal

Franklin Delano Roosevelt was carried into the White House on a massive landslide, winning 57.4 percent of the popular vote and 472 electors. FDR's victory had substantial coattails. When the 73rd Congress convened in March 1933, Democrats outnumbered Republicans by 311 to 117 in the House and 58 to 36 in the Senate.

Just how this formidable political muscle might translate was open to endless speculation. Among the many issues affecting the country at the time, there was a great deal of hope that FDR would resolve the bonus issue if he became president. The VFW's magazine, *Foreign Service*, said of the president-elect, "Hail Franklin D. Roosevelt … as a comrade, a comrade in spirit truly."

Their hope turned out to be badly misplaced. Just days after his inaugural address, FDR proposed a $460 million cut to veterans' benefits—almost the same amount submitted by Hoover—as part of the Economy Act (1933). The president intoned that "Too often in recent history, liberal governments have been wrecked on rocks of loose fiscal policy." Given the overall percentage of veterans' benefits that were part of the federal budget, the VA and veterans' programs presented a significant target indeed. In its original form, the Economy Act effectively took pensions from a half a million veterans and their families.

Both the VFW and the Legion quickly mobilized to counter the enormous impact of the Economy Act. Rank and file members pressed for a policy of confrontation with the White House, while the Legion's national leadership resisted direct intervention against the president. Faced with widespread dissent, Congress sought a compromise and returned some of the proposed cuts in the summer of 1933. In addition, lawmakers created ninety new review boards for veterans to appeal their lost benefits.

For his own part, FDR shrewdly applied both the carrot and the stick. The president spoke at the American Legion's October 1933 convention and took the opportunity to make some pointed comments to the assembled delegates. Roosevelt defended the need to address national debt by addressing the basic status of veterans:

> The first principle, following inevitably from the obligation of citizens to bear arms, is that the Government has a responsibility for and toward those who suffered injury or contracted disease while serving in its defense.
>
> The second principle is that no person, because he wore a uniform, must thereafter be placed in a special class of beneficiaries over and above all other citizens. The fact of wearing a uniform does not mean that he can demand and receive from his Government a benefit which no other citizen receives.

FDR also tried to calm the veterans' lobby with federal patronage. Roosevelt formalized the process of mitigating new federal policy by creating the Board of Veterans' Appeals. He supported an increase in disability pension rates. To ease the controversy around the Economy Act, FDR set aside places for veterans in newly created public works programs. When the Civilian Conservation Corps started operations in 1933, it offered 25,000 positions to veterans.

Congress eventually provided the remedy most veterans sought. In 1936, it overrode a presidential veto and finally provided the sought-after bonus. At a cost of $2 billion, a substantial amount at a time when the total federal budget was just $8 billion, lawmakers forced Roosevelt's hand and provided veterans with needed relief in an economic crisis.

Veterans and the Path to World War II

The nature of World War I combat had what could be best described as a chilling effect on perceptions about military service in the twenties and thirties. World War I and the Great Depression collectively challenged confidence in social and economic progress as a constant. The generation coming of age before World War II was far more jaded with respect to human nature than the men of 1917. As noted above, these men and their families were familiar with, if not well versed in, the literature of Hemingway, Remarque, Wilfred Owen, or Siegfried Sassoon. They served as a backdrop to the neutrality debates that raged in the years leading up to Pearl Harbor. For these people, the Great War offered a stark contrast between naïve romanticism and systematized horror that they had no intention of repeating. The British writer E. M. Forster understood the resulting pragmatism about war in 1940: "I don't want to lose it. I don't expect victory (with a big V!), and I can't join in any build-a-new-world stuff. Once in a lifetime one can swallow that, but not twice."

Nevertheless, and perhaps because of this pragmatism, veterans strongly supported national security and military readiness between the world wars. When Congress created the House Un-American Affairs Committee in 1938 to investigate internal threats, it was with the full support of the American Legion. After the invasion of Poland, veterans' organizations lobbied against foreign intervention, while highlighting the poor condition of US military forces. The American Legion lamented the "idealistic conception of peace" after World War I that led to wholesale disarmament and vulnerability. The Veterans of Foreign Wars warned against the "opium of neutrality" and reflected on the country's obligation to "safeguard their sons—our soldiers of the future" through military preparedness. At a meeting of its executive committee in May 1940, the Legion made its stance on war clear: "We not only believe that this nation need not become involved but insist and demand that the President of the United States and the Congress pursue a policy that, while preserving the sovereignty and dignity of this nation will prevent involvement in this conflict." They summed up their platform in the slogan "Keep out and keep ready."

In 1940, this meant more manpower, weapons, equipment, and most of all, money. As World War II raged, the VFW argued for military training through the Civilian Conservation Corps since it already contained a natural body of young men of military age. They also supported a return to the WWI "Plattsburg Idea," where civilians voluntarily trained for war under the direction of the Military Training Camps Association. For its own part, the Legion campaigned for universal military service and wholly supported passage of the 1940 Selective Service Act.

Events and public opinion aided veterans' campaigns. When Germany invaded Poland in September 1939, the US armed forces were pitifully inadequate. One week after World War II began, FDR declared a "limited national emergency" and authorized increasing Army and National Guard troop levels by 52,000 men. Standing forces were further bolstered by the nation's first peacetime draft, which inducted two million men into uniform. FDR successfully gathered public and Congressional support for this measure with the promise that draftees would serve for home defense.

Public opinion followed a path from rigid opposition to the war to a general tolerance of FDR's decision to support its teetering allies in England and France. When hostilities began in 1939, only 16 percent of Americans supported military intervention to help Poland. However, when France collapsed under the German blitzkrieg, the public consensus began to shift, with 35 percent supporting assistance to England by the summer of 1940. The subsequent German air campaign against England, the war at sea in the North

Atlantic, and the July 1941 German invasion of the Soviet Union significantly eroded opposition to US intervention. By the summer of 1941, approximately two-thirds of respondents supported varying degrees of help, from Lend-Lease aid to military force.

Military spending followed the shifting public attitude. Roosevelt began a series of defense budget increases as early as 1939, but the real surge in spending occurred after 1940, from $2.2 billion to $13.7 billion a year later. Lend-Lease assistance accounted for an additional $7 billion.

As war drew nearer, both the American Legion and VFW retreated from their earlier isolationism. At the Legion's 1940 convention, bitter floor debates broke out between advocates of neutrality and delegates who wanted condemnation of "aggressor nations." Alfred Kelly, the Oregon department commander, condemned the old policy using pointed terminology that would become familiar in the Cold War: "The people of America want courage from the American Legion, not appeasement. Strength, courage and idealism will keep us at peace; weakness, compromise and appeasement will lead us to war." In the end, the convention "roared down" a resolution calling for neutrality and endorsed a substitute offering "the fullest cooperation" to nations threatened by aggression. By its September 1941 national convention, the Legion's position was clear: "Our present national objective is the defeat of Hitler and what he stands for, and all diverting controversy should be subordinated to the main objective. We appeal for unity on this national objective."

Many of the millions of veterans who served during World War I entered into peacetime America intent on improving their country. They were heavily engaged in the rituals of patriotism, from annual parades to erecting monuments to wartime service. In the same vein, veterans' organizations were deeply engaged in a range of tangible public policy discussions that included school curriculum, immigration policy, and effective ways to foster good citizenship. When Alvin Owsley proclaimed that "a nation without heroes" would fail, he was offering veterans as both a solution and America's salvation.

Many of their activities, such as American Legion baseball, became deeply embedded in communities at the grassroots level.

The approximately four and a half million who served in World War I was the largest veterans' contingent in American history at the time and posed significant challenges to policymakers in the twenties and thirties. Federal support for health care, vocational rehabilitation, and disabilities was an expensive and daunting task at a moment in US politics when economic retrenchment was the keynote struck by a series of Republican administrations. Warren Harding attempted to take a hard line against expanding veterans' benefits at the outset of his presidency and his party paid a serious political price for its obstinance. While it started with a focus on efficiency and modernization, the new Veterans Bureau was handicapped by a penchant for corruption and mismanagement.

During the interwar period veterans' organizations—the American Legion and the VFW in particular—demonstrated political muscle reminiscent of the old Grand Army of the Republic in its heydey. As the twenties moved on, these organizations were successful in winning new reversals of policy and concessions from Washington. However, even this power had limits. When the country's economy collapsed in 1929, veterans' benefits became a prime target for Republicans during the Herbert Hoover's time in office and, despite hopes to the contrary, the incoming administration of Franklin Delano Roosevelt.

Europe's gradual slide into war during the thirties was an important reality check for American veterans. Trading on the objective value of their patriotism, as they had for the two decades following World War I, veterans possessed important influence as the United States contemplated military intervention. Yet, with that same bitter wartime experience in hand, many veterans approached the prospect of conflict with understandable wariness and serious skepticism. Like the rest of the country, this ambivalence was a recurring feature of the neutrality debate. And, as was the case with their fellow Americans, rapidly developing events soon overwhelmed their caution.

7

World War II

We were all animals, really, torn between fear—I was mostly frightened—and a murderous rage at events. One strange feeling, which I remember clearly, was a powerful link with the slain, particularly those who had fallen within the past hour or two. There was so much death around that life seemed almost indecent.

WILLIAM MANCHESTER, AUTHOR OF *GOODBYE DARKNESS:
A MEMOIR OF THE PACIFIC WAR*

The Second World War was a true global conflict, touching every continent at some point between the invasion of Poland and the final Japanese surrender. It was, and remains, America's largest war, a conflict in which forty-nine million men registered for military service and sixteen million eventually participated in uniform. The unprecedented scale of this mobilization set the tone for postwar America in terms of what that service earned and how it might reshape the entire country. In 1945, nearly every American asked what peacetime "normalcy" might bring.

Mobilization for World War II directly influenced the scope and scale of postwar expectations. Tens of millions of Americans uprooted their lives for the sake of the war effort, seeking out the opportunities presented by the wartime boom in manufacturing and industry. Women and African Americans joined in the potential bounty, challenging social norms in the workplace and neighborhoods throughout the burgeoning industrial belt. By 1945,

Americans had good reason to be optimistic. Brand-new industrial centers dotted the countryside. Personal bank accounts bulged with $140 billion in unspent money. Almost anything seemed possible in the new Pax Americana.

Victory came with a rare moment of consensus in American history. The country had served, *en masse*, on the battlefield and the production line, and defeated the fascists. For most people, World War II was indeed the "Good War." We possessed both the means and the intention to make a better future. A prevailing sense of hope drove the expectations of the privileged and the dispossessed alike.

Veterans, by virtue of their contributions to the war, occupied a prominent position in the America of 1945. They assumed a place of honor where Civil War and World War I veterans once stood. Like their past counterparts, World War II veterans were the exemplars of what a citizen could be. And also, as was the case in the past, this standing affected their perception of service and its reward. The country recognized both. One result was a piece of landmark legislation that would influence the lives of the "Greatest Generation," their children, and the country as a whole.

The Nature of Service in the Good War

As noted in the previous chapter, the men and women who served after 1941 did not have nearly as many illusions about the war as the generation that came before them. They saw service as a pragmatic, temporary, and necessary evil to combat the even greater threats posed by Nazi Germany, fascist Italy, and imperial Japan. According to historian Paul Fussell, who served as a combat infantryman in Europe: "To get home, you had to end the war. To end the war was the reason you fought it."

American officials, recognizing the potential enthusiasm gap, worked diligently at constructing linkages between military service and threats to the country. Civilian agencies like the Office of War Information (OWI) conducted a sophisticated propaganda campaign that touched print media, radio, and film. Much of the OWI's early work, expressed by Frank Capra's *Why We Fight* series, was upbeat and affirmative. At the same time, the OWI and its military counterparts also censored information related to the war effort as a matter of security and morale. The fundamental ugliness of the conflict, the boredom, suffering, and visceral terror, was never part of the initial official narrative. However, as the war progressed and the casualty lists grew, the War Department's public relations campaigns introduced increasing amounts of realism. Director William Wyler and his camera crews accompanied B-17s of the 91st Bomb Group over Germany in the *Memphis Belle* (1944). Wyler's goal was to capture the stark dangers faced by Americans at war. The film was also to appeal to an evolving audience back home. By 1945, few Americans—veterans or their families—were oblivious to the cost of victory.

In *Flags of Our Fathers*, James Bradley and Ron Powers reflected on the powerful combination of service, celebrity, and showmanship that gripped the country in the last months of World War II. The seventh and final war bond drive—the "Mighty Seventh"—"combined the old-fashioned elements of vaudeville, the country fair, the Fourth of July parade." It also put a literal human face on three veterans, John Bradley, Ira Hayes, and Rene Gagnon, who were plucked from combat on Iwo Jima and pressed into service to re-create the famous flag raising on that island. As the war wound to an unexpected close with the dropping of two atomic bombs on Japan, most Americans understood the value of sacrifice in World War II.

The Evolving Nature of Combat and Its Impact

World War II was an incredibly lethal conflict, fostered by a series of groundbreaking technological advances. Simple automotive innovations produced power plants that could propel heavily armored tanks or hold heavy bombers aloft at unprecedented altitudes for thousands of miles. Radar permitted military forces to see over the horizon. Sonar systems allowed navies the same ability to scour the seas for threats. The United States, blessed as it was with vast resources of materiel and talent, embraced military technology from the very start of the war. The Manhattan Project was the capstone of a research and development program designed to leverage science in the place of sacrificing American lives.

Military medicine also registered significant advances during World War II. During the course of the conflict, the 671,846 American wounded and injured benefited from blood plasma, elaborate evacuation systems, and frontline trauma treatment. Sulfa drugs and penicillin were instrumental in preventing infection and speeding recovery rates. Statistics tell an important story. A soldier suffering a fracture in WWI had a 46 percent of a permanent disability. In WWII, the likelihood was reduced to 10 percent.

As World War II became deadlier, it also threatened a select, and shrinking, group of combatants. One simple reason for the trend was the growing need for logistics adequate to support an increasingly complex military system. Modern armies needed medics, truck drivers, mechanics, and clerks as much as they needed infantry. One study of the US Army that divided service according "combat," "combat support," and "combat service support" assignments found that 60 percent of personnel were in the combat arms by 1944.

A further breakdown of numbers tells an important story. During World War II, there were 68 infantry divisions in the US Army, populated by 700,000 riflemen, who made up one out of fourteen soldiers overall. This one small portion of the Army experienced 70 percent of its casualties during World War II. In some elite units—like the 1st Marine Division or the 82nd Airborne Division—loss rates were on an order of magnitude larger. During the thirty-three days following their jump into Normandy, the 82nd Airborne suffered 5,245 killed, wounded, and missing, almost half its assigned strength. A 1949 War Department survey of four infantry divisions during the Normandy campaign revealed that after eight weeks in combat, 73.8 percent of officers and 59.6 percent of enlisted men assigned to rifle companies became casualties.

The changing nature of modern conflict during World War II directly impacted its veterans. Millions of Americans served during World War II and never heard a shot fired in anger. The soldiers, sailors, airmen, and marines who did fight engaged in a form of conflict that their fathers would not recognize. Death and wounds came in a growing array of forms. Paradoxically, medical remedies were reaching a point where survival, while not guaranteed, was far more likely than in past wars. The end result was a large community of veterans in need of significant help with treatment, rehabilitation, and assistance to return to civilian life. The scale of this need would seriously test existing veterans' institutions as the war came to a close.

The G.I. Bill

World War II was much like World War I and the Civil War to the extent that, while the country ramped up industry, manufacturing, and manpower for military needs, it also considered the prospects for demobilization once the conflict might end. These discussions began as early as 1942 and, from the start, policymakers saw World War I as a cautionary tale. What the country needed was an orderly process of demobilization that would avoid strikes, high unemployment, and the possibility of another economic depression once America returned to peacetime. Policymakers generally agreed that gradually drawing down active forces was the best approach. The open question was what would happen to these millions of new returnees?

FDR addressed this challenge in a July 1943 fireside chat:

> While concentrating on military victory, we are not neglecting the planning of the things to come, the freedoms which we know will make for more decency and greater justice throughout the world.

Among many other things we are, today, laying plans for the return to civilian life of our gallant men and women in the armed services. They must not be demobilized into an environment of inflation and unemployment, to a place on a bread line, or on a corner selling apples. We must, this time, have plans ready—instead of waiting to do a hasty, inefficient, and ill-considered job at the last moment.

I have assured our men in the armed forces that the American people would not let them down when the war is won.

I hope that the Congress will help in carrying out this assurance, for obviously the Executive Branch of the Government cannot do it alone. May the Congress do its duty in this regard. The American people will insist on fulfilling this American obligation to the men and women in the armed forces who are winning this war for us.

Roosevelt's call to action was poorly timed. It came at a moment when the New Deal was under attack by conservatives in both parties. Ironically, the war itself made important parts of FDR's older policies effectively obsolete. The surge in wartime production, coupled with expanding draft call-ups, made public works projects such as the Civilian Conservation Corps, the Works Progress Administration, and the National Youth Administration moot. More to the point, with returning prosperity, opponents of social welfare saw an opportunity to challenge new proposals on their costs, but also on the principle that they might create a gigantic underclass of government dependents.

In this political environment, Roosevelt had to pick his moment. The president tested the waters in an October 27, 1943, message to Congress. FDR proposed one year of post-military training for veterans: "As a part of a general program for the benefit of the members of our armed services, I believe that the Nation is morally obligated to provide this training and education and the necessary financial assistance by which they can be secured." With a nod to the needs of eventual peacetime, Roosevelt added, "We must replenish our supply of persons qualified to discharge the heavy responsibilities of the postwar world. We have taught our youth how to wage war; we must also teach them how to live useful and happy lives in freedom, justice, and decency."

These careful, tentative steps were not enough for veterans' groups. To press for additional assistance, the American Legion national convention approved a special committee on new veterans' legislation at the end of 1943. Many concerns arose in early policy discussions. The VFW pointed out an ongoing lack of coordination between the War Department and the Veterans Administration. They also noted a lack of physicians available to examine out-processing disabled service members.

Concerns like these quickly morphed into open criticism of the federal government. At the end of 1943, American Legion national commander Warren H. Atherton accused lawmakers of forgetting their obligations to disabled veterans. He referred to the latter as the "Forgotten Battalion," comprised of "the legion of the disabled, who had come home in mid-war to delay, neglect, and disillusion." In stinging testimony before Congress in November, he cited hundreds of cases of veterans forced to rely on charity because their military pay had stopped and long bureaucratic delays, lasting for months, prevented any relief. Atherton claimed there was a backlog of 70,000 cases awaited processing within the Veterans Administration. He argued for implementation of existing disability benefits and rehabilitation programs, but also saw a need to expand VA medical facilities and beds for "nervous and mental cases," tuberculosis treatment, and other needs likely to arise after demobilization. The Legion advocated for a lump sum of up to $500 as mustering-out pay (depending on length of service) for all returning veterans. To bolster its point, the American Legion began a national public relations campaign. It also recorded more than four hundred one-minute "spot announcements" for radio and produced 125 two-minute films.

Congress introduced an omnibus veterans' bill in January 1944. However, even if it was essentially presented as well-earned assistance to millions of qualified veterans, the measure did not enjoy a clean passage. Mississippi Democrat John Rankin, chair of the House Veterans Committee, stuck to familiar old territory and opposed to any legislation that might add to the federal deficit or make veterans dependent on the federal government. Rankin had an ally in Representative Andrew Jackson May, a Democrat from Kentucky and Chair of the House Military Affairs Committee, who also expressed misgivings about expense. American Legion allies in Congress soon rallied and countered with questions about the $1.3 billion approved by the House for the UN Relief and Rehabilitation Administration (UNRRA), accusing lawmakers of taking "money from the pockets of our fighting men so that UNRRA can play Santa Claus to the world." Republican Representative Edith Nourse Rogers of Massachusetts added her name to the growing list of supporters of veterans' legislation in the House. They were joined by the formidable Bennett Champ Clarke, who had served as the first American Legion commander, and represented Missouri in the Senate.

A parade of witnesses appeared during Congressional hearings on the matter. Frank T. Hines spoke for the Veterans Administration and contemplating the postwar responsibility for millions of additional clients, readily endorsed the proposed legislation. Despite some misgivings about what an influx of veterans might do to standards at colleges and universities, the American Council on Education supported the proposed program. A cluster of smaller veterans' groups, the Disabled America Veterans (DAV), the Military Order of the Purple Heart, and, most notably, the Veterans of Foreign Wars, actually opposed the bill. In a joint letter, they advised the Congress "not to be stampeded into hasty and possible unwise legislation." Omar B. Ketchum, who served as the VFW Congressional liaison, noted the potential cost of the program, but also argued that mustering-out pay, adjusted compensation, and reassimilation plans should be combined as a whole program. Eventually, the American Legion convinced the VFW to get on board. However, the DAV held out, resurrecting an old complaint when it described unemployment benefits as vulnerable to abuse by "lazy and 'chisely' types of veterans."

In the end, the Senate Finance Committee unanimously approved the Serviceman's Readjustment Bill and it went to the floor with eighty-one co-sponsors. It passed through that body without opposition. However, problems developed when the legislation reached the House of Representatives. From his seat on the House Veterans Committee, John Rankin recognized that the legislation was "the most far-reaching and most explosive bill ever to reach Congress." He went on further to say his committee was "not going to be stampeded into bringing out a half-baked bill." Rankin called for the reduction of some portions affecting unemployment and education benefits. To counter the chair's skepticism, the American Legion delivered a petition with over a million names to Congress in March 1944. The massive outpouring of support proved more than enough to finish the deal. The legislation was voted out of committee with an additional $500 million for hospital construction. Roosevelt signed the bill into law on June 22, 1944, and remarked that it was an "emphatic notice to the men and women in our armed forces that the American people do not intend to let them down."

The Serviceman's Readjustment Act of 1944 was an impressive and far-reaching program. It was also expensive, although early projections about the G.I. Bill's cost proved to be wildly optimistic from the start. By the time it reached Roosevelt's desk, estimates had almost doubled from $3.5 billion to $6.5 billion.

In part, the Serviceman's Readjustment Act was expensive because it was ambitious. Title I authorized the $500 million for hospital construction mentioned above. Title IV offered veterans job placement. However, if new veterans wanted to wait before entering the job market, Title V offered them a $20 weekly stipend for up to fifty-two weeks. Title III created a system for veterans to obtain home or business loans. Under Title II, veterans interested in furthering their education could receive money for both tuition and living expenses.

Very few people at the time understood either the strengths or inherent limits of the G.I. Bill. The law made no distinctions among veterans by sex or race and instead recognized all of them as a class of citizens protected by federal law. But this recognition did not mean veterans were granted a blank check. The G.I. Bill did not provide veterans with housing; rather it supported loans to qualified applicants. Although the law was technically color blind, it could not guarantee African American, Latino, Nisei, or any other group equal access to homes, jobs, or education. More to the point, it could not resolve generations of ingrained racism or, as we will see, bureaucratic inertia in the Veterans Administration.

Moreover, how new policy might be implemented was also unclear at the outset. The Veterans Administration was the primary federal agency responsible for the G.I. Bill, but remained, in too many ways, rooted in the past, both in terms of its staffing and its decentralized approach to management. Much of the immediate postwar would be spent reconciling the possibilities presented by the G.I. Bill with America's limited potential to achieve them.

The Rush to Demobilize

When Japan surrendered in August 1945, the sudden peace took most Americans by surprise. That summer, the country anticipated the planned invasion of the Japanese home islands and years of additional bloodshed. The War Department estimated that Operations Olympic and Coronet—which addressed the invasion of Honshu and Kyushu—might result in as many as a quarter-million American casualties. Two atom bombs made these predictions irrelevant.

Spontaneous celebrations swept through the country with the end of hostilities. A woman writing to her deployed husband captured the moment:

People outside were dancing in the streets with their nightgowns and pajamas on. Children from one year and up were running through the dark street banging pots and pans, blowing horns and ringing bells. There were some young boys on East 3rd St. that have a small band of music and they began to play in the middle of the street as everyone danced. People shouted from their windows and small bonfires were started all along the street. Victory! Glorious victory! How good it felt!

Counterbalancing this joy were dire predictions about what peacetime meant for the immediate future. The August 12, 1945, front-page *New York Times* headline read that as many as five million war production workers would lose their jobs, with aircraft construction, shipbuilding, and munitions production hardest hit. The first ten days of peace seemed to bear out these early predictions. During that short interval, 1.8 million Americans received their pink slips and an additional 640,000 filed claims for unemployment compensation. The Office of Price Administration (OPA), created during the war to keep the economy on an even keel, started removal of wage and price controls in early 1946. The OPA's timing could not have been worse. With the war at an end and restrictions fading away, the people were eager to indulge themselves, many for the first time since the Great Depression.

The results were predictable. Prices for basic market basket items, especially formerly rationed products like milk, eggs, and beef, skyrocketed, by 13.8 percent in July 1946 alone. Between February 1946 and August 1948, the CPI food index rose by 55 percent. In order to combat the skyrocketing cost of living, many unions resorted to strikes. In 1946, the country saw 4,985 work stoppages by 4.6 million workers.

While economic disruptions unfolded, pressure grew to bring the troops home. The War Department recognized growing public impatience and actually accelerated demobilization even before the war was over. Between May and September 1945, almost 700,000 men and women left the Army alone. However, early demobilization did little to placate the millions who remained in uniform. Protests and insubordination flared in both the European and Pacific theaters. In January 1946, UAW leader Emil Mazey organized a mass protest of nearly 10,000 troops in Manila and purchased a full-page ad in the United States criticizing the "hopelessly confused demobilization program." While on an inspection tour of Pacific bases, Secretary of War Robert Patterson was burned in effigy by troops stationed on Guam.

As lawmakers scrambled to head off growing discontent at home and abroad, their careful plans began to fall apart. The military streamlined the demobilization process from eighteen days to just forty-four hours. Consequently, the ongoing flow of returning veterans soon became a deluge. Finding a seat on a train or bus home developed into an ordeal as an overwhelmed transportation system struggled to cope. More importantly, the system built to receive the millions leaving the military, discussed in more detail below, began to bend and break almost as soon as the war was over.

Homecoming Expectations and Realities

For the deployed soldier, sailor, airman, or marine, absence made the heart grow fonder. Far away from families and familiar places, it was very common for military men and women to have keepsakes—photos, letters, locks of hair—close by as a way to remember life before the war. These tokens also served as symbols of future hope. This utopia counterbalanced the boredom and terror that was a daily part of life in the war zone. A 1945 War Department survey of personnel deployed to Europe recorded that more than two-thirds believed civilians had "a real sense of gratitude and appreciation for what soldiers had done."

The reality awaiting these veterans obviously was much more complicated. Friends, families, and not a few future spouses clearly celebrated their returning loved ones. As they did this, everyone had to confront unfinished business with the war's end. The immediate postwar was a tumultuous time for American society. Children met with fathers who were strangers to them. Marriages, many made in haste during the war, fractured and failed as couples reunited. The national divorce rate spiked at 31 percent in 1945, more than double the prewar percentage.

Even before Germany surrendered, a narrative appeared that identified returning veterans as a potential threat to American society. Sensational headlines tagged veterans as the perpetrators of murder, violence, and a host of bad acts. The February 25, 1945, issue of the *Boston Post* noted simply: "A great number of boys who have been educated to kill cannot, immediately upon discharge from the armed services, readjust themselves to the ways of normal life; therefore, they will lean toward a life of crime."

Despite the promises of Roosevelt's Four Freedoms—Freedom from Fear, Freedom of Speech, Freedom from Want, Freedom of Religion—racism and discrimination was alive and unfortunately well in postwar America. Approximately 2.4 million African Americans had registered for the draft and more than one million eventually served during World War II. Most were relegated to logistical work in a segregated military. However, many saw combat with distinction in units like the 99th Fighter Squadron and the 555th Parachute Infantry Regiment. Combat was a great leveler, where aptitude and not race was the determining factor in survival. Deployed abroad, African Americans came into contact with a broad variety of diverse population serving in Allied armies. Their experiences with Indian, African, and other members of the British Commonwealth and French Republic, were a revelation.

Like their fathers and older brothers at the end of the Great War, many African Americans returned home with high expectations for a job well done. The NAACP's "Double V Campaign," that victory abroad during the war must translate into victory—civil rights, job opportunities, and the vote—at home, shaped a great deal of this hope. Progress seemed to be within reach. The war had transformed the South, offering unheard-of economic opportunities in the shipyards, factories, and military boomtowns dotting the region. Thousands left the farm for the city. If they could not find work close to home, Portland, Los Angeles, Detroit, Chicago, and Philadelphia beckoned. When asked in a 1947 Roper poll, "Do you think your son's opportunities to succeed will be better than, or not as good as, those you have had," 75 percent of African Americans answer positively.

Life for many returning African American veterans was much different. When Isaac Woodard was blinded by Batesburg, South Carolina police chief Lynwood L. Shull and other officers during his arrest in February 1946, the tragedy inspired outrage and action. Harry Truman was as appalled as many Americans, especially when a jury acquitted Shull of violating Woodard's civil rights after only thirty minutes of deliberation. For the remainder of his time in office, Truman mobilized the Justice Department to assist the NAACP and other groups when they challenged segregation around the country.

Sadly, what happened to Woodard was not uncommon for African American service members traveling in the United States during and after the war. The home front was filled with examples of clashes between Black soldiers, white passengers, and police on buses and trains around the country, but particularly in the South. One study of the war years recorded thousands of confrontations. African American military personnel were particularly likely to be the victims of police violence in Texas, Louisiana, and Kentucky. In Beaumont, Texas, a Black enlisted man reportedly was shot twice by patrolmen while being arrested for taking a seat in the whites-only section of a bus. Three African Americans in the Women's Army Corps were beaten by local police in Elizabethtown, Kentucky for being in a whites-only waiting room at a bus station.

Just as it had after World War I, the NAACP intervened for African American veterans and sponsored legislation, under the so-called G.I. Assault Bill, to make attacks on military personnel a federal crime. The proposed legislation made it through the Senate, only to fail in the House of Representatives. African American veterans also organized on their own behalf. Many were encouraged to register to vote, ironically in a number of Southern states that waived the poll tax for returning soldiers. In January 1946, one hundred Black veterans marched on the courthouse in Birmingham, Alabama in uniform, with discharge papers in hand, demanding the franchise. Officials refused to even consider their request.

Segregationist obstruction did not deter them. During the course of 1946, veterans' political organizations appeared in Georgia, Louisiana, Tennessee, and Arkansas. Their members worked for themselves as citizens deserving basic rights and, as the United Registration Committee of Birmingham flatly stated, "Men who faced bullets overseas deserve ballots at home." These groups campaigned not only for the right to vote, but also against corruption fostered by political machines that dominated daily Southern life.

The African American relationship with the Veterans Administration could be best described as turbulent. It did not start that way. Borrowing from FDR's "Four Freedoms" in a March 1945 speech, Frank T. Hines promised African American veterans freedom from discrimination in the administration of the law, freedom from inequality in education, and freedom from inequality in health care and work opportunity.

Unfortunately, actual VA practice did not come close to Hines's bromides. The Veterans Administration of 1945 allowed state and regional offices considerable autonomy when it came to policy decisions, a practice that tolerated rampant segregation and discrimination within VA facilities. In 1945, the NAACP reported that seventeen VA hospitals in ten states refused to accept African American veterans. Few African Americans worked for the Veterans Administration. In Maryland, they represented 3 percent of employees. In Chicago, African Americans made up 16 percent of staff, but these jobs were mostly concentrated in clerical duties.

Faced with a familiar series of social and institutional obstacles, African American veterans took an already well-used path and organized on their own behalf. In Bennetsville, Georgia, they confronted the Klan with armed patrols.

They began voter registration drives, contested police treatment of the African American community, and sought out social norms on par with the white majority. Nationally, tens of thousands of African American veterans joined the NAACP, helping boost its membership from 50,000 in 1940 to 450,000 by 1946.

Other veterans of color mirrored these efforts. Latino veterans created the American G.I. Forum in 1949. Japanese American veterans formed the Nisei Veterans Club (1946), the Nisei Veterans Committee (1947), and joined the Japanese American Citizens League. All of these groups believed that their military service was the first stepping stone toward active participation in mainstream society and, at some point in the future, acceptance and equality. They were, like many contemporary Americans, joiners. They sponsored blood drives, scholarship competitions, and youth sports. They also lobbied federal, state, and local officials for veterans in need. In 1947, Héctor García served as an advocate for hundreds of Latino veterans who did not receive G.I. Bill educational benefits. Mike Masaoka, a combat veteran of the 442nd Regimental Combat Team, spoke for many when he said:

> I think that we persons of Japanese ancestry who served in the army, both in the Pacific and in Europe, did so because we had faith in the long-time and ultimate triumph of fair play and justice in the American way, and so we saw beyond the watchtowers of our concentration camps and we saw the kind of America that we have got to have, and we saw the kind of world that we have got to have. And so, the sacrifices of the men who died was [sic] not in vain, and I think our record is pretty well known. No other unit in American military history, for its size and length of combat, won as many decorations or suffered as many casualties.

Masaoka capitalized on this status and personally lobbied for amendments to the 1952 McCarran-Walter Immigration Act that granted Issei Japanese citizenship rights.

Being a veteran after World War II was a mix of hope, success, and frustration. Returning men and women were occupied with a sense of relief that the conflict was over, and their old civilian lives were waiting for them. Yet, things were not that simple. The war had changed them and the country. Benjamin C. Bowker's 1946 book *Out of Uniform* captures some of the real and perceived contradictions about veterans at the time:

> Veterans had lost their moral sense in battle, yet they returned highly critical of the nation's peccadilloes.
> Veterans had lost initiative in the routine of service life, yet they would organize so strongly they would dominate the nation.
> Veterans were physical and mental wrecks, yet they threatened to set up a reign of terror through cunning and brawn.
> Veterans hated the uniform, yet they tended to force universal military training on their sons and brothers.
> Veterans had gorged themselves on creature comforts denied civilians, yet they intended to seize all remaining assets through communism.
> Veterans were returning "vicious and godless," even though there had been "no atheists in foxholes."

Peace had brought with it joy, but also the potential for trouble and a prevailing sense of ambivalence. For veterans and Americans in general, the future was hopeful, but nothing was certain.

Rebuilding the Veterans Administration

At the end of World War II, the Veterans Administration comprised 65,000 employees scattered across the continental United States, roughly double the size of the agency that Charles R. Forbes presided over in the early twenties. However, despite its growth and development, the VA was an outdated and overwhelmed institution that quickly buckled under the weight of the newest generation of veterans. Problems started at the top. Historian Joseph C. Goulden described Frank T. Hines as a "fussy bureaucrat" and went on further to say that "So far as anyone could deduce, Hines ran the VA on the theory that the less he did, the better his chances of avoiding trouble."

Under his leadership, veterans' affairs became an ongoing public scandal. The *New York Times* reported instances of VA hospitals charging veterans hefty fees to cash their federal assistance checks. The *New Republic* and *Reader's Digest* published accounts of poor sanitary conditions and "perfunctory and incompetent" medical treatment. Help appeared to be nowhere in sight. During the summer of 1945, the VA was overwhelmed by tens of thousands of letters clamoring for help. One journalist described it as a "vast dehumanized bureaucracy, enmeshed in mountains of red tape, being grown with entrenched mediocrity, undemocratically operated under autocratic control centered in Washington, prescribing medieval medicine to its sick and disabled wards, highly susceptible to political pressures, rigidly resistant to proposed reforms."

Consequently, and in relatively short order, Hines was out and General Omar N. Bradley was in. He was an interesting choice by Harry Truman, who had assumed office only a few short months earlier. Bradley was a career soldier from his 1915 West Point commissioning to his rise through the officer ranks and eventual command of the 12th Army Group thirty years later. By 1945, Bradley was immensely respected by his peers and the American public. Ernie Pyle, perhaps one of the best-known war correspondents of the time, described the general in these terms: "If I could pick any two men in the world for my father, except my own dad, I would pick Gen. Omar Bradley or Gen. Ike Eisenhower. If I had a son, I would like him to go to Bradley or Ike for advice."

Bradley was horrified by the prospect of his new VA assignment. Reflecting on the moment in his 1983 autobiography, he said the news of his appointment "devastated" him. Yet, the general would dedicate more than two years to his task and he would do it well.

Bradley rapidly expanded the VA's ability to serve the massive influx of new veterans. In the year following his appointment, the number of VA employees more than doubled to 173,000. Veterans Administration field offices grew from 160 to 753. Consequently, the total number of veterans receiving service more than tripled from 400,000 to 1.5 million.

Bradley also oversaw many important qualitative improvements to the Veterans Administration. He successfully argued for changes in federal civil service law—no mean feat at the time—that allowed the VA to actively recruit medical professionals outside the established seniority system. Meantime, the general cherry-picked a cohort of staff officers and specialists to assist him. Paul Hawley, who had served as the chief surgeon of the European Theater of Operations, was put in charge of the VA Department of Medicine and Surgery.

Addressing the needs of the 671,846 Americans wounded and injured during World War II was an enormous undertaking. New technology, improved antibiotics, and timely evacuation allowed higher rates of survival, but also placed additional burdens on veterans' care for long-term treatment and rehabilitation. The intensity of modern combat also produced a significant increase in post-traumatic stress, or "battle fatigue," to use the contemporary term. The multiplying needs of American war wounded placed an escalating burden on the VA Department of Medicine and Surgery. In 1943, 71,823 military patients returned to the United States. A year later, that number grew to 172,968. By 1945, it more than doubled again to 385,972.

With Bradley's full support, Hawley introduced the VA to modern medicine. In January 1946, by virtue of Public Law 293, he was able to offer a 25 percent bonus for medical specialists and ramped up hiring. At the same time, the VA established a physician's residency program with sixty-three of the seventy-seven medical schools in the United States. Hawley was ably assisted by Dorothy Wheeler, who took charge of the VA nursing program and completely renovated both treatment and hospital administration. Mental health innovations moved in concert with these reforms. Inspired by the Menninger Clinic in Topeka, Kansas, the VA introduced a structured treatment regime that included self-governing patient wards and group therapy, a practice that encouraged veterans to discuss their problems among peers and accept support, basic steps that were often difficult for a generation of Americans for whom mental health therapy was an alien concept. Hawley took the same aggressive approach with respect to physical therapy. The VA expanded its ability to treat amputations and spinal cord injuries and forged relationships with cutting-edge institutions like the Mayo Clinic. Occupational therapy embraced what historian David A. Gerber characterized as "aggressive normalization." At Bradley's urging, major corporations like International Harvester, Ford, and Westinghouse sponsored job training programs to ease disabled veterans back into civilian life.

Journalist Albert Q. Maisel rightly described Omar Bradley as "a man who had a knack for getting at the heart of a situation," but the many reforms achieved during his tenure at the VA sadly did not outlast the general's service. At the end of 1947, he returned to active duty in the coveted role of Army Chief of Staff, pausing there before becoming the first Chairman of the Joint Chiefs of Staff. Absent his ability and formidable public standing, the Veterans Administration faltered as the forties wore on. Republicans, who surged backed into Congress after the 1946 election on the promise of reducing the cost and influence of the federal government, were shrewd enough not to directly eliminate popular programs. Instead, they cut their budgets. As early as February 1947, the VA was forced to institute a hiring freeze. By 1949, the Bureau of Budget approved the elimination of 11,000 VA positions. On the brink of the Korean War, more than 4,000 beds in the VA hospital system were empty because of staff shortages.

World War II redrew the course of history and America's place in it. Walter Lippman described the country's standing in 1945: "What Rome was to the ancient world, what Great Britain has been to the modern world, America is to be to the world of tomorrow." Victory against fascism both established American power and embellished American credibility at the same moment. The postwar was a time ripe with possibilities for both great accomplishments and hubris.

The victory that followed a hard-fought war reflected back on the men and women who accomplished it. Although their contributions varied, much like average citizens on the home front, veterans of World War II—drawn from the white mainstream of society, but also veterans of color—could look back on their service as a point of pride. This quality resembled the attitudes of almost every older generation from the American Revolution onward. But what augmented this understanding was the sheer scale of military service. No generation before or since has worn the uniform in such numbers.

With this sense of power in hand, the "Greatest Generation" who fought the Good War reentered society determined to leave their stamp on the country. Many took the individual opportunity to leverage their military experience in the booming postwar economy. Many joined the VFW, the American Legion, the new American Veterans Committee, or a growing civil rights movement to help their own cause, but also their local communities.

Landmark federal legislation helped them with these tasks. The 1944 Serviceman's Readjustment Act followed the logic of the New Deal as it wove together a social safety net for millions of veterans. Assistance for housing, education, and small business shaped and reinforced public faith in the partnership between citizens and their government. Although many contemporary Americans may have not realized it, the G.I. Bill was not an endpoint, but a wellspring for future expectations for the entire G.I. generation and their children.

8

The Early Cold War

The most significant fact about me is that for four and a half years my profession was jumping out of airplanes with a gun, and now I want to go into public relations.

SLOAN WILSON, *THE MAN IN THE GRAY FLANNEL SUIT*, 1955

As World War II ended, another global conflict began. The United States and the Soviet Union, allies of necessity in the struggle against Germany and Japan, emerged from the conflict as dominant superpowers and rivals. Over the decades that followed, the scope and scale of American commitments in service of this rivalry might have staggered the imagination of a citizen in the thirties, yet they became the new normal just a few short years after Japan's surrender.

American military forces adapted to meet the contingencies of the new Cold War against communism. Traditional conflict, where formal declarations started and finished military involvement, was a thing of the past, a point reinforced by the Korean "police action," the proliferation of nuclear threats in the fifties, and "brushfire wars" in the so-called Third World. With a host of new missions in its portfolio, the active-duty military evolved beyond its pre-1939 standard. Paradoxically, it was an institution far larger than it had been in the thirties, but at the same time inadequate for the purpose of global national security.

Sustaining America's new military obligations was a peacetime draft that moved far beyond its 1940 precedent. Between 1945 and 1973, a short stint in uniform became a routine right-of-passage for young American men. However, priorities on the home front qualified this form of permanent mobilization, much as they had during World War II. The list of deferments, particularly for educated Americans, evolved and expanded over time so that the country could simultaneously support both security abroad and the peacetime economic boom. This policy would have significant consequences once the Baby Boom generation reached draft age in the sixties.

Veterans' status during the early phase of the Cold War reflected the military's muddled mission. The strategy of containing communism was an abstract idea constructed by a diplomat. To win the new conflict with the Soviet Union, George F. Kennan proposed in 1946 "a long-term, patient but firm and vigilant containment of Russian expansive tendencies." Political scientists and government officials might understand the concept, but the average citizen did not. What the Cold War lacked were clearly delineated definitions of success or failure that had been present during World War II—surrendering armies, a captured enemy capital—important qualities determining the nature and value of victory and military service. The Greatest Generation, much like veterans of the American Revolution and the Civil War, would use these qualities as a yardstick to judge those who followed them. Rather than create solidarity among veterans as a group, distinctions drawn from Cold War military service would create and supplement the divisions that began to tear apart post-1945 America.

The Nature of Service in the Early Cold War

With Allied victory in 1945, America reverted to the traditional practice of rapidly demobilizing its military forces. By order of Congress in 1947, the Army was cut to just over a million men, with the Navy (558,000) and Marine

Corps (108,000) following suit. For the rest of the forties, the American defense establishment also underwent substantial budget cuts. From a wartime total of $350 billion in direct military spending, the Truman administration held the line for military budgets at between $10 and 13 billion annually. On the brink of the Korean War, the fiscal year 1951 request was $12.3 billion ($157.5 billion in February 2023 dollars). For 1952, the Defense Department contemplated reducing its budget to $12.1 billion.

The dominant branch of the US military was the newly created Air Force, which received the lion's share of attention and modern equipment. The newly introduced F-80 jet served alongside the venerable P-51 Mustang. The Consolidated-Vultee B-36 entered service in 1949 to supplement the aging fleet of B-29 Superfortresses. The Air Force offered policymakers the attractive option of projecting power at a distance, to substitute ordnance for American lives. For military leaders, the dawn of "push-button" war seemed at hand. In the meantime, the other branches, particularly the Army and Marine Corps, made do with an increasingly worn-out inventory of World War II weapons and equipment.

A combination of reservists, peacetime draftees, and regulars sustained military personnel needs. In an attempt to apply a lesson of World War II, Truman had asked Congress for Universal Military Training in October 1945 but failed to gather enough support for the measure. Instead, a limited version of selective service continued and proved adequate enough to sustain the small active-duty military. Over the next three decades, until its repeal in 1973, the draft spread military experience throughout much of the Baby Boom generation.

The Korean War as a Defining Moment

In June 1950, just before North Korean forces poured across the 38th Parallel, the US Army stood at 591,000, substantially below its authorized strength of

677,000. The American force closest to the conflict, the 8th Army in Japan, was an undermanned, undertrained, and poorly equipped assembly of units grown too comfortable with postwar occupation duties. With a high (43 percent) annual turnover rate, it was hamstrung by a lack of consistent leadership and institutional memory. Most of its weapons and equipment were World War II leftovers. Half of its tanks were vintage M4 Shermans. To alleviate chronic shortfalls, 8th Army commander Douglas MacArthur started Operation Roll Up, which scoured old Pacific battlefields for abandoned equipment to be shipped back to Japan for reconditioning. It was, at best, a small Band-Aid for much larger problems. Of the 13,780 two-ton trucks assigned to US forces in Japan, barely a third were in running condition. MacArthur had, according to the most optimistic estimates, a forty-five-day supply of ammunition when the North Korean invasion commenced on June 25, 1950.

The North Korean attack shocked and appalled Americans back home, although early battlefield failures were briefly reversed by the September 1950 Inchon invasion. In August 1950, months before China entered the conflict, a Gallup poll recorded that 57 percent of the public believed that the United States was already engaged in World War III. Many Americans contemplated the possibility that Korea might escalate to superpower confrontation and atomic Armageddon. When that failed to happen by the start of 1951, the home front contended with a new, unsavory development: stalemate and a grinding war of attrition that dragged on for almost two years.

The Korean War was the first chance for most Americans to understand what containment policy meant in human terms and they did not like what they saw. John Osbourn, reporting for *Life* magazine in August 1950, dwelt on the war's ugliness:

> Much of this war is alien to the American tradition and shocking to the American mind. For our men ... are waging this war as they are forced to wage it and as they will be forced to wage any war against the Communists anywhere in Asia ... This means not the usual, inevitable savagery of

combat in the field, but savagery in detail – the blotting out of villages where the enemy may be hiding; the shooting and shelling of refugees who may include [the enemy] or who may be screening an enemy advancing upon our positions.

The negative perception of the war carried over to the American fighting man. Historian Andrew Huebner explained the situation this way:

If the notion that American troops faced hardships and death had circulated during World War II, the idea that they should be pitied for it, seemed new. Bill Mauldin's Willie and Joe and the GIs of Ernie Pyle's columns had invited sympathy and gratitude, but usually not pity. During the Korean War a grimmer form of *stoicism*—born out of the dire straits in which UN forces found themselves—would become as much a part of the GI's image in American culture as his fatigue and sorrow.

Like World War II, regulars were not the only forces affected by this new Cold War battlefield. They were joined by tens of thousands of National Guard and reservists who mobilized and deployed for war in 1950. Many "Retreads," as they were known at the time, were comfortably settled into their suburban lives when the fighting began, committed to part-time National Guard weekend drills or part of the inactive reserves. In the scramble to send troops to defend South Korea, most simply shouldered their new burden and reported for duty. Some did not. When the Army appealed to reserve officers to voluntarily return to active duty, almost none did, requiring the Pentagon to force 7,862 captains and lieutenants back into uniform.

To soften the impact of unexpected mobilization, the Pentagon created an official military rotation policy. The Defense Department considered unit rotation as impractical and instead allowed individuals with thirty-six points (four points were awarded for each month in combat) to go home, usually after one year of service. In practice, policy failed to differentiate between enlistees whose terms of service were extended for Korea, reservists involuntarily recalled to active duty, and actual combat soldiers.

Casualties proved to be the final and most decisive referendum on American containment policy in Korea. Few Americans appreciated sacrificing 36,576 lives and more than twice that number wounded for the purpose of restoring the 1950 political status quo along the 38th Parallel. Polling consistently reflected widespread grievance with the war. Almost half (49 percent) of the people responding to Gallup in February 1951 considered US intervention to be a mistake.

Public discontent over Korea did take one important form. The war ended Harry Truman's political career. Hot on the heels of communist victory in the Chinese Civil War, the Soviet acquisition of the atom bomb, and multiplying spy scandals that brought Senator Joseph McCarthy to the forefront of national leadership, most Americans blamed the White House for missing key signs of the North Korean invasion, bungling mobilization, and nearly stumbling into an atomic exchange with Moscow. By February 1952, Truman's polling showed a pitiful 22 percent approval rating.

Dwight Eisenhower's promise to end the war in Korea came true, although not in the form most people might recognize in 1945. There was no exchange of surrender instruments by defeated enemy generals. There was no dramatic signing ceremony, as was the case on the USS *Missouri* anchored in Tokyo Harbor, for the cameras to record. Americans had to make do with an armistice in 1953, which ushered in a ceasefire but did not formally end the conflict. Diplomacy accomplished a limited and necessary goal, but it robbed many of the men and women in uniform of a sense of purpose and finality. David Hackworth, a highly decorated infantryman who joined the Army too late to fight in World War II, but who served in Korea and Vietnam was blunt: "*What, I asked myself, is a war without a goal?* What was victory, if not something you could taste and breathe and feel. Instead, there'd just been three years of fighting—for nothing."

Korean War veterans began making their way home, some by virtue of rotation policy, others when the armistice became official in July 1953. All told, the cohort who served—including 3.9 million enlisted men—was much smaller than the World War II generation, although 640,000 WWII veterans returned to fight in Korea. Almost 40 percent were draftees, a group supplemented by 243,000 reservists and 138,597 National Guard.

From the start, Korea veterans were perceived as a different breed than their fathers and brothers from the Good War. An August 1953 *New York Times* described them as products of the time:

> Raised as sixth-graders to family tales of the mechanized fighting of World War II, mechanically conditioned then and later to the push-button concept of living and the cosmic-ray concept of fighting, sent very young with other very young soldiers to a country they had never heard about to fight a war they did not understand, the new veterans are disquieting, machine-like products of their special time, and products particularly of the impersonalized low-pressure but deadly war that they have been waging.

The article essentially depicted them as robots, efficient corporate blanks, "an amazing amalgam of first-class fighting competence and an almost eerie disinterest in a job or surroundings or relationships."

Speaking for themselves, many Korea veterans revealed a very human side to their wartime experience. More than a few were bitter about their lost years in uniform. In a short February 1952 article titled "All's Quiet on the Home Front," Marine James C. Jones was extremely candid: "Americans in Korea have been double crossed by Americans in the United States. And some of us who have come back from that peninsula of misery are mighty ashamed of the home folks." He bridled at the indifference on display in America. While the troops fought, Jones observed, "In the vernacular, nearly everyone here is fat." Gene Gilmore expressed a common complaint in November 1952:

You find your job has shrunken in your absence, become a vestigial organ. Your take-home pay is considerably less than it was two years ago, and what is left doesn't go very far. The law that guarantees a veteran his old job and his old salary doesn't work out as intended. You are financially penalized, and not only for your time in the Army.

For too many, the problem was far more than a matter of dollars and cents. The social stigma carried by returning Korean War prisoners of war was a case in point. Veterans coming home in the fifties returned to an America caught in the throes of the Second Red Scare. Anti-communist paranoia ran amok in virtually every institution in the country. No one was truly safe. Even George C. Marshall, the five-star General of the Army who later served as both secretary of state and secretary of defense, could not escape, accused by Senator Joseph McCarthy of treason for his role in "a conspiracy so immense and an infamy so black as to dwarf any previous such venture in the history of man." McCarthy's accusations rained down on the military during the 1954 Army-McCarthy hearings, when the senator from Wisconsin decided to investigate Army dentist Irving Peress, essentially for not filling out a loyalty questionnaire after he was called into service in 1952. Although Peress was not required to do so at the time, McCarthy took his subsequent refusal as a sign of disloyalty. McCarthy expanded his accusations in February 1954 to include Major General Ralph Zwicker, who commanded Fort Monmouth, where Peress was stationed: "You are a disgrace to the uniform. You're shielding communist conspirators. You are going to be put on public display next Tuesday. You're not fit to be an officer. You're ignorant." In a speech, McCarthy described for Secretary of the Army Raymond T. Stevens, as "a fine, *innocent*, unknowing, Secretary of the Army who refuses to clean house."

This was the country awaiting the returning Korea POWs. Without question, the prisoners' ordeal did gather some sympathy, as *V.F.W. Magazine* noted in 1954: "the story we have to tell reflects a communist system which deliberately flouts every principle of morality and truth, devoting itself to one sole object, the progress of communism by any effective means, no matter how evil." Yet, there was concern that imprisonment had changed American servicemen. One author described it as the "fence-complex":

> All normal character evaluations are revised in P.O.W. camps. Because working hard means death and cheating often means life, many P.O.W.s lose their character—stability. The whole camp is reduced to a very low moral level and nobody cares much about any anything except survival.

During the war, important official sources expressed their doubts about prisoners' loyalty. The Pentagon claimed that some returning POWs had converted to communism even before the first prisoner exchange in April 1953:

> The Communists no doubt by their unremitting efforts ensnared some prisoners of war in their propaganda web. Some of them appear to have succumbed to the relentless Communist pressures, repetitious arguments, distorted and selected information and various inducements to accept, or at least repeat, many elements of Communist propaganda.

This discussion introduced a term that would never leave the American lexicon. Senior Pentagon officials expressed concerns that prisoners were permanently changed by the experience, not just by normal hardships—lack of food, adequate shelter, separation from family—but also by deliberate communist efforts to "brainwash" or reprogram them using the most advanced scientific methods available in the Cold War. All at once, veterans were caught in the worst paranoia evident during the McCarthy years. Each potentially was a "Manchurian Candidate," a term popularized by Richard Condon's 1959 book and the 1964 film version starring Frank Sinatra and Janet Leigh.

Popular media picked up on this thread and parlayed it into a larger commentary on the country:

One of the most important lessons we can learn from the red POW camps in Korea is that the softening up process was alarmingly easy with a great number of American captives. Many of our men appeared already more or less softened-up before they fell into communist hands. Somehow, we had done that part of the job for the reds. Home, school, and church had missed out somehow.

In effect, the returning POWs became a referendum on the strengths and weaknesses of American men in the fifties. Feminist writer Betty Friedan described too many of them as "apathetic, dependent, infantile, purposeless." Interestingly, as historians Richard Severo and Lewis Milford have pointed out, she had an odd ally in FBI director J. Edgar Hoover, who saw this "softness" as a gateway for communist manipulation.

In the final analysis, Korea invited both service and controversy. It was a key moment in history when American leaders applied old military tools to the new reality of Cold War international relations and found them wanting. The ambiguity of Korea's outcome carried over to its millions of veterans. Superficially, they followed the same cycle of mobilization, deployment, and homecoming familiar to World War II. But it was a process fraught with administrative blunders and an ongoing undercurrent of public resentment against US leaders that transferred over to Korean War veterans. America's "forgotten war," to use Clay Blair's term, had many casualties who struggled with their status for decades to come.

The New Look, Military Service, and Veterans Before Vietnam

Between 1953 and 1965, the American military institution sat in a holding pattern, instrumental to Cold War containment but mindful, after the Korea experience, of avoiding another land war. The armed forces of the fifties and early sixties were distinctly different from the small, backward, cloistered institution of an earlier generation. The Eisenhower administration's "New Look" emphasized technology as a way to magnify power. "Massive retaliation" via the ongoing threat of nuclear weapons became the linchpin of American Cold War deterrence. Technology also implied long-term savings, specifically with respect to personnel. Under the New Look, nuclear weapons emerged as a substitute for a large conventional military. This was a key consideration for Eisenhower, who worried in 1953 whether "national bankruptcy or national destruction would get us first."

The New Look subsequently transformed the American military. The Pentagon gutted its ground forces. Between 1953 and 1957, the Army alone shrank from 1.5 million to 998,000 personnel, beginning what Maxwell Taylor would later describe as his branch's "Babylonian Captivity." In their place, at a time when Sputnik and the space race captured the public's imagination, the American military seized upon "push-button" warfare. To maintain relevance under the new mandate, all branches gravitated to missiles, tactical nuclear weapons, and doctrine that might enhance survival in the nuclear environment.

The Americans who signed up for New Look military did so for different reasons than the World War II generation. Patriotism clearly motivated enlistments, as did the ongoing peacetime draft. However, like the all-volunteer force of the seventies, recruitment during the post-1945 era focused on the military profession more as a vocation, one that could compete with or supplement a civilian career. Military pay rates increased between 1945 and 1955. Gross compensation for all military personnel grew by 19 percent, bringing them closer to the civilian sector. Military personnel with special skills could earn even more. An airman on flight status in 1949 made more ($3,135) than the median annual income after taxes ($2,998) of an American family. The armed forces offered better pension plans to the extent that they did not require employee contributions and, by law, became available after twenty years of service. A young man or woman right out of high school could leave the service in their late thirties and enjoy their freedom or start a whole new career. Better compensation also allowed service members to support their families. The Cold War witnessed an enormous increase in "dependents," spouses and children, from only 67,000 in 1940 to 500,000 by 1971.

Not surprisingly, the military culture in the fifties increasingly resembled the civilian world. An endless stream of short-term draftees fostered a military that one 1960 publication described as "marginal and ambiguous." David Hackworth, who continued as an officer in the New Look era, took the military to task for one of its remedies:

> Name tags were all very well for the new-style officer who stayed in a peacetime command only long enough to jockey his way into a better, career-furthering slot: why bother memorizing names, went his thinking, he'd never use again? But for the trooper, personalized uniforms were just another gimmicky example of an increasingly impersonal, almost corporate Army—one difficult to love, let alone have the allegiance to that would serve him and the country well in the event of war.

Veterans Activism and Generational Friction

The post–World War II era saw a familiar pattern of veterans' activism as younger groups challenged their older counterparts. At the time, the American Legion was the dominant veterans' organization. In 1946, it had two million constituents scattered throughout the country. Most were average citizens, but the Legion also included 195 members of the House of Representatives and forty-four senators.

The postwar Legion repurposed many of its traditional causes for the Cold War. It supported Truman's campaign for universal military training in 1945 and returned to the same policy, again, unsuccessfully, during the Korean

War. As tensions with the Soviet Union rose, a point sharpened by Moscow's successful acquisition of the atom bomb in 1949, the Legion lobbied for a reliable system of civil defense.

At the same time, the American Legion added to its long record of community activism. One area of interest was the national housing shortage, which plagued the country after the war. In Baton Rouge and New Orleans, American Legion posts formed corporations to develop hundreds of housing units in suburban subdivisions. To supplement health care for veterans and their dependents, the Legion also purchased and rehabilitated community hospitals in Louisiana. In 1949, the American Legion began the Community Development Program, which focused on both sustainable employment and affordable housing.

Postwar veterans' organizations devoted considerable energies to American children. Both the VFW and American Legion sponsored local chapters of the Boy Scouts, Boys Clubs, 4-H Club, and Girl Scouts. In 1954, the Legion created the Child Welfare Foundation, a project dedicated to medical and educational research that would "collectively fight the many ills confronting our nation's young people." Veterans were also concerned about some of the social problems rooted in the World War II home front: teenage delinquency, the breakdown of the family, and sexual promiscuity. The American Legion sponsored state and national chapters of Boys' State, which provided instruction in citizenship, governance, and trips to Washington, DC. In 1960, 18,000 boys visited the nation's capital under Legion sponsorship.

As they had in the twenties, many veterans saw a potential solution to the country's problems in the national sport: baseball, which continued to enjoy massive popularity. On the brink of World War II, the country was captivated by Joe DiMaggio's fifty-six-game hitting streak. The same audience followed the "Yankee Clipper" when he enlisted in February 1943 and started playing baseball in Army exhibition games for the troops. According to a War Department survey, 75 percent of service members played or watched the game during the war. When these men came home, they introduced their young sons to the sport through the most familiar institution available to them. By 1947, approximately five million boys played in American Legion leagues.

For the Legion, baseball meant more than just play. The sport offered a chance to mentor young boys into adulthood. Coaches stressed good sportsmanship, leadership, and physical achievement. They emphasized that the "spirit of competition" was more important than winning on the field: "when an attempt is made by some leader to take all the stars from a group of teams and with them form a team solely for the purpose of winning championship honors, it destroys the very foundation upon which the program is built." Legion baseball also wanted to shape better citizens: "The good sportsman has learned teamwork. The good citizen has also learned teamwork, which is merely another name for co-operation. A nation of individualists would pass swiftly into anarchy."

Of course, whether it applied to public policy or charity, veterans' groups did not move in lock step. Newer organizations like the American Veterans Committee (AVC) challenged the political and social status quo much more readily than their older peers. Young veterans chafed at the conservative values of the VFW and American Legion and the fact that they had little voice in these organizations. Bill Mauldin characterized speeches made by Legion leaders as "a mixture of National Association of Manufacturing advertising and a Hearst editorial page." The old groups offered few apologies. For a senior delegate to the American Legion 1946 national convention in San Francisco, the reason was simple: "This is a billion-dollar corporation. You don't turn something like that over to a bunch of inexperienced kids."

After World War II, the AVC became deeply involved in the civil rights movement, forming a strong, long-term alliance with the NAACP. It advocated for minority veterans and their surviving family members who were denied disability benefits by the Veterans Administration and state governments. The American Veterans Committee Legal Aid Project assisted Black veterans to navigate the medical claims process, often allying with their NAACP counterparts by filing *amicus curiae* briefs in federal court.

The AVC also fought against racism embedded within national veterans' organizations. As noted in an earlier chapter, state leadership in the American Legion and the Veterans of Foreign Wars normally determined membership standards, which included segregated posts. Times were changing, however. The cumulative effect of FDR's Four Freedoms speech, The NAAP's "Double V" campaign, and the military service of one million African Americans in the Good War had shifted both national norms and expectations. Many white veterans were not prepared for a new era, one that was capped by the landmark 1954 *Brown v. Board* decision. In response to *Brown*, the VFW Clark-Lyon Post No. 4731 of Indianola, Mississippi embraced the past, pledging:

> To aid all Races but not at each others expense. To provide equal but separate schooling for the Black and White Races. To prevent mongrelization of our nation by avoiding conditions that foster and promote intermarriage of races. To uphold Segregation in the states that desire it and whose social structure requires it.

The American Veterans Committee did not shrink from challenging this stance and made its disdain public. In 1955, the AVC attacked the American Legion for its "false patriotism" because the latter tolerated ongoing segregation through its affiliate organization, the Forty & Eight.

Younger veterans in the AVC were also deeply enmeshed in the anti-communist debates of the early Cold War. As was the case in many American organizations at the end of World War II, communists were part of the AVC's original membership. Official AVC policy was to allow communists to run for office, publicly oppose them, and let rank-and-file members decide through the ballot process. However, as tensions with the Soviet Union escalated, this position proved untenable. At its national convention in November 1948, the AVC decided to ban communists from the organization.

Even as the American Veterans Committee backtracked, the FBI started an in-depth investigation of the organization between 1947 and 1950. An official report noted that the AVC had been "subjected to Communist infiltration in local chapters." It was a dangerous moment, coming at a time when Senator Joe McCarthy was approaching the apex of his political power and causing havoc across the American landscape.

Undeterred, the AVC doubled down and counterattacked against its critics. In June 1950, the AVC National Planning Committee demanded McCarthy's impeachment "for high crimes and misdemeanors" committed during his anti-communist investigations. It called out McCarthy's irresponsibility and subsequent harm to free speech, civil liberties, and overall American resilience in the Cold War. The AVC counseled the incoming Eisenhower administration to make a distinction between "undesirables" who threatened national security and loyal government employees.

Young veterans hammered away at the older groups, especially the American Legion, which had thrown its support behind McCarthy and other red-baiting politicians. When Bill Mauldin took over national leadership of the AVC, he flagged the "antics of certain self-styled 'veterans leaders' who were sounding off in all directions," acting like "Junior FBI, amateur GPU, or hooded Dick Tracys." In 1954, the AVC attempted to heal the increasingly bloody rift between itself and other veterans groups by proposing a joint code of conduct. Both the American Legion and the Veterans of Foreign Wars rejected the proposal, leading Mauldin to comment that the latter organization "appears committed to continuing this 'now you see it, now you don't' spook hunt as an out-and-out publicity gimmick to gain new members."

The Korean War G.I. Bill

In the years following World War II, the American Legion and the VFW became the guardians of the original 1944 Serviceman's Readjustment Act.

Despite ongoing Republican campaigns to retrench benefits as too expensive and unsustainable, veterans' groups rallied again and again to flex their political muscle and beat back the fiscal conservatives. Once the United States went to war in Korea, these organizations saw an opportunity to expand the veterans' safety net further. With the precedent set by World War II, they successfully shepherded the 1952 Veterans' Readjustment Assistance Act (PL 82-550) through Congress.

While the 1952 G.I. Bill rested on past policy, it contained many compromises on spending that hurt Korean War veterans. The new legislation provided slightly more money ($26 a week instead of $20) for unemployment insurance but reduced its availability from one year to six months. Lawmakers also cut funds for the Veterans Employment Service, whose overall number of field offices declined throughout the fifties. One of the most important changes to the Veterans' Readjustment Assistance Act was to educational benefits. The original G.I. Bill had paid up to $500 annually for tuition in addition to $75 monthly allowance to single veterans without dependents. The 1952 G.I. Bill allowed for a lump sum for all expenses; $110 a month for individuals, $135 for veterans with one dependent, and $160 for veterans with two or more dependents. For unmarried veterans, this was a significant reduction even before inflation. The Chancellor of Syracuse University, William P. Tolley, characterized the benefits plan as a "shabby deal." The Association of American Colleges voted unanimously, and unsuccessfully, in January 1954 to urge lawmakers to increase the subsistence allowance for veterans.

Two trends characterized veterans' policy in the decade following the Korean War. Like the World War II generation, they expected social approval and generous benefits. According to an October 1954 Roper survey of veterans, a strong majority favored special additional consideration from lawmakers. The poll noted the preference for expanding service-connected disability payments, civilian employment security upon returning from the Korea deployment, veterans' preference in federal civil service applications, and improved VA payments for school and training.

These expectations clashed with the Eisenhower administration's basic understanding of the federal budget. Dwight D. Eisenhower was a hero to veterans, a relationship that partially explained his landslide victory over Adlai Stevenson in 1952. Yet, one of his concerns was federal spending, much of it related to the military, which he believed threatened to bankrupt the country. By extension, the billions committed to veterans' programs, supplemented by the 1952 G.I. Bill, presented significant concerns to fiscal conservatives interested in preserving the postwar economic boom.

Such were the circumstances in 1955 when Eisenhower appointed Omar Bradley to chair a commission on veterans' benefits. Bradley, who had retired from the Army two years earlier, answered his former commander's call, although his new mission was much different than it had been a decade earlier. When the Bradley Commission started its work, the main problem was not building a system adequate to the task of serving a massive influx of new veterans. On the contrary, his job was to address the escalating expenses of two G.I. Bills, now covering almost twenty-two million individuals, and veterans' rising expectations, fostered by the likes of the American Legion and VFW, that additional help was on the way. Eisenhower's 1956 budget message pointedly identified veterans' benefits as an ongoing and increasing expense that needed "constructive reconsideration." In particular, the White House balked at the idea of a full retirement pension for all veterans regardless of service in peace or war. Administration analysts estimated the new costs for this program alone might be as high as $762 billion, more than ten times the 1956 fiscal year budget.

Bradley's purpose in 1955 was to put his own popularity and political capital behind the possibility of cutting veterans' benefits. As it navigated the thicket of government priorities and the powerful veterans' lobby, the Bradley Commission was cautious. It had good reason to be. The Disabled American Veterans (DAV) attacked the commission even before it issued its final report, warning Bradley against "A disgraceful campaign for economy in government, mostly at the expense of all our war-disabled."

To make its case, the Bradley Commission argued for the prioritization of veterans' benefits rather than their expansion. It made a distinction between "programs which take care of the needs arising directly out of military service" and other normal problems associated with aging and infirmity. In other words, Bradley proposed a basic division of labor between the Veterans Administration and the existing civilian social welfare system against inefficient and extremely costly duplication.

Criticism rained down upon the Bradley Commission as soon as its report became public. Omar B. Ketchum, the VFW's legislative director, wrote in May 1956 that his organization "staunchly defended liberalization and expansion of compensation and pension program and denied that changing social and economic conditions had any bearing upon the need for veteran pensions." The strongest negative response came from the American Legion, which attacked the commission's report as "filled with cliches [sic], self-contradictions, inaccuracies, looseness of expression, non-sequitors [sic], statistical monstrosities." For its own part, the Veterans of Foreign Wars characterized commission recommendations as "impractical, contrary to national tradition and replete with distortions and exaggerations" and an "attempt to reverse the traditional national policy of the United States with respect to those who have served in the Armed Forces."

Collectively, veterans' groups managed to stymie the Eisenhower administration's attempted economy drive. The Veterans Administration saw a few small cuts, to educational funding and VA bed space, but overall, the 1957–64 period actually witnessed a series of modest budget increases, from $4.8 billion in 1957 to $5.3 billion in 1960, and $6.0 billion in 1964. Gone for good was the proposed lifetime pension for all veterans.

Unexpected, tragic, and inconclusive, the Korean War left a mark on America. In his 2007 work, *The Coldest Winter*, David Halberstam captured

This vast disconnect between those who fought and the people at home, the sense that no matter the bravery they showed, or the validity of their cause, the soldiers of Korea had been granted a kind of second-class status compared to that of the men who had fought in the previous wars, led to a great deal of quiet—and enduring—bitterness.

Much of this bitterness was actually expressed during the war and it remained part of the deep undercurrent of discontent that followed in the years after the 1953 armistice. Americans might have considered the Korean War the "forgotten war," as journalist Clair Blair described it, but its veterans did not forget.

As a whole, the veterans community represented an enormous part of the country by the fifties. The accumulation of service from both World Wars, the peacetime draft, Korea, in addition to surviving nineteenth-century veterans (the last Civil War veteran died in 1956) amounted to tens of millions. According to the Bradley Commission report, both veterans and their families affected by the 1944 and 1952 G.I. bills accounted for a total of eighty-one million people, or almost half of the country. Years before the Great Society became a reality and ushered in a new wave of social welfare programs, continually expanding veterans' programs were already solidifying the expectation that federally funded benefits were the rule rather than an exception to national policy.

Cold War era veterans remained deeply involved in post-WWII American society and many of their efforts followed traditional paths. The VFW and American Legion expanded their philanthropy to the point where it touched millions of homes. Other organizations, most notably the American Veterans Committee, embraced some of the most controversial features of the postwar "rights revolution," delving into issues of race, segregation, and right-wing politics. As they did so, groups like the AVC, working in concert with the NAACP, helped set the stage for ever greater campaigns for social justice in the sixties.

9

Vietnam

At the age of twenty-four, I was more prepared for death than I was for life.

PHILIP CAPUTO, 1981

Vietnam was as a dividing point for Americans; Democrat versus Republican, "hawk" versus "dove," and, most importantly for the Baby Boom generation, as Robert Timberg wrote in *The Nightingale's Song*, those who stayed home and "those who went." Like Korea, Vietnam was yet another undeclared Cold War conflict. However, unlike Korea, Vietnam was a combination of civil war, insurgency, and proxy war abetted by the United States, the Soviet Union, and China. As the war progressed, this new form of American containment policy had even less clarity, a quality that cost troop morale on the ground and public support back home.

Vietnam divided veterans just as much as the public. The American Legion and Veterans of Foreign Wars were early and consistent supporters throughout most of the conflict. They constituted the hardliners, the hawks who saw the war as our best line of defense against the communist menace. Official authority rewarded their allegiance. American Legion and VFW leaders received regular briefings from the Department of State, Navy, and the Marine Corps and open access to the White House.

In a clear echo of the American Veterans Committee, a young generation of veterans challenged both the old guard and the Cold War status quo in the sixties. African American veterans formed the Deacons for Defense and Justice to protect civil rights workers who confronted an increasingly violent landscape in the American South. Veterans also joined the early antiwar movement, lending their experience and agency to a growing opposition against the military establishment. By the beginning of the seventies, the Vietnam Veterans Against the War was a permanent fixture in mass protests. Its members provided some of the most poignant and heartbreaking moments in American history.

The divisiveness plaguing the country bled over into official veterans' policies. When Congress decided it was time to debate an updated version of the G.I. Bill, it was clear that lawmakers did not consider all military service to be equal. Representative Olin Teague of Texas finished World War II with three Silver Stars and three Purple Hearts after serving in the 79th Infantry Division. As the powerful chair of the House Committee on Veterans Affairs, he used his service as a yardstick to justify reduced benefits for Vietnam era veterans. It was a deliberate decision that had a serious long-term impact of the postwar transition of millions of young men and women back into normalcy.

Service in the Age of Counterinsurgency

The sixties were a time of violent, global change. At the start of the decade, some of the last vestiges of Europe's old colonial empires began their final slide into collapse. By 1960, all of French West Africa and French Equatorial Africa were free. Seventeen new African nations emerged between 1960 and 1961 as Europe withdrew from the continent. Guerrilla war followed the end of French dominion in Southeast Asia. Communist-backed insurgents threatened the stability of Laos. In South Vietnam, the Diem government in Saigon was under siege by a resurgent Viet Cong. America's backyard in the Western Hemisphere did not escape unrest. Latin America saw ten military governments toppled between 1956 and 1960. When the sixties began, Fidel Castro and a young cohort of Cuban revolutionaries were an inspiration for a new generation ready to challenge US power.

A new American administration saw these turbulent times as a mandate for action.

As a senator, John F. Kennedy made his stance clear in 1959:

> So, in practice, our nuclear retaliatory power is not enough. It cannot deter Communist aggression which is too limited to justify atomic war. It cannot protect uncommitted nations against Communist takeover using local or guerrilla forces. It cannot be used in so-called brush-fire wars ... In short, it cannot prevent the Communists from nibbling away at the fringe of the free world's territory or strength.

Kennedy's version of Cold War containment involved developing what policymakers called "flexible response." In part, this meant economic aid and technical assistance. Billions went into the Alliance for Progress in Latin America to address the potential foundations—poverty, disease, housing, education—for Cuban-inspired revolutions. Kennedy also invested additional billions in nuclear, conventional, and special forces. Much like the Eisenhower administration, the White House endorsed and expanded covert operations on a global scale.

The war in Vietnam was the largest and bloodiest proof of the concept of American Cold War commitments. The war tested abstract Cold War principles—containment, escalation, massive retaliation, mutually assured destruction—and revealed their underlying complexities and contradictions. When the United States launched Operation Rolling Thunder (1965–1968), its strategic bombing campaign against North Vietnam, the goal was reducing Hanoi's ability to support the insurgency in South Vietnam. At the same time, target selection was also dictated by concerns about Chinese or Russian intervention and domestic political support for the war. On the ground,

American commanders constructed rules of engagement against communist guerrillas (otherwise known as the Viet Cong, or VC) and North Vietnamese regulars that were designed to protect civilians caught in the crossfire. However, American command also demanded a "body count" as it pursued a war of attrition. These circumstances placed the American military in an impossible position, something illustrated in Philip Caputo's memoir of his experience as a Marine officer in 1965:

> The day before, a rifleman from B Company had shot a farmer, apparently mistaking him for a VC. To avoid similar incidents in the future, brigade again ordered that [rifle] chambers be kept clear except when contact was imminent, and in guerrilla-controlled areas, no fire be directed at unarmed Vietnamese *unless they were running*. A running Vietnamese was a fair target. This left us bewildered and uneasy. No one was eager to shoot civilians. Why should the act of running identify someone as a Communist? What if we shot a Vietnamese who turned out to have a legitimate reason for running? Would that be a justifiable act or grounds for a court martial?

Responding to his men's questions, Caputo's company commander said, "Look, I don't know what this is supposed to mean, but I talked to battalion, and they said as far as they are concerned, if he's dead and Vietnamese, he's VC."

However, it is important to remember that, given the force structure in Vietnam, the overwhelming majority of Americans avoided Caputo's experience. Unlike Korea, neither the National Guard nor the reserves deployed to serve in Southeast Asia. Deployed units were regularly replenished by a stream of draftees who carried most of the weight of the war effort. Even among this group, selective service was not the same system it had been in either world war. The number of exemptions and deferments available to Baby Boomers had expanded beyond essential defense skills, marital status, children, or religious beliefs. During the Cold War, education was another important condition that took young men off the draft rolls. Millions completed the

Selective Service College Qualification Test (SSCQT) for reclassification to 2-S (deferred for college). By December 1965, Selective Service granted 1.8 million student deferments.

Young Boomers who lacked any of these options could find other ways to beat the system. During the sixties and early seventies, a fairly sophisticated network of "draft counseling" emerged to help construct physical or mental ailments that might disqualify a young man from service. Overall, during the Vietnam era, fifteen million American men received deferments.

The rest, unmarried young men who could not afford college or a convenient medical diagnosis, carried the brunt of the draft. Consequently, the units deploying to South Vietnam included large numbers of the working-class and a disproportionate number of racial minorities. According to Charles Moskos's well-known study of race in the military, between 1960 and 1970, African Americans represented 16 percent of Army draftees.

One of the most infamous results of US military manpower policy was Project 100,000. When it began in 1966, the Defense Department promoted Project 100,000 as a way to help disadvantaged men through military service and education. Specifically, it invited individuals previously rejected for low scores on the Armed Forces Qualification Test (AFQT) that placed them in Category IV (scoring between 10 and 30 percent on the test) to join.

The Pentagon added the caveat that these individuals would receive additional remedial training in the service. Defense secretary Robert S. McNamara praised the program for giving these generally poor and uneducated inductees "an opportunity to return to civilian life with skills and aptitudes which for them and their families will reverse the downward spiral of decay." Between 1966 and 1968, Project 100,000 added approximately one quarter of a million men to the US military through the selective service system. In 1966, 25 percent of the Army's recruits came from Category IV inductees. That same year, a full third of Project 100,000 men were African American. Lacking skill levels adequate for most occupational specialties, approximately

37 percent of the so-called New Standards Men were assigned to the combat arms, a rate more than a third higher than other recruits. Civil rights leaders almost immediately attacked the initiative for the disproportionate burden it placed on the Black community. Floyd McKissick, national director of the Congress of Racial Equality, called the program "a cynical method to punish black youths for the social ills imposed on them by the major society."

America and the Vietnam Veteran

Approximately 2.7 million Americans served in the Vietnam War between 1961 and 1975. It was a smaller force than the one that fought in Korea and far more reliant on new technology. Vietnam eventually saw regular use of laser-guided munitions, infrared optics, satellite communications, and a host of innovations. Consequently, the military of the sixties relied on an increasing proportion of specialists necessary for its day-to-day management. One result was an ongoing decline of combat personnel. By 1968, only 29 percent of all personnel in the Army were assigned to the infantry, artillery, armor, and air defense artillery. Taking into account units actually deployed to South Vietnam, only 7.2 percent of all Army forces directly engaged the enemy in Vietnam.

The amount and type of public support for these forces fluctuated throughout the war. Americans generally favored a strong military response to communist aggression in the early stages of the conflict. In early 1966, 61 percent of those polled agreed with escalating Operation Rolling Thunder if a bombing halt failed to bring Hanoi to the diplomatic table. A year later, 67 percent still supported strategic bombing of North Vietnam.

Public attitudes about the ground war were a different story. When conventional forces deployed to South Vietnam, support for this action was relatively strong. In August 1965, shortly after Marines began Operation

Starlite around Danang, only 24 percent of respondents indicated that "the US had made a mistake sending troops to fight in Vietnam."

However, escalating troop deployments and concurrently increasing casualties seriously eroded public tolerance of military operations. Almost two thousand Americans died in South Vietnam in 1965. Two years later, combat deaths grew on an order of magnitude to 11,363. By February 1967, 32 percent of poll respondents believed the war was a mistake. By October it was 46 percent. After the Tet Offensive, victory seemed far beyond reach and a stalemate the most likely outcome. In August 1968, for the first time a majority of Americans (53 percent) thought that sending troops was a mistake. By May 1971, after the Nixon administration announced the invasion of Cambodia, that majority had grown to 61 percent.

Like Korea, the emerging condemnation of the war carried over into a negative public perception of the military and its membership. According to a March 1971 Harris poll, 82 percent of respondents believed that the draft had produced soldiers who did not want to fight, 61 percent responded that drugs had broken down military discipline, and only 59 percent believed that the American Army could "outfight any other army in the world."

More ominous was the impact of atrocities on the public mindset. Allegations of war crimes had surfaced as early as 1966 when retired Special Forces Sergeant Donald Duncan revealed US involvement in torture as well as operations in Laos and North Vietnam. Writing in *Ramparts*, Duncan questioned "whether communism is spreading in spite of our involvement or because of it." Revelations about the 1968 My Lai Massacre deepened public concerns. In a series of stories for the *St. Louis Post-Dispatch*, Seymour Hersh investigated deliberate acts by soldiers of 23rd (Americal) Division that resulted in the rape, mutilation, and deaths of hundreds of South Vietnamese men, women, and children. Myrtle Meadlo, the mother of one of the soldiers, lamented, "I sent them a good boy and they made him a murderer."

Not everyone condemned My Lai. The American Legion archives include one reference to the massacre, a press statement regarding Army efforts to improve its image in August 1970. When Lieutenant William F. Calley was convicted for his part in My Lai, the American Legion began a campaign to raise $100,000 for his appeal and a petition to collect ten million signatures to protest the conviction. The national commander of the VFW said "There have been My Lais in every war. Now for the first time we have tried a soldier for performing his duty."

Veterans' Activism in the Sixties

Veterans' groups followed divergent trajectories during much of the sixties. On the one side were the older organizations, which aligned with many of the traditional interests of the generation that had fought World War II. The American Legion and VFW in particular were consistently friendly outlets for Richard Nixon and Spiro Agnew. As a candidate for president in March 1968, Nixon announced his plan for peace in Vietnam at a New Hampshire American Legion Hall. Agnew made a characteristically clumsy attempt to speak about racial equality before the VFW in August 1968 when he said that "Law and order must mean to all our people the protection of the innocent—not to some the cracking of black skulls."

The older veterans' organizations generally supported both American policy toward the Vietnam War and the war effort in general. In a call back to the World War II experience, the Legion conducted morale building campaigns like "Call Vietnam," which sent thousands of Christmas cards to deployed troops. As the war became increasingly controversial, they organized overt patriotic displays and direct support for the Nixon administration. The Legion presented Richard Nixon with its Distinguished Service Medal in June 1969. That fall, following massive Moratorium to End the War in Vietnam marches around the country, the VFW and American Legion held a counterprotest in Washington on Veterans Day that drew approximately 10,000 people. Just a few months after the shootings at Kent State, the Legion national commander endorsed the invasion of Cambodia.

Nixon recognized this special relationship when he appointed Donald E. Johnson, a former Legion national commander, to head the VA in June 1969. Johnson held the position throughout Nixon's time in office, but eventually resigned under the weight of a scandal involving VA appointments, mismanagement of programs, and political fundraising for the administration. His departure in 1974 came only a few months before Nixon's resignation.

For their own part, the new veterans' groups that emerged in the sixties joined a path already blazed by organizations like the NAACP and the American Veterans Committee (AVC). Self-defense in the pursuit of civil rights was an unfortunate and well-established tradition after World War II. During the bloody 1946 election year, as white extremists wreaked havoc in African American communities, some returned World War II veterans refused to passively accept aggression. Klan harassment in Bennetsville, Georgia, prompted African American veterans to form armed patrols. The *Atlanta Daily World* described them as "a proud restless group" that was "tired of being booted about."

A generation later, the same cycle of violence against civil rights workers produced a similar result, specifically the Deacons for Defense and Justice. First formed in 1964 to counter officially sanctioned brutality against civil rights workers and the local population of Jonesboro, Louisiana, African American veterans made up the Deacons' membership. They acquired weapons and ammunition and assigned shifts to ensure round-the-clock security for civil rights workers. Historian Lance Hill notes that the Deacons for Defense addressed the immediate need for safety rather than long-term strategy, a feature that defined the group for most of its existence.

The Deacons presented civil rights leaders with an interesting dilemma. One marcher commented in a 2013 interview that he felt "rather reassured" by their armed presence. Another civil rights activist spoke to the need for peace of mind in the violent, militarized context of the American South of the early sixties: "The Deacons took the fear out of it, because they taught them [civil rights workers] that the same bullet that will kill you is the same bullet that will kill somebody else. There's no difference. There's no difference. But it also shows that you don't look for trouble, all you do is protect yourself."

However, having armed veterans accompanying marchers and organizers was a problem for what leaders like Martin Luther King, Jr., intended as a peaceful movement. The Deacon's militancy and the prospect of armed self-defense openly alienated many members of the Congress on Racial Equality (CORE) active in the South at the time. Martin Luther King was reported to have been "deeply upset and concerned" about Deacon activity. In contrast, Jackie Robinson, writing for the *Chicago Defender*, was "1,000 percent" in favor of the Deacons.

The Deacons for Defense and Justice were not alone among new activist veterans' organizations in the sixties. When it was founded in 1967, the Vietnam Veterans Against the War (VVAW) was a marginal addition to the antiwar movement. Initially, members took a fairly conservative approach to protest. In public, they sported suits and ties and projected a clean-cut appearance. They attempted redress by conventional political organizing and voting. VVAW members volunteered for Eugene McCarthy in 1968 when the antiwar candidate challenged Lyndon Johnson for the Democrat nomination. Richard Nixon's subsequent victory was a serious blow to these hopes.

At the end of the sixties, the VVAW changed its tactics. It joined the Serviceman's Link to the Peace Movement (or LINK), which fostered antiwar activity, from coffeehouse discussions to dozens of underground newspapers, throughout stateside and overseas military bases. At home, VVAW protests developed into exercises in counterculture street theater to attract media attention. In September 1970, it staged Operation RAW (Rapid American

Withdrawal), which involved a "tactical" march by 200 veterans from Morristown, New Jersey to Valley Forge, Pennsylvania. The theme, according to a *New York Times* account, was re-creating the Vietnam experience "as realistically as possible without actually shooting anyone." As they marched, veterans handed out pamphlets to people who collected along their route. One of them said

> We might have burned your house
> We might have shot your dog
> We might have shot you …
> We might have bombed out bridges you use every day
> We might have raped your wife and daughters
> We might have turned you over to your government for torture
> We might have taken souvenirs from your property
> We might have shot things up a bit …
> We might have done *all* these things to you and your neighbors
> If it doesn't bother you that American soldiers do these things every day to the Vietnamese simply because they are gooks, then picture YOURSELF as one of the silent victims.
> HELP US END THE WAR BEFORE THEY TURN YOUR SON INTO A BUTCHER OR A CORPSE.

Two Americas followed the VVAW on its journey to Valley Forge. Antiwar politicians like George McGovern and Edmund Muskie (both World War II combat veterans) sent messages in support. Celebrity activists Donald Sutherland and Jane Fonda were present when they arrived, with Fonda giving a welcoming speech to the footsore marchers. In contrast, World War II veterans from VFW Douglas MacArthur Post 1507 also waited for their military comrades. A forty-eight-year-old former paratrooper who had fought in the Battle of the Bulge expressed their attitudes very well when he called the VVAW "a disgrace to everything we stand for."

In February 1971, the VVAW staged the Winter Soldier Investigation, a conference held to discuss and provide testimony on alleged war crimes in Vietnam. Over the course of three days, more than a hundred veterans offered firsthand accounts of murder, rape, and torture committed against both Viet Cong insurgents and innocent civilians. An interesting thing occurred during Winter Soldier. Although most media outlets ignored the event, the *New York Times* sent Neil Sheehan, a reporter with a long track record in Vietnam as well as healthy skepticism regarding US policy. However, when he tried to verify Winter Soldier claims, he found a clear pattern of inaccurate and uncorroborated information. Sheehan believed that "The country desperately needs a sane an honest inquiry into the question of war crimes and atrocities in Vietnam by a body of knowledgeable and responsible men who are not beholden to the current military establishment."

Perhaps the best known VVAW protest was Operation Dewey Canyon III in April 1971. Assembling a "full division of Vietnam veterans" that included "combat veterans, wounded and decorated, maimed in body and spirit," the VVAW promised a "limited incursion" into Washington, DC. Their mission was to "override Nixon's blood lust" and end the war. Almost a thousand veterans eventually attended the event.

History remembers two very different parts of Dewey Canyon III. When hundreds of veterans attempted to enter the Capitol Building to meet with legislators, they confronted a series of wooden barricades that blocked their entrance. Undeterred, dozens assembled in front of the barrier and took turns throwing an assortment of campaign ribbons, Purple Hearts, medals for valor, and even certificates of honorable discharge, over it. Many took the moment to denounce the war and remember fallen comrades.

One day earlier, a much quieter, but important VVAW protest took place in front of the Senate Foreign Relations Committee. John Kerry, a decorated Navy veteran who served in South Vietnam in between 1968 and 1969, addressed the needless sacrifice of American lives for the "mystical war against communism." More importantly, he spoke to the consequence to the country and his generation:

> The country doesn't know it yet, but it has created a monster, a monster in the form of millions of men who have been taught to deal and to trade in violence, and who are given the chance to die for the biggest nothing in history; men who have returned with a sense of anger and a sense of betrayal which no one has yet grasped.

Kerry finished his testimony to loud and enthusiastic applause from veterans in the audience.

VVAW leader Jan Crumb saw his group breaking new ground during Dewey Canyon III. He claimed that veterans "were neither the trashers, passive marchers, nor the usual nonviolent civil disobedience types. We followed our own instincts and did things our own way. There was a great deal of humor and a great deal of seriousness about what we did."

The VVAW carried this momentum into protests at the 1972 Republican Convention in Miami, Florida. Hunter S. Thompson, who covered the event for *Rolling Stone* magazine, witnessed their arrival: "There is no anti-war or even anti-establishment group in America today with the psychic leverage of the VVAW... They are golems, come back to haunt us all—even Richard Nixon, who campaigned for the presidency in 1968 with a promise that he had 'a secret plan' to end the war in Vietnam."

However, for all the gravity that Vietnam veterans lent to the antiwar movement, it did not last. Understanding the vast unpopularity of selective service, the Nixon administration issued the last draft call in December 1972. The policy officially lapsed just six months later. More importantly, the administration announced a formal end to the war at the end of January 1973 with the conclusion of the Paris Peace Talks. In one fell swoop, the reason for being for both the antiwar movement and the VVAW was gone.

The Cold War G.I. Bill

The Vietnam War, like the conflict in Korea, generated a new round of veterans' programs that unfortunately saw federal support deteriorate even further. When the Veterans Readjustment Benefits Act (PL 89-358), popularly known as the Cold War G.I. Bill, became law in 1966, it significantly cut support for education. Like the previous World War II and Korean versions, veterans could receive funding for a total of thirty-six months of training. However, the Cold War G.I. Bill offered only $100 a month (down from $110) for tuition, fees, and "subsistence" for a full-time student with no dependents. Veterans attending classes with two or more dependents received a monthly stipend of $150 (down from $160). With these cuts and fourteen years of inflation, most private colleges and a few public ones were effectively out of reach for most Vietnam-era veterans.

A prolonged and controversial debate among veterans in Congress ultimately produced this policy. Cost was an ongoing concern, particularly with respect to the millions of new veterans entering the system as the Vietnam War escalated and draft calls grew. Combined with the massive commitments of new Great Society programs like Medicaid and Medicare, coupled with war spending, lawmakers were increasingly reluctant to add to the list.

A most abstract, but familiar, discussion about the value of military service also shaped the Cold War G.I. Bill. Many World War II veterans, like Olin Teague, opposed even the notion that his experience was the same as any form of Cold War service, whether it was in Vietnam or otherwise. He maintained, along with the American Legion, that that it was fundamentally less risky and disruptive to both volunteers and draftees who, as a group, deserved less.

Teague did not represent all veterans in congress. Senators Ralph W. Yarborough of Texas, George McGovern (D-SD), and Daniel Inouye (D-HI), all of whom served with distinction in World War II, allied with

Representatives Frank Horton (R-NY) and Philip Burton (D-CA) to argue for parity between present and past veterans. Yarborough believed that all military service, regardless of its type, deserved both official recognition and benefits. During debates on the 1966 law, he noted that amendments to the Korean Veterans Assistance Act extended the window for eligibility to 1955, two years after the official armistice. Moreover, in testimony before Teague's committee, Yarborough detailed the number of World War II veterans who qualified for the original G.I. Bill, but never saw combat. In the end, Yarborough failed to convince enough legislators to restore generous original benefits to Vietnam veterans.

This failure was tragic, especially with respect to educational benefits. Of the three cohorts of veterans, World War II, Korea, and Vietnam, men and women returning to civilian life in the sixties made up one of the best educated militaries in American history. Vietnam veterans earned high school diplomas at twice the rate of the World War II generation (59.1 percent to 26.3 percent). Thirteen percent of Vietnam veterans had some college credit, more than both World War II (9.6 percent) and Korea (11.1 percent) veterans. However, given the cuts imposed by the 1966 G.I. Bill, the broad array of private and public colleges available in 1945 was not available to Baby Boomers returning home from Vietnam.

Despite the shortfalls of the 1966 legislation, the Veterans Administration and other federal agencies introduced a series of programs designed to ease the transition from the Vietnam era military to civilian life. Operation Outreach sent VA counselors directly to South Vietnam as early as 1967 to address topics such as job placement for wounded veterans and provide guidance about navigating VA medical care and rehabilitation. Between 1968 and 1970, representatives met with approximately 1.1 million veterans. Project Transition was a Defense Department initiative that offered counseling on military installations in the United States and around the world. By 1969, DoD officials claimed that 250,000 personnel received job training and an additional

1.5 million personnel had undergone counseling. The Pentagon also struck up relationships with defense contractors, such as IBM, to employ discharged veterans. In June 1971, the Nixon administration went a step further by encouraging the National Alliance of Businessmen, which represented almost 30,000 companies, to provide 100,000 jobs for Vietnam veterans.

Unfortunately, the economic prospects for Vietnam veterans proved even more limited than their educational opportunities. As the Vietnam War wound down, the post-1945 American boom was ending, ushered in by foreign competition, rising inflation, and declining employment, particularly in traditional manufacturing and industry. Between 1969 and 1970 alone, 1.2 million people lost their jobs, increasing the national unemployment rate from 3.5 percent to 4.9 percent. Joblessness was magnified by Nixon's intentional military downsizing. The number of personnel discharged from the military increased from 496,000 in 1965 to over one million by 1970.

Some Vietnam era military policies actually worsened many veterans' transitions back into civilian life. In the closing years of the war, all branches struggled with escalating disciplinary problems as well as a significant increase in drug use. One consequence was a spike in other than honorable discharges. Between June 1970 and June 1971, for example, almost one in five sailors left the Navy under terms that were "general," "undesirable," "bad conduct," or "dishonorable." These distinctions were important because dishonorable discharge automatically forfeited readjustment benefits under the Cold War G.I. Bill.

As a result of these factors, Vietnam veterans often struggled when they returned to "The World," in the United States. Veterans' unemployment was only 4 percent in late 1969, but, by 1971, in the teeth of a recession, the rate for younger veterans aged twenty to twenty-four was 12.4 percent. The economic possibilities for minority veterans were even worse. The National Urban League estimated that Black veterans' unemployment was 22.4 percent in the first quarter of 1972.

The Vietnam War represented a broad spectrum of conflict that was typical of the Cold War at that time. It was at once a conventional conflict and an insurgency. It reflected the elements of both a civil war and a geopolitical contest between superpowers. While many of these elements were present in the Korea War, the conflict in Southeast Asia took them and magnified each.

The generation gap that divided America in the sixties and seventies was equally present among contemporary veterans. The men who fought the "Good War" never fully accepted Vietnam veterans as peers in terms of service or earned benefits. Both the American Legion and Veterans of Foreign Wars were intent on protecting their 1944 version of the G.I. Bill, often literally at the expense of the next generation of American veterans. The 1973 Nader Report constantly identified the generation gap between World War II and Korea veterans and younger men and women exiting the Vietnam era. It noted in particular that "the larger part of the benefits go to veterans who never saw combat, at ages when their readjustment needs have passed, and for problems unrelated to military service."

The generational divide informed veterans' activism during the Vietnam era. The old guard lent its energies to traditional causes and kept faith with leadership in Washington. Throughout the Vietnam War, both the American Legion and VFW were consistent pillars of support for US containment policy in Southeast Asia. In contrast, veterans in the VVAW became some of the most vocal and effective contributors to the antiwar movement in America, partly because of their status, but also because they never endorsed violence against the establishment. In the aftermath of the Kent State massacre, the VVAW provided "strike marshals" to prevent clashes between protestors and local authorities.

For all the obvious reasons, Vietnam left deep scars on America and its 2.7 million veterans did not escape this fact. They carried the burdens of a confused and ambiguous battlefield home to a reception that was supportively ambivalent at best or openly hostile at its worst. Official authority did not help their transition in any way resembling what awaited veterans of the Good War. While some leaders fully believed that their service placed them on the same level as the men and women of 1945, a critical mass did not, a decision that limited help at a point where these millions of young veterans needed it the most. As Robert Timberg has pointed out in the *Nightingale's Song*, the consequences of these decisions would last for decades.

10

The All-Volunteer Military

For years there was a popular belief that the Vietnam War destroyed the U.S. Army, but it didn't. Our Vietnam experience simply cut away the façade and exposed a cancer-riddled interior.

DAVID H. HACKWORTH, 1989

The early seventies witnessed significant changes in modern American military history. The Cold War transformed from ongoing brinksmanship to open diplomacy between the superpowers, a process encouraged by Nixon's historic opening of relations with China in 1972. Less than a year later, Washington and Hanoi officially ended America's direct role in the Vietnam War. Without the need for massive commitments of force in South Vietnam, the Pentagon began a program of deliberate retrenchment of the US military establishment. Accordingly, the draft ended in 1973, ushering in a new generation of peacetime military service.

For the first time since 1940, the US military subsisted on an all-volunteer force. In many ways, it resembled the smaller, more insular military of the era before World War II. Service was less a routine part of life for the children of the Baby Boomers, much like earlier peacetime American society. Yet, the post-1973 military was also distinct in many ways. Racial minorities, particularly African Americans, joined the all-volunteer military in numbers far larger than their civilian proportion. Like the rest of the country, gender norms were also changing. Freed from federally mandated limits and actively recruited by the Pentagon, more women entered the ranks than at any time in American history.

The veterans of the final decades of the Cold War reflected both the times and their changing missions. Peacetime routine dictated the tempo of most military service before September 11. However, conflict was not completely a thing of the past. Operation Desert Storm (1991) resulted in the largest deployment of US forces since Vietnam and the first mass introduction of the reserves and National Guard since Korea. As peacekeeping and peace enforcement missions escalated in the nineties, a growing body of active-duty and part-time soldiers was exposed to the prospect of combat.

The country that welcomed veterans home in the decades after Vietnam was also evolving. Hard economic times and public skepticism about military service established the boundaries for military service throughout much of the seventies. However, both of these issues eased during the Reagan era. Massive increases in defense spending addressed poor pay, obsolescent weapons and equipment, and the need for upgraded training. Morale across the service branches improved, augmented by a new version of the G.I. Bill and increasingly better educated and invested cohorts of recruits. Public attitudes also generally shifted to a positive perception of the military. Although fewer people served and the country was ambivalent at best about conflict abroad, civil-military relations in America experienced a renaissance in the eighties.

The End of the Draft

By the end of the sixties, the vastly unpopular selective service system was on its last legs, pushed in that direction by the escalating need for manpower in Vietnam. Inductions rose from 103,328 in 1965, to 343,481 in 1966, to 298,559 in 1967, and 383,000 in 1968. Pressed for more personnel, federal officials took a harder look at the range of deferments, particularly personal health and educational status, to meet their quotas. Eventually, this search reached into the American middle class, which had the resources for its sons to avoid the risks of war. As draft calls grew, public opinion was badly divided on the equity of the system. In April 1968, fewer than half (48 percent) of people asked by Gallup considered the draft fair. That same month, 54 percent of respondents to a Roper poll opposed extending the draft lottery to nineteen-year-olds whether they were enrolled in college or not.

When Richard Nixon formed the President's Commission on an All-Volunteer Armed Force in late 1969—otherwise known as the Gates Commission—it was intended to reduce political controversy as it crafted manpower policy for a smaller US military. Without the mandate to prosecute an active war in South Vietnam, the Nixon administration deliberately drew down active-duty forces, a process that shed 1.2 million personnel between 1969 and 1973. In a callback to the fifties, the largest cuts came from the Army (47 percent) and Marine Corps (37 percent).

What might replace the old selective service system was a question of significant debate within the US military establishment. The Gates Commission promoted an idea that gained increasing traction among conservative policymakers: privatizing a formally public process. Essentially, the commission advised Pentagon leaders to treat military service as a job subject to market forces. In their future scenario, the service branches would be compelled to compete for young men and women just like the rest of the private sector, where wages, benefits, and working conditions dictated the success or failure of recruiting campaigns.

Initially, the Joint Chiefs and senior military leaders rejected the idea of reducing a citizen's duty to what was primarily a vocational decision. They expressed concerns that a volunteer military might actually be less democratic as it jettisoned the selective service system, regardless of its many inherent faults. Shortly after his retirement as Army Chief of Staff, William Westmoreland noted, "I deplore the prospect of our military forces not representing a cross section of our country."

The Nixon administration brushed past these concerns and implemented many of the Gates Commission's recommendations. Military pay rates briefly improved and recruiters emphasized service as an adventure with the potential to improve future civilian job prospects. Slogans like "Navy. It's Not Just a Job, It's an Adventure" was a common approach. The 1981 Army "Be All That You Can Be" campaign emphasized high-tech training and equipment that young people associated with the new information economy.

Regardless, whether it was incentivized or not, military service was a hard sell in the seventies. The bitter conflict over the Vietnam War remained strong. According to a 1971 Harris poll, most Americans characterized Vietnam veterans as "suckers, having to risk their lives in the wrong war, in the wrong place, at the wrong time." A survey of young men in 1971 indicated that 88 percent "probably" or "definitely" would not consider military service.

Economic circumstances actually helped the all-volunteer military in its first few years. Inflation and recession dominated the landscape in the decade after Vietnam. The rust-belt region of the United States shed manufacturing and factory jobs by the tens of thousands as businesses shuttered in the face of cheaper foreign competition and two oil crises. As late as 1982, when unemployment reached almost 11 percent, a military career looked like a good choice for a young man or woman.

During these times, recruiters largely met their goals, but at the cost of quality. An early indicator was educational standards, which clearly suffered at the outset of the all-volunteer force. In 1961, for example, 18 percent of enlistees had some college credits. By 1973, only 3 percent of new recruits had this same academic experience. Similarly, fewer Army and Marine entrants had completed high school. In 1973, only 54 percent had their diplomas. By 1980, the number of Army recruits with four years of high school had declined to 38 percent. The impact on the military was widespread and negative. A 1976 study of trainees at Ft. Benning revealed that 53 percent had a reading level of fifth grade or lower. Between 1978 and 1982, approximately one-quarter of Navy enlistees were classified as Category IV, reflecting the lowest test scores allowable for military service.

For all its institutional challenges, the post-1973 military did record some important advances. It was, by many measurements, a far more diverse organization. In part, this was deliberate. Recruitment campaigns after the Vietnam War were designed to be race neutral. "All Marines are Green" and "One Navy" were common contemporary slogans. By 1974, almost a third of new recruits were African American. The number of African Americans subsequently increased in all branches. In 1964, they were 9.7 percent of the enlisted ranks in the military. By 1974, this had increased to 15.7 percent. In the early seventies, African Americans were most prevalent in the Army (19.9 percent) and Marine Corps (17.7 percent).

The new military was also increasingly female. Prior to the Nixon administration, the Women's Armed Forces Integration Act (1948) had restricted females to 2 percent of total US enlisted personnel. With the end of selective service, the military branches prepared plans to at least double this number.

Women did not disappoint. They joined for many of the same reasons as men, because they were patriots, or looking for a new skill, or simply seeking out a challenge. Constance Anderson, an Army nurse during the Korean War, recalled that service offered exciting possibilities: "I was always looking over the hill for a greener pasture ... I felt maybe there was something out there that I haven't seen or needed to see." In terms of quality, women substantially improved the potential recruiting pool. According to standardized testing, in 1972, there were more than twice as many women in Category I and II than male recruits.

Military pay and benefits were also an attractive way for women to overcome the long-standing civilian wage gap with men. In 1970, a brand-new private

(E-1) made $5,419.17 a year. This compared very favorably with professional ($5,099), clerical, ($4,451), crafts ($4,557), and "operatives" ($4,309) positions available at the time for women between the ages of eighteen and twenty-four. Military benefits—a housing allowance, pension contributions, the G.I. Bill, and health care made a military career appealing to women. Consequently, female recruiting far exceeded Pentagon expectations. By the end of the seventies, 7.6 percent of all enlisted personnel were female, increasing to 11 percent by 1990.

Although motivated by patriotism or the simple desire for self-improvement, a stigma clung to women in the military. Reflecting on her own enlistment in 1969, Ann Powlas later lamented, "in my mom and dad's day, during World War II, women in the service were considered to be bad people. They just knew I was going to come out a whore." While on recruiting duty in 1971, Marine Captain Maureen Fullerton was compelled to assure parents that if their daughters "might encounter Lesbianism," the perpetrators would be immediately discharged from the military.

Regardless of these doubts, women became a permanent asset within the US military. Retention rates gradually improved to the point that by 1977, the military kept women at about the same rate as men and at a higher rate in the medical, administrative, intelligence, and communications specialties. A 1978 Defense Department manpower study noted that women were applying to recruiters at a much higher rate than men and their process had become increasingly more selective.

Military Missions before September 11th

In the aftermath of the Vietnam War, the Pentagon embarked on a period of significant soul searching and began the slow and deliberate process of reconstructing the American military establishment. Part of this involved new doctrine that abandoned the many hard-won lessons of counterinsurgency in favor of conventional conflict in Western Europe. Other measures were structural. To compensate for massive cuts to the active-duty military, Army Chief of Staff Creighton Abrams introduced the "Total Force" concept. Abrams's original plan was an echo of military reorganization during World War I, whereby regular units formed the backbone of national defense, directly supplemented by the National Guard and reserves. Guard divisions would bolster combat power, while reserve units accounted for combat support, transport, engineers, civil affairs, military police, and the like. This planning was informed by two important caveats. First, the "Total Force" would be deployed gradually to large-scale conflicts. Second, the main battlefield for planning purposes was Western Europe, specifically for a major war between NATO and the Warsaw Pact.

Absent a hot war, the US military focused instead on training, with an emphasis on conventional operations against the Soviet Union. When it was created in 1973, Training and Doctrine Command (TRADOC) formulated new ways to defeat the massive Communist Bloc forces poised to invade West Germany. In the search to orchestrate armored striking power, air mobility, and air power, the AirLand Battle was born. Exercises like REFORGER [Return of Forces to Germany] allowed the US military to practice and refine its post-Vietnam theories to the point where they were effectively ingrained in the force structure. Concurrent with REFORGER, the Air Force participated with annual Cold Fire exercises with its NATO partners. Contemporary Navy training exercises followed the same format. Operation Northern Wedding (1970–1986) practiced resupplying American forces in the event of a war with the Warsaw Pact.

In the meantime, the military added new missions to its portfolio. As part of the US commitment to peace between Egypt and Israel in the Camp David Accords, American units rotated into the Sanai as peacekeepers in Operation Bright Star. Initially 1,400 soldiers deployed for joint training exercises in 1980. By 1982, 4,000 US troops were committed to the mission.

American participation in peacekeeping missions involved real-world risks. This was clear when the 32nd Marine Amphibious Unit arrived in Lebanon in 1982 as part of a multinational force. Working with the British, French, and Italian militaries, the Marines' initial mission was the evacuation of the Palestine Liberation Organization (PLO) from the southern part of the country. US actions were dictated by strict rules of engagement (ROE) that limited peacekeepers to self-defense. In practice, as one Marine officer explained, "If a guy shoots at you and you feel it is directed fire... then you use minimal force necessary to take care of the situation. If he is shooting at you with small arms, you can return the fire with small arms." Americans trained with the Lebanese military, manned checkpoints, and conducted patrols, occasionally contending with unexploded ordinance, small arms, and indirect fire. As violence escalated in 1983, the Marines modified their ROE to allow loaded weapons and proportional responses against a "hostile act."

Sentries guarding American facilities in Lebanon were unprepared for the suicide truck bomb that destroyed a US barracks and killed 241 US servicemen on October 23, 1983. A subsequent Defense Department investigation faulted the chain of command for contributing "to a mindset which detracted from the Marines' readiness to respond to the type of terrorist attack which occurred on 23 October," according to one official history. However, the tragedy illustrated the potential ambiguities and dangers that inhabited the modern operating environment. What constituted a "hostile act" normally fell under conventional definitions, not what Marines experienced in Lebanon. Rather than risk additional casualties, US forces departed the region in February 1984.

Short, sharp direct military interventions were a recurrent theme in the eighties. American naval units periodically clashed with the Libyan military around the Gulf of Sidra. In August 1981, this resulted in Navy fighters shooting down two Libyan jets. American forces invaded Grenada as part of Operation Urgent Fury (1983). During Operation El Dorado Canyon (1986), the United States conducted airstrikes against Tripoli, Benghazi, and other military targets in Libya. The eighties ended with the invasion of Panama during Operation Just Cause (1989).

Despite the growing penchant for flexing military muscle, the Vietnam War clearly overshadowed American thought during the Reagan years. Secretary of Defense Caspar Weinberger followed the logic of decisive use of force, clear exit strategies, and deliberately limiting American losses. In the last days of superpower brinksmanship, casualties were comparatively smaller than in past wars. Operation Urgent Fury cost nineteen killed and eighty-nine wounded in action. Operation Just Cause resulted in 23 combat deaths and 325 wounded. In comparison, during the 1968 Tet Offensive, US and South Vietnamese forces suffered approximately fifteen thousand casualties.

The First Gulf War (1990–1991) significantly altered the course of US military affairs.

With the collapse of the Soviet Union and the end of the Cold War, the global order at the start of the nineties was in a state of flux. Regional powers, to include Saddam Hussein's Iraq, saw the changing times as a mandate to increase their hegemony. One result was the August 1990 Iraqi invasion of neighboring Kuwait.

Hussein's ambitions directly threatened American strategic access to oil. As Iraqi forces consolidated their occupation of Kuwait, the George H. W. Bush administration ordered the immediate deployment of US forces to the Persian Gulf. Elements of the 82nd Airborne were among the first units to arrive in what became known as Operation Desert Shield (August 1990–January 1991). Eventually, almost 500,000 personnel and 2,000 US aircraft were dispatched to the region in the largest mobilization of American military power since the Vietnam War.

The rapid success of Operation Desert Storm was a surprise and a relief for American leaders and citizens alike. In roughly one week, using the same AirLand Battle Doctrine created and implemented in the eighties, coalition forces expelled the Iraqi military from Kuwait. Victory served as a vindication for military reformers and promoted a sense of confidence in military intervention. Back home, commentators speculated about how victory in the desert had dealt a decisive blow to the "ghosts" of Vietnam. The *South Florida Sun Sentinel* applauded, "Schwarzkopf Exorcised the Demon of Vietnam."

American military commitments subsequently multiplied after Desert Storm. As the sole remaining superpower tasked with overseeing what Bush defined as the "New World Order," US forces participated in a series of missions involving humanitarian assistance, peacekeeping, and peace enforcement. Immediately after the First Gulf War, the United States led Operation Provide Comfort, which offered aid to nearly two million refugees, primarily Kurds, in northern Iraq. By the end of 1992, attention turned to the Horn of Africa, where approximately 300,000 Somalis died of famine and an additional 1.5 million were at risk of starvation. The United States joined the Unified Task Force (UNITAF) and forty-two countries to use "all necessary means" to deliver humanitarian aid to Somalis. According to the White House, Operation Restore Hope (1992–1993) was a limited commitment to "create security conditions which will permit the feeding of starving Somali people and allow the transfer of this security function to the UN peacekeeping force."

Unfortunately, events on the ground proved difficult for the world's only superpower.

Instability prompted the mission to shift from humanitarian relief to the early stages of nation building. At the start of 1993, under the renamed Operation Continue Hope, the incoming Clinton administration focused on disarming militias and creating "credible police forces in large cities and towns." This process led to a series of clashes with local warlords in Mogadishu, which climaxed in a running battle throughout the city in October. After suffering ninety-one casualties (eighteen dead and seventy-three wounded), US forces withdrew early the following year.

Despite the controversy resulting from the Battle of Mogadishu, US policymakers continued military intervention for the sake of humanitarian causes. This was clearly the case with respect to the former Yugoslavia, where ethnic and religious conflict ravaged the region. Operation Joint Endeavor (1995) saw the United States contribute one-third of the 60,000 personnel sent for peace enforcement duties under the UN Implementation Force (IFOR). The US unit taking the lead was the 1st Armored Division, which arrived in Bosnia as part of Task Force Eagle.

The mission was more complicated than overseeing humanitarian aid or simply interposing neutral forces between combatants as dictated by traditional peacekeeping. Task Force Eagle was in the former Yugoslavia to oversee the surrender of heavy weapons, mine removal, monitoring of police equipment and vehicles, and prisoner release. Additional duties involved securing mass grave sites, controlling black market activities, apprehending war criminals, providing civilian medical care, as well as security operations during elections.

"Peace enforcement operations" also meant that the Americans sent to the former Yugoslavia came ready to fight. Task Force Eagle arrived with its organic armored vehicles and weapons. The massive show of force was intended to deter violence against both local citizens and US soldiers and demonstrate NATO's will to retaliate against aggression, as it did in 1999 when air units began a bombing campaign against Serbia. As far as units on the ground were concerned, "force protection" was the watchword of the moment. New doctrine required strict rules of engagement to guard against escalation. Personal body armor came into more common use in order to limit harm to American personnel.

America's ongoing commitments to peacekeeping and peace enforcement missions placed substantial strains on the "Total Force" structure. Operation Desert Shield and Operation Desert Storm reintroduced the Guard and reserves to overseas contingency operations, a trend that escalated for the remainder of the nineties. After the 1st Armored Division rotated home, units from the Georgia, North Carolina, Oklahoma, Texas, and Virginia National Guard all served in Bosnia-Herzegovina. By 1997, 15,000 Army reservists alone were deployed in over a hundred countries. These deployments returned a degree of valuable practical experience to the US military lost after Vietnam. However, the rapidly rising tempo of operations came at a cost to personnel, equipment, and training. Service within the Total Force was no longer a matter of one weekend a month and two weeks during the summer. At the beginning of 2001, the dilemma prompted one military journal to ask the simple question: "Are We Wearing Out the Guard and Reserves?"

Veterans Come Home: From Vietnam to September 11th

The words Warren Harding spoke in 1920 seemed perfectly appropriate to the country's struggles after the Vietnam War: "America's present need is not heroics, but healing; not nostrums, but normalcy." The war in Southeast Asia, and all the attendant controversies of the sixties, had roiled the country and left it bitterly divided. Healing was the order of the day.

World War II veteran Gerald Ford inherited Vietnam after Richard Nixon's resignation in August 1974 and America's only unelected president approached the issue with understandable caution. Military assistance, much less any form of American intervention, was out of the question. In terms of the war's legacy, Ford said in April 1975, days before the final collapse of South Vietnam, that "Today, Americans can regain the sense of pride that existed before Vietnam. But it cannot be achieved by refighting a war that is finished—as far as America is concerned." Ford's counsel was for the country to shed the harsh memory of the conflict for the sake of unity and the future.

Jimmy Carter understood the problem very well when he spoke before the American Legion national convention in August 1976: "Where I come from, most of the men who went off to fight in Vietnam were poor. They didn't know where Canada was, they didn't know where Sweden was, they didn't have the money to hide from the draft in college. Many of them thought it was a bad war, but they went anyway." Carter followed his acknowledgement of Vietnam's bitter social legacy with a bold promise. "But I think it is time for the damage, hatred and divisiveness of the Vietnam war to be over. I do not favor a blanket amnesty, but for those who violated Selective Service laws, I intend to grant a blanket pardon."

Even the best-intended solutions invited controversy. As a presidential candidate, Jimmy Carter had not shied away from one of the highest profile disputes of the moment: amnesty for young men who had actively dodged the draft during Vietnam. For the thousands who had fled the country and actively avoided service, he offered a clean slate. *New York Times* columnist James Reston captured Carter's dilemma:

> There was no honorable way the new President could avoid this decision about Vietnam, or keep it from breaking the unity he sought in his first speech as Chief Executive. He had spoken in the campaign with more eloquence on the need for forgetting or forgiving—unfortunately he confused the two—than on anything else except keeping his promises.

Not surprisingly, traditional veterans' groups opposed the plan. In a January 1977 conference call with his American Legion leadership, the national commander was clear: "The American Legion and the American Legion Auxiliary vehemently protest and unalterably oppose your proposed pardon/amnesty plan for draft evaders, military deserters and those receiving less than honorable discharges during the Vietnam period. We continue to urge that each case be judged on an individual basis through the existing judicial and administrative channels currently open to those individuals."

Carter temporized on presidential action for approximately 100,000 deserters who had fled service after entering the military. The administration promised to "initiate a study" on what actions it might take for this group. For its own part, the American Veterans Committee challenged Carter to "fulfill his inaugural promises of compassionate justice."

Public commemoration of Vietnam was rare after the war. The ongoing debate about the origins and conduct of the conflict undercut any possible consensus on just how the country might recognize military service, much less celebrate it. There were exceptions. In a reversal from the Korean War, the fate of approximately 2,500 American prisoners and personnel missing in action attracted a great deal of public interest and sympathy. When it was formally created in 1970, the National League of Families of American Prisoners and Missing in Southeast Asia wanted their loved ones accounted for and returned home. As part of its ongoing campaign, the League created an image that captured the attention of the nation: the silhouette of an emaciated prisoner against the backdrop of a guard tower. When the country celebrated its first National POW/MIA Recognition Day in 1979, the iconic black-and-white flag could be seen throughout the country.

Private groups of veterans pressed forward with additional initiatives. Jan Scruggs, Robert Doubek, and John Wheeler founded the Vietnam Veterans Memorial Fund (VVMF), a nonprofit dedicated to raising funds and lobbying for a site in Washington, DC. Notable individuals such as H. Ross Perot and organizations like the Gold Star Mothers provided funds, which eventually grew to $8 million. The American Legion donated $1 million. The VVMF was ultimately successful. In July 1980, President Carter signed the Vietnam Memorial Bill that allocated a 6.5-acre site on the Washington Mall to construct a monument. During the signing ceremony Carter returned to the theme of reconciliation: "In honoring those who answered the call of duty, we do not honor the war. But we honor the peace they sought. the freedoms they fought to preserve, and the hope that they held out to a world that's still struggling to learn how to settle differences among people and among nations without resorting to violence."

The design for the Vietnam War Memorial was open to a public competition, which was ultimately won by Maya Ying Lin, a twenty-one-year-old undergraduate at Yale University. Lin's selection was an interesting testament to the memorial's ultimate goal. She had no direct, personal link to the war. Perhaps more importantly, her design was less about commemorating the conflict or any particular subset of individuals. It was for the sake of healing and reconciliation. "I felt a memorial should be honest about the reality of war and be for the people who gave their lives... I didn't want a static object that people would just look at, but something they could relate to as on a journey, or a passage, that would bring each to his own conclusions." People visiting the memorial could literally reflect on themselves in polished black granite as they read the list of lives lost in Vietnam.

The subsequent public discussion of the memorial reflected the lingering cleavages about the Vietnam War. Some of the criticism focused on artistic aesthetics. The *National Review* described the monument as "Orwellian glop." Other barbs were personal. Writing an opinion piece for the October 24, 1981, *New York Times*, Vietnam veteran Tom Carhart expressed his own disdain: "I believe that the design selected for the memorial in an open competition is pointedly insulting to the sacrifices made for their country by all Vietnam veterans. By this will we be remembered: a black gash of shame and sorrow, hacked into the national visage that is the Mall." Despite the ongoing controversy, construction moved forward on schedule.

Formal dedication of the memorial was the capstone of a five-day "National Salute to Vietnam Veterans" in November 1982. Events included a three-day vigil at the National Cathedral for service members killed or missing in Vietnam. There were workshops for individuals suffering from Agent Orange exposure. When 15,000 veterans marched down Constitution Avenue, "roaring crowds and an outpouring of gratitude" from as many as 150,000 spectators following their progress. Among the marchers was William Westmoreland, who described it as "quite an emotional experience—something I never thought would take place." Ronald Reagan was not present, instead busying himself with White House events.

The eighties were a clear turning point for Vietnam veterans and the country. A 1985 CBS/*New York Times* poll indicated that 84 percent of respondents thought that Vietnam veterans did not receive the same respect as World War II veterans, but 94 percent believed they deserved it. In May 1985, 25,000 Vietnam veterans received a tickertape parade in New York City before thousands of cheering spectators. Even larger celebrations followed in Chicago and Houston that year, where hundreds of thousands cheered on the marchers. Military themes—from the *Rambo* series, to *Aliens* (1986), *Top Gun* (1986), *The Delta Force* (1986), and *The A-Team* (1983–1987), dominated popular culture and ranged from cartoonish caricatures to deeply scarred victims of an unwinnable war. Regardless, veterans were heroes again.

Ronald Reagan eventually came around to national sentiment. In November 1984, he made a speech during the dedication ceremony on the National Mall for a statute depicting three soldiers who served in Vietnam. The president commented on this new addition, but also recognized the original memorial:

> It's almost 10 years now since U.S. military involvement in Vietnam came to a close. Two years ago, our government dedicated the memorial bearing the names of those who died or are still missing. Every day, the families and friends of those brave men and women come to the wall and search out a name and touch it.
>
> The memorial reflects as a mirror reflects, so that when you find the name you're searching for you find it in your own reflection. And as you touch it, from certain angles, you're touching, too, the reflection of the Washington Monument or the chair in which great Abe Lincoln sits.
>
> Those who fought in Vietnam are part of us, part of our history. They reflected the best in us. No number of wreaths, no amount of music and memorializing will ever do them justice but it is good for us that we honor them and their sacrifice. And it's good that we do it in the reflected glow of the enduring symbols of our Republic.

> The fighting men depicted in the statue we dedicate today, the three young American servicemen, are individual only in terms of their battle dress; all are as one, with eyes fixed upon the memorial bearing the names of their brothers in arms. On their youthful faces, faces too young to have experienced war, we see expressions of loneliness and profound love and a fierce determination never to forget.

In his speech, Reagan essentially sidestepped the divisiveness that had characterized so much of the debate about Maya Lin's creation. The president's rhetoric at once ignored the underlying problems that persisted a decade after the war was over, while it gave agency to a renaissance in public support for veterans of Vietnam.

These sentiments took a tangible form in 1984. Ironically, as a new, updated version of the G.I. Bill was reported out of the House Armed Services Committee in 1982, it was opposed by both the White House and Defense Department as too expensive and unnecessary. This changed once it became clear the Montgomery G.I. Bill was immensely popular among potential recruits. According to a 1986 report, 85 percent of Army volunteers cited it as a key reason for enlistment. Unfortunately, continuing a trend evident since the Korean War, new educational benefits were inadequate for tuition and housing at most contemporary state colleges.

The First Gulf War (1990–1991) was an important benchmark in American military affairs following the end of the Cold War. At the start of the conflict, while hundreds of thousands of American personnel deployed to Saudi Arabia in the fall of 1990, no one knew what the cost of expelling Iraq from Kuwait might be. Casualty estimates ran from 20,000 to 100,000 personnel, figures that gave citizens, the Bush administration, and Congress a reason to pause as the country debated war.

Motivating celebrations of the military in 1991 was a sense of relief that the experts and their casualty figures were wrong. Compared to previous

American conflicts, Operation Desert Storm came at a relatively low cost for the United States. Of the approximately half a million American troops deployed, US forces suffered 382 dead and 467 wounded in what became known as the "Hundred-Hour War."

In the national victory celebrations that followed Iraqi surrender, the yellow ribbon became the symbol of the moment. Although it was originally intended as a way to recognize returning Iranian hostages, it took on a much broader meaning for veterans and the military after the First Gulf War. Antiwar protestor Trish Shuh framed the issue in 1991 with a turn of phrase possessing even more traction ten years later: "You can oppose the policy but still support the troops." The yellow ribbon allowed Americans what they sought after Vietnam: a way to celebrate individual sacrifice without engaging any of the controversies surrounding the war.

A certain ambivalence settled over the First Gulf War that determined just how much it might heal American civil-military relations after Vietnam. Yellow ribbon celebrations proved short-lived as the country eventually turned to a host of unresolved domestic problems ranging from crime rates to illegal drugs, and an emerging economic recession. The catch phrase of post–Cold War America in the nineties was how best to spend the "peace dividend" as the country shed its obligation to contain communism. In relatively short order, Gulf War veterans would add their own voices to this discussion.

Healing Wounds from Vietnam to September 11th

For veterans, modern warfare often reflects the relationship between increasingly lethal military technology and its impact on the human body. Breakthroughs like the proximity fuse, poison gas, incendiaries, anti-personnel mines, and cluster munitions created horrific wounds that frequently outpaced the capabilities of contemporary military medicine. Coping with the mental and physical consequences of the gap between lethality and healing was a defining lifetime experience for thousands of veterans.

The gap between weapons systems and healing is sometimes also a function of comprehension. Rapid advances in military technology often overtake the conventional wisdom about war. For example, few policymakers or citizens understood the implications of nuclear weapons as they entered the US inventory in the early fifties. Consequently, fundamental ignorance shaped nuclear tests conducted on military personnel between 1945 and 1962. In the same way, social norms also affected the mental toll exacted on the military, from shell shock, to combat exhaustion, to post-traumatic stress disorder (PTSD).

The gaps between injury and comprehension shaped both the timeliness and application of veterans' health policy. Individuals suffering from radiation effects caused by nuclear testing spent decades fighting for compensation. Although clearly a problem during the Vietnam War, PTSD did not appear in psychological service protocols until the late seventies.

This was the case with Agent Orange. During the Vietnam War, US military planners saw an opportunity to leverage applied science against Viet Cong guerrillas. Operation Ranch Hand (1962–1971) conducted aerial spraying of a variety of defoliants to reduce the cover available for ambushes and destroy food crops that sustained the communist war effort. In 1967 alone, Ranch Hand destroyed 1.5 million acres of vegetation. During the war, the Air Force sprayed an estimated twelve million gallons of Agent Orange alone on locations throughout South Vietnam.

Agent Orange was dangerous and initially linked to birth defects, a fact revealed by the National Cancer Institute as early as 1968. During the war, physical problems manifested among South Vietnamese civilians and later began appearing among US military personnel who were part of Ranch Hand or operated in sprayed areas. Veterans complained of skin lesions, cysts, immune disorders, and cancer. They also reported increasing incidents of birth defects, such as spina bifida, experienced by their children.

Getting help for Agent Orange–related problems involved a long and difficult campaign. Many lawmakers balked at the prospect of adding billions of dollars to the long-term cost of Vietnam veterans' medical care. The Veterans Administration stonewalled claims for years. According to J. C. Peckarsky, director of the VA Compensation and Pension Service, in a 1979 interview, "Absolutely nobody had an Agent Orange disability."

Faced with these obstacles, veterans resorted to litigation. One class action lawsuit filed in 1979 claimed that 2.4 million personnel who served in Vietnam were affected by the spraying program. In 1984, these efforts resulted in an out-of-court settlement and the creation of the $180 million Agent Orange Settlement Fund.

The American Legion threw its full weight behind Vietnam veterans seeking compensation and treatment for Agent Orange illnesses. The Legion sponsored its own investigation, conducted through Columbia University in 1988, that linked dioxin in Agent Orange to twenty-one diseases, most involving cancer. When the government proved reluctant to launch an independent study of the problem, the Legion filed its own lawsuit. Congress finally settled the matter of disability compensation in 1991 when it passed the Agent Orange Act. By 2005, the Agent Orange Registry contained the names of 420,055 veterans who had requested physical examinations. More recently, the 2022 PACT Act, passed to address new illness resulting from Iraq and Afghanistan service, also expanded Agent Orange benefits.

The debate over Gulf War Syndrome followed a similar track. In the years following the war against Iraq, Desert Storm veterans began complaining about a range of problems that included joint pain, difficulty focusing, insomnia, and depression. Within a few years, thousands reported "chronic fatigue syndrome, multiple chemical sensitivities, and fibromyalgia."

The possible cause of these ailments was the subject of significant speculation and investigation. Was it a side effect of an experimental drug to combat nerve gas administered to 400,000 US troops during Operation Desert Shield? Or was it the accumulation of toxins in Kuwait, which included low levels of nerve agents and other chemical weapons, residual radioactivity from depleted uranium munitions used by the US military, and tainted air from oil fires lighted by retreating Iraqi forces? For its own part, the Pentagon initially attributed Gulf War Syndrome to post-traumatic stress.

Regardless of potential causes, the number of veterans claiming the effects of Gulf War Syndrome grew. By 1995, 29,000 were on the VA Persian Gulf War Health Registry, a list that was growing by 1,000 people a month. By 2003, it included 70,000 veterans. As was the case with Agent Orange, Gulf War Syndrome extended to veterans' families. A Mississippi National Guard unit reported that of fifteen children born to its members after redeployment from Desert Storm, thirteen had birth defects.

Like Agent Orange, the US government evaded the issue for years after the First Gulf War. The Department of Veterans Affairs delayed researching low-level chemical agent exposure. As late as 1997, only a dozen investigators were assigned to Gulf War Syndrome complaints.

Once the federal government finally recognized the legitimacy of Gulf War Syndrome, it created a mechanism for disability benefits in the same manner as Agent Orange, a process that remained open until 2021. However, gaining official recognition of a Gulf War–related illness proved very difficult. Between 2010 and 2015, the VA approved fewer than one in five applications for disability benefits.

The history of PTSD is longer than ailments like Agent Orange or Gulf War Syndrome, but it follows much the same path. Each war had its own label for the mental toll inflicted on combatants. During the Civil War it was called "nostalgia" or "soldier's heart." During the twentieth century, the terms evolved into "shell shock" and "combat fatigue." During the Vietnam War, manifesting behavioral problems were simply called "post-Vietnam Syndrome." The first formal clinical diagnosis of PTSD had to wait until 1978 when it appeared in the *Diagnostic and Statistical Manual of Mental Disorders* (*DSM-III*), which defined it as a "psychologically traumatic event that is generally outside the range of usual human experience."

There were a number of tangible reasons for the long delay. In the thirty years between World War II and *DSM-III*, military medicine focused on returning troops back to combat duty. Doctors deliberately treated mental breakdowns as close to the front lines as possible. The Pentagon eventually instituted the one-year rotation in part to reduce the toll of combat on the mental well-being of troops. These policies worked well between 1945 and 1975. Mental breakdowns accounted for 10 percent of casualties in WWII, but just 4 percent in Korea. In Vietnam, they averaged 1.2 percent each year.

Long-term care was a much different story. During Vietnam, the veterans' health care system lacked diagnostic tools to understand post-traumatic stress. VA doctors generally relied on civilian protocols, which lacked proper context. Many assumed that mental trauma predated military service. When the House Committee on Veterans Affairs debated the matter, World War II veterans led by Olin Teague used their own experience as a frame of reference and opposed changes to counseling and treatment. What had been good for their generation seemed appropriate for younger Vietnam veterans.

That is not to say progress was at a standstill. In the years following Vietnam, the civilian medical community developed an increasingly sophisticated understanding of combat trauma. Studies considered the types of combat ("heavy" versus "light"), the type of war (conventional versus unconventional), the relationship between physical wounds and mental trauma, and the impact of veterans' reception upon returning home (the so-called life course theory). When the Department of Veterans Affairs created the National Center for PTSD in 1989, research was already well advanced for the hundreds of thousands of Vietnam veterans in need of help.

The New Generation of Women Veterans

As the all-volunteer military evolved, the number of women in uniform grew. The female enlisted ranks significantly increased in the seventies and peaked at 195,532 in 1989, encouraged by a force structure that opened an increasing array of occupational specialties for women. By 2018, 16.5 percent of enlisted personnel were female, with the largest percentage in the Air Force (24.9 percent) and the lowest in the Marine Corps (9.5 percent).

At the same time, while more women joined the ranks of American veterans, the system struggled to incorporate them. The problem of equal or even adequate facilities for female veterans was highlighted by Lynda Van Devanter and the Vietnam Veterans of America Women's Project as early as 1980. Institutional culture proved to be a significant obstacle. Historically, veterans' services were overwhelmingly male. It was not uncommon for a female veteran seeking out help at the VA to be asked, "Who's your husband?"

What the VA could offer women veterans also boiled down to matters of practicality. Medical specialties relevant to women were difficult and sometimes impossible to find. The VA did not furnish prenatal services even if the pregnancy occurred while in the military. Routine gynecological care was often referred to fee-for-service private providers, but the VA would not reimburse female veterans because it was not considered service related. A 1982 General Accounting Office report indicated that VA hospitals failed to provide women with complete physical exams, domiciliary care, or psychiatric treatment. Other studies found that female veterans tended to use VA health services less than men, in part because women enjoyed better private insurance. Regardless, progress was slow. A 1992 GAO report identified many of the same problems as its predecessor, VA hospitals and medical centers that lacked segregated female wards or basic amenities like separate bathrooms and showers for women.

The nineties saw some attempts at remedying this situation. In 1998, the Department of Veterans Affairs budgeted $67 million to improve facilities for women and address privacy concerns. The department also created a Women Veteran Coordinator in each VA medical center to be an advocate for female veterans. Officials increased outreach through seminars and town meetings as well as the annual conventions of the American Legion, the Women's Army Corps, Women Marines, and Disabled American Veterans, following the theme "Women are Veterans, Too." A January 1999 GAO report noted that the "VA has made considerable progress in removing barriers that prevent women veterans from receiving care."

The all-volunteer military also confronted the worsening quandary of sexual assault. In 1988, the Defense Department indicated that at least 5 percent of military women were raped on active duty. This was likely a low estimate, challenged two years later by a study that found that at least a third of women experienced some type of sexual harassment or assault while in uniform. Senate hearings on sexual abuse during and after the Gulf War and the 1991 Tailhook scandal reinforced public concerns. In her testimony before the Senate Veterans Affairs Committee, Jacqueline Ortiz reported being "forcibly sodomized" by one of her sergeants during Operation Desert Storm. Barbara Franco, an Army veteran assaulted twice during her career, testified that "Most women veterans do not go to the V.A. because it is the same male-dominated, abusive system and environment which hurt us before."

Military Sexual Trauma (MST), as it became known, was a serious and epidemic problem within the military. According to one 1995 Defense Department report, 23 percent of women veterans reported at least one sexual assault to the VA after leaving the military. Consequently, as the Clinton administration mandated additional attention to women veterans, the Department of Veterans Affairs devoted new resources to MST. The number of women receiving counseling through the VA for military sexual trauma subsequently increased from 2,350 in 1993 to almost 9,000 in 1997. A 2003 VA study reached the optimistic conclusion that the data showed "unprofessional, gender-related behaviors" declining significantly between 1995 and 2002. This optimism proved premature.

A new American military greeted the final stages of the Cold War. Until the advent of the First Gulf War, the rhythms of peacetime defined most military service. This changed in 1990 when the United States and its coalition partners successfully liberated Kuwait from Iraqi occupation. As the nineties progressed, peacekeeping and peace enforcement missions added additional risks to a diversified force structure comprised of regular units, reservists, and the National Guard. While the country applied the post–Cold War peace dividend and significantly cut back on military personnel, the burdens of the world's only remaining superpower fell upon a shrinking body of Americans.

The all-volunteer military was at once less representative of society as a whole, yet more diverse than it had been in the past. Women and minorities entered uniform in unprecedented numbers after 1973. Together, they transformed the culture of the modern American military as it redefined its post-Vietnam mission.

While veterans of the all-volunteer military aspired to many of the same things as their predecessors, the social and economic environment was at times far less welcoming. The specter of Vietnam hung over civil-military relations even after the troops came home from Operation Desert Storm. The first serious signs of American post-industrial decline—two oil crises and a rising tide of foreign imports—signaled profound difficulties for veterans' employment. Although public acclaim for the military and economic prospects brightened in the eighties, it was not the same country that had welcomed back veterans from the Good War in 1945.

Many veterans of the Vietnam War and later conflicts also struggled with new sicknesses and injuries. The successive impacts of nuclear testing, Agent Orange, Gulf War Syndrome, and the lingering accumulation of PTSD and MST left tens of thousands in need of long-term help. Although young veterans affected by these illnesses sometimes found common cause with established veterans' groups like the American Legion, action often proved grudging and incomplete.

Faced with these familiar obstacles, veterans did what they had always done: acted as their own advocates. Lynda Van Devanter was a pioneer of contemporary women veterans' causes and prompted the first of many cycles of revelations and reform. The costs and consequences of gender integration in the military became an important part of the policy discussion as the twentieth century came to a close. However, the tentative progress made on this issue and many others would soon be overshadowed by a national catastrophe and new rounds of global conflict.

11

After September 11th

This is our war: we can't shoot at every target, we can't always tell who is a target; but we look out for one another and we don't mind doing the nation's dirty work. Air Force pilots and Army majors expert in Microsoft PowerPoint have a perfectly clean view of it. We won't get support if it makes a mess.
Bring it.
We're the infantry.
War's a bitch, wear a helmet.

STAFF SERGEANT DAVID BELLAVIA, 1ST INFANTRY DIVISION, IRAQ

America began the new millennium with a war. Although the warning signs were there, based upon reporting by intelligence agencies and federal law enforcement, the conflict took the people and the incoming Bush administration almost by complete surprise. Few people at the time could imagine the events of September 11 or the scope and scale of the subsequent Global War on Terror (GWOT).

The world's only superpower—a status that it would soon share with an emerging China—found itself committed to a composite of conflicts both conventional and unconventional. First in Afghanistan, then Iraq, and a dozen other places scattered around the world, American forces deployed against al-Qaeda, the Taliban, and their evolving offshoots. In 2001, the US defense establishment was convinced a combination of old doctrine (local alliances) and new technology (precision guided munitions), popularly known as "shock and awe," would be adequate to the task of prosecuting contingency operations abroad. However, the unfolding conflicts in Afghanistan and Iraq later proved their optimism was unfounded. As the wars dragged on, a few pundits and academics invoked the memory of Vietnam, although comparisons were problematic as best.

The twenty-first-century veteran was as much a composite as their war. They remained the same volunteers as the post-Vietnam military with important caveats. The Global War on Terror saw the first sustained deployment of the reserves and National Guard since Korea. The contemporary force structure reflected increasing racial diversity and included an unprecedented number of women, many directly involved in combat whether they were assigned to combat branches or not.

Veterans of the "Forever War" also faced a series of challenges particular to their conflict. The most obvious was the grinding, exhausting nature of repeated deployments. Unlike Korea and Vietnam or the peace enforcement duties of the nineties, service was not limited to a one-year term of duty. Without the option of a draft or meaningful national mobilization, the Pentagon was forced to improvise. "Stop loss," the controversial policy to withhold discharges for some personnel at the end of their enlistment contracts, was implemented by the time the United States invaded Iraq. In other cases, American policymakers resorted to private contractors to supplement the war effort. In the meantime, regulars and reservists alike confronted the prospect of a war without end.

In many respects, the Forever War uniquely defined twenty-first-century veterans.

Wounds and post-traumatic stress compounded by constant deployments took a definite toll on them, a problem perhaps best illustrated by escalating suicide rates. While the public was far more sympathetic to their plight than it had been during the Vietnam era, fewer people had direct military experience and understood its consequences. With the Greatest Generation passing from the scene, the civil-military link was increasingly superficial. Moreover, for all the hundreds of billions spent on the Global War on Terror, resources for veterans were inadequate and poorly managed in too many cases.

Contemporary veterans responded to these challenges in ways already illustrated throughout this book. Where government, specifically the Department of Veterans Affairs failed, they pursued solutions through their own advocacy. When they could not reach a consensus with older veterans, a situation resembling the past experiences of the American Veterans Committee, the Vietnam Veterans Against the War, and the Vietnam Veterans of America Women's Project, they struck out on their own. The contemporary veterans' movement is more fragmented but proved no less dedicated to improving policy and general conditions than it was in the past.

The Nature of the Forever War

The so-called Forever War, which raged from September 11, 2001, to the final withdrawal of US forces from Kabul almost twenty years later, took many forms. The initial invasion of Afghanistan involved special forces and CIA paramilitary operatives working with Afghan tribes loosely grouped around the "Northern Alliance." For the most part, Operation Iraqi Freedom was conventional, although the United States fielded roughly a third of the forces deployed for Desert Storm in 1991. After regular operations ceased in May 2003, and the coalition shifted to "stability operations," the situation deteriorated into a full-blown insurgency.

At that point, the American war on terror became increasingly complicated. Like much of the war in South Vietnam, winning local support was a key mission. Unlike Vietnam, this required restraint, expressed in elaborate and constantly evolving "Rules of Engagement" (ROE). The rules dictated that US forces discriminate between civilian and military personnel and exercise appropriate use of force in all contacts. Troops were issued ROE Cards that distilled the law of war into a series of guidelines. They included rules such as "a. Positive identification (PID) is required prior to engagement. PID is a reasonable certainty that the proposed target is a legitimate military target. If no PID, contact your next higher commander for decision."

This was clearly a form of war far removed from the past. In a Fall 2008 article for *Military Review*, the US commander in Iraq (and eventual CENTCOM commander), General David H. Petraeus spoke of the Iraqi people as the "decisive terrain" in the war. To secure their loyalty, he emphasized a constructive "non-kinetic" (noncombat) methodology designed to preserve reconciliation and civil stability. Petraeus was asking the soldiers to follow a doctrine that combined contradictory practices: "pursue the enemy relentlessly," while, at the same time, building support within the civilian community by utilizing restraint.

Policies like these caused a great deal of confusion for rank-and-file soldiers and Marines in Iraq and Afghanistan. Even so, as US and coalition forces reconstructed largely forgotten counterinsurgency doctrine to build popular support in occupied territory, they were also increasingly enmeshed in a vicious conflict with insurgents. Iraq and Afghanistan developed into wars of ambush, sabotage, and intimidation. Troops, vehicle convoys, and bases were constantly exposed to small arms fire, mortars, and rocket attacks. The most lethal weapon of choice was the improvised explosive device (IED). In Iraq, it was the single greatest cause of casualties, accounting for 61 percent of all coalition fatalities in 2009.

IEDs defined much of the cost of the Forever War for its veterans. As the dual conflicts in Iraq and Afghanistan continued, military medicine contended with the effects of Traumatic Brain Injury (TBI), as well as infections caused by foreign material embedded in wounds. To compensate, the Pentagon embarked upon extensive research for better ways to protect combatants. The process eventually cocooned soldiers in layers of ceramic and flame-resistant synthetics that added greater protection at the cost of heat and limited mobility.

It took the Defense Department years to catch up to troop needs, a point driven home in 2004 when Secretary of Defense Donald Rumsfeld visited troops at Camp Buehring, Kuwait. Tennessee and Idaho Army National Guard soldiers challenged the Secretary on "shortages and antiquated equipment" as well as "hillbilly armor" scavenged from garbage dumps to upgrade vehicles. Rumsfeld's response, while pragmatic, perfectly captured the chasm between leadership and the combat soldiers: "You go to war with the Army you have, not the Army you might want or wish to have at a later time."

The military that went to war after September 11 was a small regular force, pared down by years of defense cuts in the nineties. The total active-duty military headcount peaked at approximately 1.5 million in 2011 before dropping back to 1.3 million in 2018. The Army remained the largest component (476,000), followed by the Navy (327,000), Air Force (325,000), and Marine Corps (185,000). With the exception of the Marine Corps, all the active service branches were smaller than they were before the start of the Korean War.

To compensate for the lack of adequate regular forces, the American military fell back on old policy and even older tradition. Overseas contingency operations leaned heavily on the modern-day equivalent of the militia: the National Guard and reserves. Through post-Vietnam "Total Force" doctrine, the Pentagon incorporated the National Guard and reserves directly into the US defense structure, not for conventional war in Western Europe against the Soviet Union but for a broad spectrum of missions necessary for the Global War on Terror. Function followed this intent, with the National Guard comprising half the Army's combat units after 2001. Combat support—transport, engineers, civil affairs, military police—were drawn almost entirely from the reserves.

However, the Total Force concept was never realized during the Cold War. Desert Shield/Desert Storm (1990–1991) served as a brief stress test of US policy, when one in four US soldiers deployed to the Middle East was a reservist of one form or another. Most of these individuals performed combat support missions. The handful of Army National Guard combat brigades mobilized to fight were not deployed by the time Desert Storm kicked off in January 1991, largely because they were not ready for deployment. After 1991, the reserve components provided increasing numbers of personnel for peacekeeping and peace enforcement, disaster aid, humanitarian relief, post-conflict reconstruction, and other missions categorized under the contemporary label of Military Operations Other than War (MOOTW).

To make up for personnel shortages, the US military leaned heavily on military contractors. Private Military Companies (PMCs) were made up of a hodgepodge of veterans drawn from dozens of countries. Whether they were employed as logistical support or security functions, "force protection" of base facilities, checkpoints, and convoys, contractors were usually led by Americans, expatriate European and South African veterans. However, the bulk of personnel were made up of "local nationals" (Iraqi and Afghani) and "third country nationals" (Gurkhas, Fijians, Kenyans, Colombians, etc.). Contractors covered a broad array of logistical tasks that ranged from food service to basic maintenance. They carried out limited combat duties, manning security checkpoints and guard towers. It was not uncommon for private military contractors to accompany VIPs as bodyguards. By July 2007, there were 190,000 contractors of all types in Iraq, compared to 160,000 US troops.

Part-Time Soldiers and the Forever War

As noted above, the National Guard and reserves were an integral part of the contemporary American military after September 11 and remain so today. In 2018, almost a million personnel served in all military reserve components, approximately 45 percent of US forces. In the four years after planes struck the Pentagon and World Trade Center, 150,289 of 558,000 Americans serving in the reserve components were on active duty, the most since the Korean War. The Army National Guard and Reserves provided the largest contingent, 38 percent of the deployed service branches.

Part-time soldiers were deeply involved in the Iraq and Afghanistan missions. They were instrumental in counterinsurgency operations, civil affairs, and combat support. Regardless of their specific missions or specializations, by 2010, half of all Army reserve units saw some type of combat. Between 2001 and 2021, when the United States finally departed Afghanistan, National Guard and reserve forces suffered approximately one-fifth of the total US casualties in overseas contingency operations.

Throughout this time period, the US military was heavily dependent on its citizen soldiers. In 2000, the Army National Guard fielded a total of forty-six brigades or their equivalents, providing half of that branch's combat capability. After September 11th, these units were regularly deployed alongside active-duty units fighting insurgents in Iraq and Afghanistan. Air National Guard pilots made significant contributions to the war, flying almost one-third of fighter and attack aircraft in 2007.

Reservists were critical to military logistics. In 2017, Army Reserve units provided 82 percent of civil affairs, 56 percent of transportation, and 50 percent of medical support units. Air Force reserve components were responsible for aerial refueling, tactical reconnaissance, military airlift, and command and control. Air National Guard personnel handled approximately one quarter of remotely piloted aircraft sorties in 2010.

The nature of this contribution magnified the burden carried by the reserves. Units with critical skillsets experienced repeated deployments after 2001. The Maryland Army National Guard's 115 Military Police Battalion was called up three times in a two-year period, for example. Oftentimes, units were mobilized too quickly for personnel to get their affairs in order. Members of one Michigan Army National Guard unit shipped out for Iraq with only forty-eight hours' notice.

The system designed to protect reservists when they became veterans buckled and broke under the weight of the Forever War. One basic problem involved the massive scale of mobilization. Between 2001 and 2014, 815,000 reservists served on full-time active duty. These numbers quickly overwhelmed a structure built around one weekend a month and two weeks of annual training, usually in the summer months. Part-time soldiers fighting after September 11 too often arrived home to what one historian simply called "antiquated policies." According to a 2003 GAO report, 93 percent of Guard and reserve soldiers reported pay problems.

The wounded and injured had a worse time of it. By a quirk of the military bureaucracy, reservists and National Guard casualties were frequently removed from active duty rolls during treatment and recovery, a status that resulted in stoppages of pay and benefits for them and their families. Many wounded were stuck in limbo in medical holding units because of chronic management failures. Representative Tom Davis (R-VA), Chair of the House Committee on Government Reform, commented during a February 2005 hearing, "Frankly, I am appalled that these men and women not only have had to face the recovery from their war wounds, but are simultaneously forced to navigate a confusing and seemingly uncaring system of benefits." Two years later, a *Washington Post* exposé of Walter Reed Army Hospital spoke volumes about an ongoing unsolved problem:

> Life beyond the hospital bed is a frustrating mountain of paperwork. The typical soldier is required to file 22 documents with eight different commands—most of them off-post—to enter and exit the medical processing world, according to government investigators. Sixteen different information systems are used to process the forms, but few of them can communicate with one another. The Army's three personnel databases cannot read each other's files and can't interact with the separate pay system or the medical recordkeeping databases.

Many National Guard and reserve veterans faced significant problems when they attempted to reclaim their old civilian jobs. Federal law designed to protect reservists proved outdated and ineffective. The Uniformed Services Employment and Reemployment Rights Act (USERRA) of 1994 was a modern update of one part of the original G.I. Bill and predated the surge in overseas contingency operations. According to the USERRA, all deployed service members had a right to their original jobs back once they returned home. The law protected employment for activated National Guard and reservists for up to five years. It was built around the baseline assumption that most deployments would last just one year, as they had during Vietnam and the Korean War.

Unfortunately, lawmakers never anticipated multiple or multi-year deployments that became the norm after 2001. In fact, USERRA included the exception that waived employer responsibility if "circumstances have so changed as to make such reemployment impossible or unreasonable." Other provisions of the USERRA simply shifted the costs of military deployments from private businesses to the individual reservist. While the law mandated that deployed individuals could keep their employer health insurance and pension plans, it made the soldier responsible for payments, a difficult prospect for reservists on a military pay scale.

None of these concerns were theoretical. In 2011, the National Guard Bureau estimated that 20 percent of returning soldiers were unemployed, twice the rate for all veterans in the 2000s. During the first two years of the war, 5,690 veterans lost their jobs after returning home or were fired before deploying. Thousands of men and women filed complaints with the Veterans' Employment and Training Service in the Department of Labor. In 2004, approximately 1,500 did so, a number that remained consistent until 2011. To bypass this process, many businesses simply required new hires to sign preemployment agreements to take any disputes to binding arbitration. This tactic survived subsequent challenges in federal courts.

The Forever War took a heavy toll on America's citizen soldiers. It resulted in a laundry list of social and economic calamities, lost jobs, bankruptcy, and divorce. All of these problems accompanied the wounds, injuries, and mental stress experienced overseas in Iraq, Afghanistan, and dozens of other locations around the world. In his 2005 testimony before the House Committee on Government reform, a Pennsylvania reservist noted, "The Reserves and Guard are fighting next to the active duty and we still treat them like second class citizens."

These failures impacted the National Guard and reserves to a degree that still lingers today. Signs of trouble appeared as early as 2005, when the Army missed its recruiting goal by 80,000 personnel, or 8 percent. The situation in the Army National Guard was worse. That component failed to meet its own recruiting targets each year between 2003 and 2005 by 13 percent. By 2022, the deficit had considerably deepened. Army recruiters fell short of their quotas by 25 percent that year. For its own part, the Army National Guard missed its goal by 5 percent.

Women and the Forever War

As noted in the previous chapter, women were a rarity in the American military prior to 1968 by virtue of federal law. However, the Nixon administration and the all-volunteer military changed that status for good after the Vietnam War. In the aftermath of September 11, their numbers continued their rapid increase in all the military branches.

Because official Defense Department policy regarding women serving in the combat branches did not change until 2015, most served in support roles during the Forever War. In practice, they worked in a variety of important specialties such as military police, civil affairs, medical, and transportation. All of these carried substantial risk in an insurgency without a front line or any defined borders. Women suffered casualties along with their male comrades. Between 2001 and 2020, a total of 161 female military personnel were killed in Iraq and Afghanistan, 2.4 percent of the total deaths suffered by US forces. Between 2001 and 2017, slightly more than one thousand women were wounded in both countries.

Beyond the risks involved in ongoing insurgencies, contemporary American military culture posed a separate and distinct threat to women. Ongoing revelations about Military Sexual Trauma (MST) appeared with increasing frequency in the twenty-first century. In 2007, 3 percent of women indicated that they were sexually assaulted with more reporting sexual coercion (8 percent) and unwanted sexual attention (27 percent). According to the Department of Veterans Affairs in 2002, 22 percent of women reported MST along with 1 percent of men. However, these statistics were almost certainly too low. Subsequent academic studies indicated MST rates between 20 percent and 43 percent for female veterans. Affected individuals demonstrated higher rates of substance abuse, anxiety, depression, fatigue, gastrointestinal distress, and pelvic pain. In just two years, from 2016 to 2018, the VA processed 36,000 claims of PTSD related to Military Sexual Trauma.

There are two separate but related tragedies in these numbers. In terms of sheer quantity, it is clear that one of the greatest sources of injury to women veterans was the American military establishment. The second problem is difficult to objectively measure but likely more profound. Sexual assault in the military is, at its foundation, a betrayal of trust. It is a rejection of the comradeship essential to unit cohesion and integrity. When committed by leadership against subordinates, it reflects a failure of fundamental responsibilities owed to individuals and the military as an institution. For their service in the Global War on Terror, America's military women went above and beyond the call, but paid an additional heavy price for their service, something that set them apart from their male peers and redefined their status as contemporary veterans.

"For the Troops, but against the War": Civil-Military Relations in the New Century

Civil-military relations in the twenty-first century continued along a path of reconciliation and support that started in the Reagan era. Although the country never recaptured the atmosphere evident in the heyday of World War II, the ongoing friction commonplace during the Vietnam War had retreated, at least to a degree. At the same time, the number of veterans in the general population, which peaked in 1980, began a slow decline as the century ended. With their passing, and the reduction in forces made throughout the nineties, American connection to military service and war became increasingly tenuous.

Commemoration became a routine and expansive part of post–September 11th America. Military themes and patriotic displays were incorporated into sporting events, particularly professional baseball and football. Pageantry related to the national anthem, which often included aircraft overflights, parachute jumps into stadiums, or a giant American flag spanning the whole playing field, were regular features for the national television networks. Product marketing also leaned into military themes and highlighted links to veterans. The term "tactical" applied to a broad variety of items from clothing to baby carriers. Companies like Black Rifle Coffee became million-dollar concerns by leveraging veterans' status to market their products.

Yet, civil-military relations in the new century also reflected a growing separation. The obvious reason for this distance was the end of the draft, which had resulted in two generations of self-selected military service. Unlike the Baby Boomers, fewer members of Gen X (1965–1980) and Millennials (1981–1996) chose enlistment and represented a shrinking portion of society as a whole. As fewer Americans joined a smaller military, the overall number of veterans in the country was also fading. Time and mortality eroded the World War II generation from 9.2 million in 1990 to just 2.1 million by 2010. The end result was a country that valued military service in an abstract, but uninformed way. A 2013 Pew Research Center study punctuated this new reality. In the twelve years following the September 11 attacks, only 0.5 percent of the American public served in the active-duty military.

The insular nature of the American military had many consequences after 2001. Without a draft, the Pentagon had to rely upon volunteers for the duration of the war, a practice that became increasingly difficult as controversy about stop-loss policy, the treatment of mobilized reservists and National Guard, and the general lack of success in Iraq and Afghanistan soured public opinion. A June 2006 Youth Poll indicated that only 14 percent of young men expressed an interest in joining the military, down 33 percent from the previous year.

Surveys also recorded a significant decline—from 70 percent in 2001 to 40 percent in 2002—in parents likely to recommend military service to their children.

Not surprisingly, in a situation that recalled the early days of the all-volunteer force, the military—especially the Army—struggled with recruit quality. A 2015 Congressional Research Service study noted that the individual military branches generally were able to sustain two qualifications: 90 percent possessing a high school diploma and 60 percent scoring above average on the Armed Forces Qualification Test (AFQT). However, in 2013 and 2014, the components most heavily deployed after September 11, the Army National Guard and Reserves, struggled with these standards. To compensate, the Army raised its maximum enlistment age from 35 to 42 and increased waivers for preexisting medical conditions, drug use, and criminal offenses. Exceptions for prior drug use became more common, both before enlistment and while in uniform. In his 2019 annual report, the Marine Corps Commandant noted:

> I remain troubled by the extent to which drug abuse is a characteristic of new recruits, and the fact the vast majority of recruits require drug waivers for enlistment. I am equally troubled by the fact that we do not specifically monitor personnel for continued substance abuse while in-service.

Portions of military culture were also an increasing point of contention. For the uninitiated, it was alien to twenty-first-century sensibilities, at once brutal, intolerant, and incomprehensible. Sebastian Junger's writing about the contemporary military exposed many of these features in startling detail:

> "I used to score three hundreds on my PT tests shit-canned ... just drunk as fuck," O'Bryne told me. "That's how you get sober for the rest of the day. I never got in trouble, but Bobby beat up a few MPs, threatened them with a fire extinguisher, pissed on their boots. But what do you expect from the infantry, you know? I know all the guys that were bad in garrison were perfect fucking soldiers in combat. They're troublemakers and they like to fight. That's a bad garrison trait but a good combat trait—right?"

Junger's *Tribe: On Homecoming and Belonging* (2016) spoke directly about the chasm between a tiny military subculture and the vast majority of society. The common cause of World War II and all its components—rationing, censorship, and conscription—was a thing of the past. Ironically, we were victims of our own success. Junger notes, "The beauty and tragedy of the modern world is that it eliminates many situations that require people to demonstrate a commitment to the collective good." Today, the military has the same status as police and firefighters. They are specialists providing a service that civilians accept as long as it does not intrude on their own sense of normalcy.

Preserving this normalcy was a major policy goal after September 11. Full-scale, national mobilization was never a serious option. In fact, the president signaled the opposite track in an October 2001 news conference:

> Now, the American people have got to go about their business. We cannot let the terrorists achieve the objective of frightening our nation to the point where we don't—where we don't conduct business, where people don't shop. That's their intention. Their intention was not only to kill and maim and destroy. Their intention was to frighten to the point where our nation would not act.

This approach preempted necessary military reforms, particularly with respect to the personnel shortages plaguing US overseas contingency operations. Reconstituting selective service was a dead issue as far as elected officials were concerned. According to an August 2007 Gallup poll, 80 percent of respondents rejected the idea outright.

The inconclusive nature of the war on terror also eroded public support. Americans are not patient people in general and policymakers had long recognized the need for plausible military "exit strategies" in the post-Vietnam era. The small-scale military interventions of the eighties, Desert Storm, and the many peacekeeping/peace enforcement missions of the nineties were built around the decisive use of force or, lacking that, holding casualties to a bare minimum. Iraq and Afghanistan defied this approach. The regular drumbeat of IEDs, ambushes, and subsequent dead and wounded, all without a conclusive end in sight, created a creeping sense of disillusionment. By March 2008, a *Washington Post*/ABC poll indicated that 63 percent of Americans believed the war in Iraq was not worth fighting.

Unfortunately, the American military also earned some of this disdain. Revelations about civilian deaths in Haditha in November 2005, attributed to US Marines, and the treatment of prisoners in Abu Ghraib created shockwaves around the country. By June 2006, 57 percent of the people polled by the Opinion Research Corporation believed American troops had committed atrocities.

An incident in July 2011 illustrated the nature of the civil-military gap. A video, posted on YouTube six months after the fact, revealed four Marines urinating on Taliban dead, a violation of the rules of engagement. The incident immediately went viral and inhabited cable news and tabloid television for days. Commentators in the United States and the Middle East expressed their outrage. Secretary of Defense Leon Panetta called the act "deplorable" and launched an investigation. Although the Marines pled guilty to a variety of charges, none expressed any regrets. One interviewed by *ABC News* simply said, "These were the same guys that were killing our family, killing our brothers, but do I regret doing it? Hell no."

Veterans' Activism in the New Century

Veterans' organizations carried forward into the new century much as they had for most of the post–World War II era. The American Legion and the Veterans of Foreign Wars kept their dominant position, at their apex comprising one-third of the total US veterans' population. However, time and advancing age would diminish their ranks by September 11th. When the terrorist attacks occurred, the Legion could count approximately three million members, although that number would shrink by one-third over the next two decades. For its own part, VFW membership peaked in 1992 at approximately two million and subsequently entered a period of decline. By 2019, it was comprised of just 1.2 million members.

Although well-established groups like the American Legion, VFW, or even the American Veterans Committee ran recruiting drives for the successive waves of veterans returning to the civilian world after Vietnam, it was a case study in diminishing returns. Robert D. Putnam's excellent 2000 book *Bowling Alone: The Collapse and Revival of American Community* identified declining interest in established civic organizations around the country. However, Putnam argued that the decline was less about interest in social activism than it was a rejection of traditional ways to pursue change.

This seems to be the case with veterans who followed Baby Boomers into military service. The men and women who served in the Forever War have become advocates, although on their own terms. Some of the earliest post-2001 veterans' groups embodied the spirit of the Vietnam Veterans Against the War in that they leveraged military service to augment their criticism of the wars in Iraq and Afghanistan and US policy in general. When Operation Truth was launched in 2004, it provided a platform for veterans to express their discontent regarding the lack of adequate body armor, the military's stop-loss program, and incoherent US counterinsurgency efforts in occupied countries.

Also founded in 2004, the Iraq Veterans Against the War (IVAW) was a regular fixture in the small antiwar movement. Borrowing a page from the past, it sponsored Winter Soldier: Iraq and Afghanistan in March 2008, which brought together two hundred active-duty military and veterans to talk about their wartime experiences. In public forums, they discussed civilians allegedly killed by 1st Cavalry Division in Abu Ghraib in the first year of the war as well as the abuses committed by US forces against innocent Iraqis during counterinsurgency sweeps. While it exposed possible war crimes, the 2008 Winter Soldier meeting also illustrated the costs to veterans who fought in a conflict without clearly defined sides. Adam Koresh, a Marine who served in Fallujah in 2004, put the Forever War in stark terms: "It's criminal to put such patriotic Americans… in a situation where their morals are at odds with their survival instincts." As the war progressed and the Obama administration began troop withdrawals, the IVAW shifted its focus from potential human rights violations to issues prevalent among veterans such as suicide prevention, PTSD, and veterans' health care.

Other veterans' groups focused specifically on educational support, which experienced something of a renaissance following the Montgomery G.I. Bill. Between 1985 and 2011, Congress passed no fewer than seven separate programs. The 2005 Reserves Educational Assistance Program addressed veterans' transition from the military to the civilian work force by offering up to thirty-six months of vocational training or college to the National Guard, active reservists, or members of the Individual Ready Reserve (IRR). The Veterans Retraining Assistance Program (2011) provided one year of instruction for unemployed veterans.

The capstone of veterans' education was the post-9/11 G.I. Bill (2008), which paid up to $25,000 for tuition and books and a housing stipend. Like the 1966 and 1984 versions of the G.I. Bill, this put many public universities well within the reach of most veterans. However, private institutions, with an average tuition of $42,000 in 2019, remained far outside the scope of the program without additional student loans or grants. The one major change to policy was an allowance for veterans to transfer these benefits to their family members.

Overall, these combined programs proved to be extremely popular. In Fiscal Year 2018 alone, 800,000 veterans received education benefits at a cost of $12 billion to the federal government. But progress came with consequences.

One was the fact that the Department of Veterans Affairs could not keep pace with college enrollment and benefits applications. More than half of the 167,000 veterans who used their education benefits for the fall 2009 semester experienced delays. Promises of additional staff did little to affect the backlog. As late as October 2018, the VA still wrestled with 120,000 unfilled applications. Some veterans had to wait up to sixty days to received finished paperwork for school.

Veterans found additional problems as they navigated the college experience. Individual schools lacked the proper metrics to transfer military training or courses into academic credit. Many veterans discovered, upon presenting their Joint Services Transcript, that university registrars tended to go for low-hanging fruit, translating basic training into a physical education credit. More advanced military training rarely made it on to official college course records. Repeated deployments also posed unforeseen difficulties for student veterans when they interrupted college and triggered loan repayments. Todd Bower discovered that his student loans were referred to a collection agency only after he was wounded by a sniper near Fallujah in 2004 and returned home.

For some veterans, the transition from military to campus culture was particularly jarring. Discharged men and women entered higher learning in numbers not seen since the Vietnam War. As a group, they tended to be older—the average was 33 in 2012—than most undergraduates. Many had seen combat over multiple tours, and their experiences did not mesh well with normal university students. One veteran reflected on his own encounter:

> Some guy in my class came up to me and told me he really supports the troops and thank you for your service. I was just back and I was in one of those moods. So, I said, oh yeah, so what do you do to support the troops? He kind of looked at me ... that attitude ... they are kind of stumped and stare at you. Do you buy a bumper sticker? Do you join a Facebook group? I was upset with the whole thing.

College faculty and staff agencies presented separate difficulties. Few twenty-first-century teachers had the military experience common to the World War II generation. Although colleges could accommodate wounded and injured veterans because of the Americans with Disabilities Act, they lacked psychological counseling expertise for PTSD, Military Sexual Trauma, and the problems associated with Traumatic Brain Injury.

The Student Veterans of America (SVA), incorporated in 2008, emerged to address these and other concerns. The SVA committed to "empowering veterans" and "providing an educational experience that goes beyond the classroom." It sponsored scholarships, hosted mentorship programs with the private sector, offered leadership training, and conducted annual conferences for its campus affiliates. By 2019, the SVA claimed 1,583 chapters and advocacy for 700,000 "military affiliated students" in all fifty states and four countries.

Women veterans joined the SVA but also created their own purpose-built organizations. The Service Women's Action Network (SWAN), founded in 2007, promised to "Support, Connect, Advocate" for a series of issues ranging from health care and housing to financial advice, employment counseling, and legal services. SWAN sued the Defense Department in 2012 to allow women into the combat arms. As late as June 2020, the SWAN Twitter feed covered military access to birth control, body armor specifically for women's physiology, and LGBTQ rights. During the COVID-19 crisis, women veterans' organizations offered direct support for individuals affected by the disease. Both SWAN and Women Veterans Interactive created links to VA health resources, domestic abuse counseling, and ongoing fundraising for COVID relief.

Veterans and Public Policy in the Twenty-First Century

The surge in military operations after 2001 prompted a rapid development of veterans' programs. Some of these, like education policies, continued and expanded on past practice dating back to World War II with a few modern updates. In other cases, particularly with respect to medical treatment, programs reflected both the contingencies of modern insurgency abroad and badly needed reforms to the Department of Veterans Affairs at home.

Post-2001 veterans' health care presented its own special challenges. Although the Forever War was not as costly as Vietnam or Korea, US casualties were not insignificant. As of July 2024, the American military forces suffered 7,085 killed and 53,531 wounded, a total that did not include contractors or local nationals in US service. Wounded troops benefited from improved body armor and advances in trauma care—blood coagulants, routine use of tourniquets, frontline diagnostic equipment—as well as rapid access to air evacuation and surgery. Consequently, the survival rate for US forces was 90.7 percent in 2007.

However, although soldiers survived burns, traumatic amputation, or traumatic brain injuries (TBI) that might have killed them a generation earlier, this fact presented significant long-term commitments to veterans' medical care. After 2001, the Department of Veterans Affairs also had to contend with a spectrum of problems ranging from severe wounds to respiratory illnesses and rashes caused by military burn pits, to military sexual trauma, PTSD, and escalating suicide rates.

The VA lacked adequate facilities to address these new responsibilities. One basic, systemic problem was a lack of bed space. In 1998, as a result of the "peace dividend" and years of budget cuts, there were only 45,303 beds for all living veterans in the entire VA system. Incredibly, four years into the Global War on Terror, there were actually fewer spaces (41,731) with more than a third (15,109) designated for long-term nursing home care.

Much like the rest of the country, the Department of Veterans Affairs suffered its own opioid crisis. In too many cases during the Forever War, the VA horribly mismanaged the use of prescription drugs. Department of Veterans Affairs doctors, encouraged by companies like Perdue Pharma, issued painkillers for both physical injuries as well as PTSD. Between 2001 and 2013, opioid prescriptions from VA doctors increased by 270 percent. According to a 2012 study published in the *Journal of the American Medical Association*, veterans with post-traumatic stress disorder (PTSD) were three times more likely to be prescribed opiates for pain than other veterans.

However, the opioid scandal was not the only one buffeting the veterans' medical system in the new century. In 2007, Walter Reed Army Medical Center came under siege after the *Washington Post* reported that the "crown jewel" of military facilities was an unhealthy hulk:

> Behind the door of army specialist Jeremy Duncan's room, part of the wall is torn and hangs in the air, weighted down with black mold. When the wounded combat engineer stands in his shower and looks up, he can see the bathtub on the floor above through a rotted hole. The entire building, constructed between the world wars, often smells like greasy carry-out. Signs of neglect are everywhere: mouse droppings, belly-up cockroaches, stained carpets, cheap mattresses.

It was a situation made worse by staff shortages and indifferent management.

In 2014, the issue of lengthy wait times for medical care, a fact deliberately hidden from federal regulators, further tarnished public faith in the Department of Veterans Affairs. The focal point was the Phoenix VA, where some veterans waited up to 115 days before seeing a doctor. As many as forty died during these delays in this one facility alone. Subsequent investigations revealed what the American Legion called "an epidemic of mismanagement" in at least a dozen states.

Each round of scandals has produced concurrent reforms. VA head Eric Shinseki was forced out in 2014, as was the commander of Walter Reed, Major General George W. Weightman. Public outrage has also produced a blizzard of new federal law. The Choice Act (2014) opened up veterans' access to private medical care. It was followed by the Clay Hunt Suicide Prevention for American Veterans Act (2015). Senator John McCain introduced the Veterans Overmedication Prevention Bill in 2017, which would require the VA to "to review the deaths of all covered veterans who died by suicide during the last five years, regardless of whether information relating to such deaths has been reported by the Centers for Disease Control and Prevention." The recent PACT Act (2022) qualified hundreds of thousands of veterans exposed to toxins in Vietnam, the First Gulf War, and post-2001 operations for VA care.

Veterans' health resources have multiplied accordingly. Thousands of new staff hires followed the Walter Reed scandal. To ease the passage from military to civilian life, the military created Warrior Transition Units for out processing personnel. In 2010, as part of a joint private and public sector initiative, the National Action Alliance for Suicide Prevention was created to coordinate strategy and resources for veterans.

Not surprisingly, the Department of Veterans Affairs budget has ballooned in recent times. Between 2001 and 2011, it more than doubled from $61.4 billion to $124.3 billion. By 2023, federal funding for veterans accelerated to 308.5 billion. Expanding access to civilian medical care and the inclusive nature of the PACT Act account for a significant proportion of these increases.

Post-2001 contingency operations were, in many respects, a compendium of America's past history of warfare. Operation Iraqi Freedom largely succeeded on the basis of conventional force doctrine honed over a generation of training and practice. When the situation in the country deteriorated, coalition forces stumbled into a war of counterinsurgency. "Rapid decisive operations" took a less conventional path in Afghanistan, but again, US forces found themselves fighting an elusive enemy in a conflict defined by raids, ambushes, and a slow, steady accumulation of both civilian and military casualties.

There were many costs to the Forever War. Beyond the trillions spent on the conflict, its veterans bore the brunt. As noted above, tens of thousands suffered wounds and physical injuries. The mental burdens endured by the men and women who served was also significant. According to a 2008 study made with the help of American Legion posts in six states, severe PTSD symptoms persisted in 10 percent of veterans. Five years later, the VA published a report that indicated the prevalence of combat trauma among 11 percent of male veterans and 7 percent of women.

Civil-military relations were generally positive in the new century, but superficial and consequently fickle. Ironically, public access to the war, via cable news, the internet, and a host of platforms, did not translate into a greater understanding of the conflict or its participants. Journalist Sara Corbett observed in 2004 that veterans "must live with the confounding mix of anonymity and exposure wrought by surviving the war." For all the good intentions demonstrated by Americans throughout the conflict, the fundamental lack of understanding undercut meaningful connections with veterans. As the war continued, the gap between the respective civilian and military worlds grew.

Veterans' programs did not keep pace with the surge in US global commitments. As deployed men and women returned for care or to receive earned benefits, they found an overwhelming bureaucratic labyrinth that too often failed to meet its basic obligations to them. Cycles of public outrage and reform prompted larger VA budgets to meet these expanding obligations. This is a necessary trend given the millions of new veterans who are joining older cohorts left over from World War II and the Cold War. However, given recent scandals, it remains to be seen if the system will be able to conform to the needs of this new generation.

When faced with obstacles at home, Veterans of the Forever War, like their counterparts in generations past, struck out to become their own advocates. This young cohort, while less interested in joining traditional veterans' groups like the American Legion and VFW, nevertheless used their leadership and organizational skills to lobby for their specific interests, a diverse collection of causes emanating from the men and women tasked with fighting their country's most recent war.

Conclusions

Did I see those brave and noble countrymen of mine laid low in death and weltering in their blood?
Did I see our country laid waste and in ruins?
Did I see soldiers marching, the earth trembling and jarring beneath their measured tread?
Did I see the ruins of smoldering cities and deserted homes?
Did I see the flag of my country, that I had followed so long, furled to be no more unfurled forever? Surely, they are but the vagaries of mine own imagination. But hush! I now hear the approach of battle.
That low, rumbling sound in the West is the roar of cannon in the distance.

SAM R. WATKINS, COMPANY H, 1ST TENNESSEE, 1882

The Nature of American War

War is a crucible for countries and citizens alike. Nations fight, as they always have, to survive as political entities. When they are successful, nations persist and may grow. In other cases, like East Prussia in 1945 or portions of Ukraine today, countries or parts of them may simply disappear never to be seen again.

For the people who fight, war is not just a political abstract. True belief in a particular system of government, be it for democracy or king and country, clearly motivates many individuals. However, other human features also apply to service. The men and women who join may do so out of boredom, or curiosity, or obligation to family tradition. They may seek out social recognition for heroism based upon a long line of archetypes, some real and some imagined. Audie Murphy and John Wayne motivated Vietnam veterans like Phil Caputo or Ron Kovic to serve their country as young men growing up in post-1945 America.

The historical record demonstrates that not all American wars are created equal. The Revolution, the Civil War, and World War II were definitive, positive moments for America, each serving as a major milestone marking victory against both internal and external threats. The objective value of these wars is evident by their outcome. However, even when it comes to just wars, the historical record evolves over time. Americans have intentionally curated their military experiences, a process that often created an idealized version of what constituted a "good" war. This definition served as a standard, as historian Eleanor L. Hannah observes, for what later generations would aspire to when their time to fight arrived.

In contrast, more than a few American wars were cautionary tales. Prolonged conflicts lacking a clear point of origin, identifiable sides, and what would later be called an "exit strategy," were correspondingly unpopular with the public, something that framed the reception for their veterans. The so-called Banana Wars in Central America and the Caribbean in the 1920s, Korea, and Vietnam all fall into this category. The more recent wars that followed September 11 began with significant public support that diminished as deployments dragged on for decades. America's final, calamitous withdrawal from Afghanistan is still a raw wound that we live with today.

The actual conduct of American wars also defined them. Over more than three hundred years of history, American military operations covered the entire spectrum of conflict. Conventional doctrine has guided much of this effort, from the Continental Line at Cowpens in 1781 to 73 Easting, where the 2nd

Armored Cavalry Regiment faced the Iraqi Republican Guard in 1991. In the meantime, and, at some points concurrent with these operations, the United States has fought unconventional enemies for centuries. The ongoing conquest of the American West involved thousands of clashes with Native Americans. In the modern era, US forces fought with and against rebels, insurgents, and a panoply of irregulars. It was not uncommon during these operations to refer to hostile territory as "Indian Country."

The twenty-first-century war against terror contained elements of virtually all of America's past wars and introduced a few of its own. As US forces struggled to contain the Taliban, ISIS, and their many offshoots, the Pentagon joined every major power in developing information warfare systems that address every place the internet might touch, from military logistics to crucial infrastructure, to presidential elections.

In the end, veterans are a composite of their institutions and their experiences. These are what separate the former soldier, sailor, Marine, or Airman from the civilians who wait for them when they come home. The veteran is attuned to the consequences of service and war. They are not abstract like lines on a map. Death, wounds, sickness, and trauma are real, life-changing, and permanent artifacts that follow the veteran long after the headlines fade and their uniforms are consigned to mothballs. As one story ends another begins.

The Changing Nature of American Veterans

Veterans embody the best and worst of what an American can be. At points, they are the exemplars of citizenship, who embraced sacrifice for the greater good. During the colonial period, as colonial communities fought for survival, this was literally true. Whenever the country faced challenges to its existence or centered its efforts on a universally held principle (abolishing slavery) or alleviating oppression (during World War II) this same metric returned again and again.

However, just as consistently over the course of American history, veterans were perceived as a threat. Many believed that a body of trained men, bloodied by war and returned home, was not a far step from an armed mob and a threat to American democracy. This was true during Shays' Rebellion and equally so in the words of the 1944 book, *When Johnny Comes Marching Home*: "A civilian can be licked into shape as a soldier by the manual of arms and a drillmaster, but no manual has ever been written for changing him back into a civilian." In this context, veterans were a dangerous, permanent subculture embedded in American society, one that might easily translate their experience into lawlessness and criminal behavior. Predictions of postwar crime waves regularly appear in American history, even after World War II. In *The Veteran Comes Back* (1944), Willard Waller believed that "Sometimes the veteran has been so completely alienated from the attitudes and controls of civilian life that he becomes a criminal."

Whether applied to positive or negative tropes, it is important to consider that veterans do not belong to a monolithic bloc. They many share general experiences—the decision to enter military service, first impressions of boot camp, deployment overseas—consolidated under a group identity. However, individual service is a unique composite of a particular branch of the military, an occupational specialty, and a unit, among many other factors. In the end, a "former Marine" infantryman often has very little in common with a Navy technician.

Additional separations and subcultures within the military accumulate with individual and collective experiences. The wounded, "men dealing with every combination of physical catastrophe," in the words of historian Thomas Childers, exist in a class all by themselves. In *Soldier from the War Returning*

(2009), Childers reflects on the shock of being wounded and the excruciating process of recovery that dictated the terms of transition back into civilian life. Endless and exhausting rounds of surgery and rehabilitation, each with their own moments of progress and setbacks, left an imprint that reshaped the veteran's identity.

Civilians at home could and often did struggle with these complexities. Their task was easier during colonial times when constant mobilization was the norm and most adults—men and women alike—shared the burden of frontier survival. Even when danger shifted west with settlement, many communities maintained their military ties in a different manner. The muster became an anticipated social event even as the militia practiced for war.

The Civil War ripped away this gloss and introduced the citizen soldier to the brutal realities of mass mobilization augmented by industry and the resulting charnel houses at Antietam, Shiloh, Gettysburg, and more than a dozen other battlefields. Heroes still inspired the forces on contested ground, but their value shrank in the wake of modern wars of constant attrition. Although the western frontier briefly rekindled belief in the romanticized frontiersman, and the Spanish-American War produced its own legendary acts of valor, the new twentieth century began with the realization that military service was a necessary, albeit temporary, obligation of gargantuan, conscripted citizen armies serving at the behest of the nation-state. Teddy Roosevelt's transition from a national hero after his gallant and foolhardy ride up San Juan Heights to a father grieving the loss of his son Quentin in the skies over France was a testament to the new order of the world.

The term "selective service" precisely described military participation from the civilian domain. During both world wars and the subsequent Cold War, an increasingly complex system of deferments—physical and mental capacity, critical skills, marital status, education, and a host of other exceptions—filtered a citizen's military obligation. By the time that manpower needs for the

Vietnam War began ramping up, the deferment system began to break down under the weight of its problematic utility and, more importantly, the social controversies it was provoking.

The advent of the all-volunteer military in 1973 made this elaborate system, and the concurrent debate, moot. Service became a self-selecting process, dictated by personal interest and market forces. This milestone produced two consequences for both the military as an institution and society as a whole. When it invoked the all-volunteer force after Vietnam, the country never looked back, consistently refusing to return to conscription regardless of need. Secondly, military service became an increasingly rarified part of being an American citizen. By virtue of law, circumstance, and choice, contemporary veterans belong to their own tribe.

Civil-Military Relations and the Moral Callus

In his 2012 book *The Last Full Measure: How Soldiers Die in Battle*, Michael Stephenson observed that "To survive a great battle was to be elected to an elite." It is a simple, hard reality, that the transition from civilian life to the military, comes at a cost. Combat is the capstone of a process that starts with enlistment and ends when the newly minted veteran returns home.

Throughout, a moral callus begins to grow around the prospective recruit when they first enlist. The first layer is the deliberate product of training. Combining tradition with modern scientific methodology, the military experience is designed to desensitize and reshape the individual. During the Korean War, the Defense Department's Research and Development Board commissioned a series of papers that examined the broader application of fear to individuals and units in combat. In a 1951 report for the board, Yale psychologist Neal E. Miller framed the problem in terms of encouraging an "adaptive response" through training. Military doctrine needed to consider "not how afraid a man is, but what fear motivates him to do." The end goal, as explained by historian Gwynne Dyer, follows:

> In basic training establishments, however, the malleability is all one way: in the direction of submission to military authority and the internalization of military values. What a place like Parris Island produces when it is successful, as it usually is, is a soldier who will kill because that is his job.

Once a person enters a war, the moral callus becomes a product of circumstance. The contingencies of war take military training and transform it in ways that alter the nature of the combatant, a process James Jones described as "The Evolution of a Soldier." A lifetime of moral training and social norms may fall away in the moments dictated by war. After killing a Japanese sniper, William Manchester recalled, "I can remember whispering foolishly, 'I'm sorry' and then just throwing up ... I threw up all over myself. It was a betrayal of what I'd been taught since a child." The act of combat, stripped of rhetoric and propaganda was, in the words of Marine veteran Eugene Sledge, an act of "brutal, primitive hatred."

Veterans have attempted to explain this transition in literature. In *All Quiet on the Western Front*, there is a passage where Paul Bäumer and his unit returned from the trenches to discover a field kitchen ready to feed the full complement of men listed on the roster, not understanding that half of them were wounded or dead. Remarque presented the survivors celebrating a "stroke of luck" that doubled their rations. For the combat veteran of 1918, full bellies held precedence over lost comrades.

Yet, it is hard to explain this transition to a layperson. Any number of euphemisms have appeared over time such as "seeing the elephant" or "losing your cherry." More recently, a veteran described experiencing combat as "passing through a door." An infantryman attempted to convey the complex sense of pride, fatalism, and comradeship developed in combat: "Nobody gets out of a rifle company. It's a door that only opens one way, in. You leave when they carry you out, if you're unlucky, dead, or if you're lucky, wounded. But nobody just walks away. That was the unwritten law." In the end, it is clear that veterans, particularly their most recent incarnation, constitute a separate social group that will always be separated from the larger public.

Veterans' Advocacy and the Evolution of Policy

American society generally has understood its obligation to veterans. However, fulfilling this obligation has been a matter of ongoing debate for literally centuries. Opinion has divided over many factors: some philosophical, some practical. The public discourse has repeatedly returned to concerns that veterans' programs might foster dependency upon the state. Exactly what part of the state also enjoined much discussion. In the beginning, responsibility fell to local and state authorities. Over time, as the scope and scale of the veterans' population grew, the federal government took primary responsibility for them. Even so, the process was never entirely divorced from the people. What Omar Bradley made clear in December 1945 applied before World War II and afterward:

> While we can assist with benefits and offer guidance, it is the community that must do the grassroots work. For it is in his daily association with his neighbors that the veteran rubs shoulders with so many troublesome problems Washington cannot hope to solve.

A separate hurdle has always been cost. For a young republic emerging from its revolution, crafting a national system for any form of social welfare was a daunting task. However, even when the country enjoyed prosperity, as was the case after the Civil War or World War II, the massive commitments to veterans caused public official to pause. The original G.I. Bill was both generous and successful, but it was not endless as the Bradley Commission demonstrated in 1955. Contemporary veterans' benefits have seen a massive increase since September 11 but will likely run afoul of the same concerns that defined the funding debate in generations past.

All of these factors have affected the ebb and flow of veterans' programs. Lawmakers were remarkably proactive in the early stages of the Civil War when they crafted the General Pension Act of 1862. In the years that led to the Gilded Age, the system of identifying injuries, disabilities, and recipients grew increasingly elaborate and complex, establishing an early precedent for nationally funded social welfare. Yet, even as accumulating layers of federal largess increased, they attracted criticism for waste and fraud—many times rightly so—from Progressives intent on breaking the power of political machines in American life. The original 1944 Serviceman's Readjustment Act (G.I. Bill) took up the practice of earned social welfare benefits and amplified it beyond the original New Deal standard. At the end of World War II, its contagious popularity spawned a variety of versions at the state level. Pennsylvania made veterans' preference part of its state hiring practices. Louisiana offered homestead land. Many Southern states waived the poll tax for veterans. However, the half-life of this generosity proved to be very short. On the advent of the Korean War a fiscally conservative Congress began making major cuts to the Veterans Administration. Subsequent versions of the G.I. Bill were much less generous by design.

Into this reoccurring breach stepped veterans, at points husbanding new policy commitments, in other cases filling the gaps left by it. This role took time to develop. When the Society of Cincinnati formed in 1783, it primarily was a social organization for American officers. The Aztec Club of 1847 served the same basic function. It was not until the creation of the Grand Army of the Republic (GAR) that veterans engaged in serious political lobbying. For more than a generation, the GAR successfully organized Civil War veterans for the sake of shaping elections and government policy. Both the Veterans of Foreign Wars and the American Legion followed this template and became enormously influential in elections and social welfare programs for their members and veterans as a whole.

Into the Future

The deployments following September 11 are long gone, but our obligations to the men and women who made them will remain with Americans for decades to come. At 4.2 million, the individuals who served in US overseas contingency operations are second in size only to Vietnam veterans. At the start of the twenty-first century, the early waves of returning veterans were a prominent new part of classrooms, workplaces, and medical facilities. Over the last two decades they have assumed familiar roles in American communities and the political landscape.

Veterans of the Forever War will take their own unique attributes, talents, and troubles into the future. The all-volunteer force that welcomed women and minorities has produced and will continue to produce an increasingly diverse cohort of veterans. Even as the number of veterans in the United States continues to decline, the overall proportion of women with military service grows. By 2040, they are projected to be approximately 16 percent of veterans overall. The women who served are just as susceptible as men to the physical and mental toll of repeated deployments, a situation made worse by the ongoing problem of Military Sexual Trauma. Suicide rates for veterans steadily rose between 2005 and 2018. For individuals between eighteen and thirty-four, the rate was three times higher than non-veterans.

In a country where veterans of the Forever War constitution about 1 percent of the population, the ongoing gap between military and civilian cultures will be shaped by sincere recognition shrouded by a prevailing ambivalence. One veteran spoke for many when he commented that "I realized that whatever friends I had made before the Army no longer really existed. The only friends that I now have are the ones I made while I was in." Our ability to bridge this gap will be an important component of success or failure in the future. It will likely be determined by how well we remember the past and apply its lessons to the persistent struggles of the present day.

BIBLIOGRAPHIC ESSAY

Historical Sources

There are a number of essential readings on American military history, civil-military relations, and veterans' affairs. They include Walter Millis, *Arms and Men: A Study in American Military History* (New Brunswick: Rutgers University Press, 1981); Paul Fussell, *Wartime: Understanding and Behavior in the Second World War* (New York: Oxford University Press, 1989); Thomas Childers, *Soldier from the War Returning: The Greatest Generation's Troubled Homecoming from World War II* (New York: Houghton Mifflin Harcourt, 2009); and Sebastian Junger, *Tribe: On Homecoming and Belonging* (New York: Twelve, 2016). A classic source on American military veterans' benefits is William Henry Glasson, *History of Military Pension Legislation in the United States* (New York: Columbia University Press, 1900).

Introduction

The quote at the start of the chapter is from Therese Benedek, *Insight and Personality Adjustment: A Study of the Psychological Effects of War* (New York: The Ronald Press Company, 1946), 298.

The field of veterans' history is significant and continually growing. Some examples of this work include Stephen R. Ortiz, *Beyond the Bonus March and GI Bill: How Veteran Politics Shaped the New Deal Era* (New York: New York University Press, 2010); James Wright, *Those Who Have Borne the Battle: A History of America's Wars and Those Who Fought Them* (New York: Public Affairs, 2012); and Benjamin Cooper, *Veteran Americans: Literature and Citizenship from Revolution to Reconstruction* (Amherst: University of Massachusetts Press, 2018).

Historians have addressed the evolution of veterans' benefits in the modern era. See David A. Gerber, "Disabled Veterans, the State, and the Experience of Disability in Western Societies, 1914–1950," *Journal of Social History*, vol. 36 (Summer 2003): 899–916; and Mark Boulton, *Failing Our Veterans: The G.I. Bill and the Vietnam Generation* (New York: New York University Press, 2014).

Chapter One
The Revolutionary War

The quote at the start of the chapter is from Natasha A Larimer, "Step Forth Like Men: Negotiating Manhood and Military Service in Revolutionary Pennsylvania, 1775–1790" (Ph.D. dissertation, University of Wisconsin, Madison, 2003), 242.

There are a number of useful general histories of European and colonial military affairs. See Theodore Ropp, *War in the Modern World* (New York: Macmillan, 1962); Allan R. Millett, Peter Maslowski, and William B. Feis, *For the Common Defense: A Military History of the United States from 1607 to 2012* (New York: Free Press, 2012); and Don Higginbotham, *The War of American Independence: Military Attitudes, Policies, and Practice, 1763–1789* (Boston: Northeastern University Press, 1983).

For general histories of veterans during colonial times, readers may consider Ricardo A. Herrera, "Self-Governance and the American Citizen as Soldier, 1775–1861," *Journal of Military History*, vol. 65 (January 2001): 21–52, John Resch, *Suffering Soldiers: Revolutionary War Veterans, Moral Sentiments, and Political Culture in the Early Republic* (Amherst: University of Massachusetts Press, 1999).

Individual states pursued a variety of policies toward their soldiers and veterans. See Joseph Seymour, *The Pennsylvania Associators, 1747–1777* (Morrisville: Westholme Publishing, 2012); Albert H. Tillson, "The Militia and Popular Political Culture in the Upper Valley of Virginia, 1740–1775," *Virginia Magazine of History and Biography*, vol. 94 (July 1986), 285–306; Gregory T. Knouff, *The Soldiers' Revolution: Pennsylvanians and the Forging of Early American Identity* (University Park: Pennsylvania State University Press, 2004); F. W. Anderson, "Why Did Colonial New Englanders Make Bad Soldiers? Contractual Principles and Military Conduct during the Seven Years War," *William and Mary Quarterly*, vol. 38 (July 1981): 395–417; Laurel Daen, "Revolutionary War Invalid Pensions and the Bureaucratic Language of Disability in the Early Republic," *Early American Literature*, vol. 52 (2017): 141–67; Kristin A. Collins, "'Petitions without Number': Widows' Petitions and the Early Nineteenth-Century Origins of Public Marriage-Based Entitlements," *Law and History Review*, vol. 31 (February 2013): 1–60; Thomas R. Saxton, "'In Reduced Circumstances': Aging and Impoverished Bucks County Continentals and Their Families in the Young Republic," *Pennsylvania History*, vol. 74 (Winter 2007): 21–73.

Useful recent dissertations on colonial American veterans and civil-military relations include Natasha A Larimer, "Step Forth Like Men: Negotiating Manhood and Military Service in Revolutionary Pennsylvania, 1775–1790" (Ph.D. dissertation, University of Wisconsin, Madison, 2003); and Charles P. Neimeyer, "No Meat, No Soldier: Race, Class, and Ethnicity in the Continental Army" (Ph.D. dissertation, Georgetown University, 1993).

There is extensive scholarship on African Americans in uniform during the colonial era and afterward. See Errol A. Henderson, "Slave Religion, Slave Hiring, and the Incipient Proletarianization of Enslaved Black Labor: Developing Dubois' Thesis of Black Participation in the Civil War as a Revolution," *Journal of African American Studies*, vol. 19 (June 2015): 192–213; Pete Maslowski, "National Policy Toward the Use of Black Troops in the Revolution," *South Carolina Historical Magazine*, vol. 72 (January 1972): 1–17; Robert A. Geake, *From Slaves to Soldiers: The 1st Rhode Island Regiment in the American Revolution* (Yardley, PA: Westholme Publishing, 2016); Judith L. Van Buskirk, *Standing in Their Own Light: African American Patriots in the American Revolution* (Norman: University of Oklahoma Press, 2017); Karen E. Sutton, "The Nickens Nine: Free African Americans in Lancaster and Northumberland Counties, Virginia, During the Era of the American Revolution" (Ph.D. dissertation, Morgan State University, 2021).

Chapter Two
The Early Republic

The quote at the start of the chapter is from A Sermon of the Mexican War: Preached at the Melodeon on Sunday June 25, 1848, by Theodore Parker, Minister of the XXVIII, Congregational Church in Boston. https://library.uta.edu/usmexicowar/transcription?content_id=455.

As a young country, the United States struggled to construct a military adequate to its national defense. See J. C. A. Stagg, "Soldiers in Peace and War: Comparative Perspectives on the Recruitment of United States Army, 1802–1815," *William and Mary Quarterly*, vol. 57 (January 2000): 79–120; William B. Skelton, "The Confederation's Regulars: A Social Profile of Enlisted Service in America's First Standing Army," *William & Mary Quarterly*, vol. 46 (October 1999): 770–85.

There is a large body of excellent histories of the American military in the nineteenth century. Three standouts are Edward M. Coffman, *The Old Army: A Portrait of the American Army in Peacetime, 1784–1898* (New York: Oxford University Press, 1986); William S. McFeely, *Grant: A Biography* (New York: W. W Norton & Company, 1982); and James M. McPherson, *Battle Cry of Freedom: The Civil War Era* (New York: Oxford University Press, 1988).

Debates regarding how to both recognize and compensate veterans carried into the formation of the United States. See C. Edward Skeen, *Citizen Soldiers in the War of 1812* (Lexington: University Press of Kentucky, 1999); John Hay, "Broken Hearths: Melville's 'Israel Potter' and the Bunker Hill Monument," *New England Quarterly*, vol. 89 (June 2016): 192–221; Edward Tang, "Writing the American Revolution: War Veterans in the Nineteenth-Century Cultural Memory," *Journal of American Studies*, vol. 32 (April 1998): 63–80; Ann M. Becker, "The Revolutionary War Pension Act of 1818," *Historical Journal of Massachusetts*, vol. 47 (Summer 2019): 98–137; Matthew Pinsker, "The Soldiers' Home: A Long Road to Sanctuary," *Washington History*, vol. 18 (2006): 4–19; Michael D. Hattem, "Citizenship and the Memory of the American Revolution in Nineteenth-Century Political Culture," *New York History*, vol. 1010 (Summer 2020).

The sociologist and political scientist Theda Skocpol produced an important body of work regarding veterans. See Theda Skocpol, *Protecting Soldiers and Mothers: The Political Origins of Social Policy in the United States* (Cambridge: Belknap Press of Harvard University Press, 1992); Theda Skocpol, "America's First Social Security System: The

Expansion of Benefits for Civil War Veterans," *Political Science Quarterly*, vol. 108 (Spring 1993): 85–116.

The Antebellum era saw distinct approaches to race and military service in America. See Mark E. Neely, "Guerrilla Warfare, Slavery, and the Hopes of the Confederacy," *Journal of the Civil War Era*, vol. 6 (September 2016): 376–412; Ashley K. Schmidt, "Black Revolutionaries: African American Revolutionary War Pensioners in the Early Republic, 1780–1850" (Ph.D. dissertation, Tulane University, 2018); Lee W. Eysturlid, "'An Opportunity to Show Their Epaulets and Feathers': The South Carolina Militia During the First Secession Crisis, 1848–1851," *Armed Forces & Society*, vol. 20 (Winter 1994): 306–16, Joyce Tang, "Enslaved African Rebellions in Virginia," *Journal of Black Studies*, vol. 27 (May 1997): 598–614; Carol Anderson, *The Second: Race and Guns in a Fatally Unequal America* (New York: Bloomsbury Publishing, 2021).

There were a variety of Spanish legacies present as America expanded west across the continent in the nineteenth century. See Kimberly S. Hanger, "*Personas de Varias Clases y Colores*: Free People of Color in Spanish New Orleans, 1769–1803" (Ph.D. dissertation, University of Florida, 1991); Eric Herschthal, "Slaves, Spaniards, and Subversion in Early Louisiana: The Persistent Fears of Black Revolt and Southern Collusion in Territorial Louisiana, 1803–1812," *Journal of the Early Republic*, vol. 36 (Summer 2016): 283–311, John Lynch, *The Spanish American Revolutions, 1808–1826* (New York: W. W. Norton, 1986); James E. Wainwright, "William Claiborne and the New Orleans Battalion of Color, 1803–1815: Race and the Limits of Federal Power in the Early Republic," *Louisiana History*, vol. 57 (Winter 2016): 5–44; Robert L. Paquette, "A Horde of Brigands? The Great Louisiana Slave Revolt of 1811 Reconsidered," *Historical Reflections*, vol. 35 (Spring 2009): 72–96.

Chapter Three
The Civil War

The quote at the start of the chapter is from Sarah E. Gardner, "When Service is Not Enough: Charity's Purpose in the Immediate Aftermath of the Civil War," *Journal of the Civil War*, vol. 9 (March 2019): 36.

For treatments of American civil-military relations during and after the Civil War see Eric Foner, *A Short History of Reconstruction, 1863–1877* (New York: Harper & Row, 1990); A. James Fuller, "Oliver P. Martin and the Politics of Historical Memory," *Indiana Magazine of History*, vol. 110 (December 2014): 324–56; Fred Arthur Bailey, "Mildred Lewis Rutherford and the Patrician Cult of the Old South," *Georgia Historical Quarterly*, vol. 78 (Fall 1994): 509–35; Elaine Frantz Parsons, *Ku-Klux: The Birth of the Klan During Reconstruction* (Chapel Hill: University of North Carolina Press, 2016); Richard Zuczek, "The Federal Government's Attack on the Ku Klux Klan: A Reassessment," *South Carolina Historical Magazine*, vol. 97 (January 1996): 47–64.

There is some excellent scholarship on Civil War veterans. See Paul A. Cimbala, *Veterans North and South: The Transition from Soldier to Civilian After the American Civil War* (Santa Barbara: Praeger, 2015); Larry M. Logue and Peter Blanck, *Race, Ethnicity, and Disability: Veterans and Benefits in Post-Civil War America* (New York: Cambridge

University Press, 2010); Gene Klein, "Confederate Monuments and Their Impact on the Collective Memory of the South and the North," *Southeastern Geography*, vol. 61 (Fall 2021): 241–57; Randall G. Holcombe, "Veterans Interests and the Transition to Government Growth, 1870–1915," *Public Choice*, vol. 99 (June 1999): 311–26; M. Keith Harris, *Across the Bloody Chasm: The Culture of Commemoration Among Civil War Veterans* (Baton Rouge: Louisiana State University Press, 2014); Russell L. Johnson, "'Great Injustice': Social Status and the Distribution of Military Pensions after the Civil War," *Journal of the Gilded and Progressive Era*, vol. 10 (April 2011): 137–60.

Studies specific to Northern veterans are Stuart McConnell, *Glorious Contentment: The Grand Army of the Republic, 1865–1900* (Chapel Hill: University of North Carolina, 1992); Jonathan D. Neu, "From Civil War to Civic Reform: Grand Army Veterans in the Progressive Era, 1890–1920" (Ph.D. dissertation, Carnegie Mellon University, 2018).

Conversely, the scholarship on Southern veterans is equally large. See Gary W. Gallagher, *Lee and His Generals in War and Memory* (Baton Rouge: Louisiana State University Press, 1998); Shari Eli and Laura Salisbury, "Patronage Politics and the Development of the Welfare State: Confederate Pensions in the American South," *Journal of Economic History*, vol. 76 (December 2016): 1078–1112; Herman Hattaway, "Clio's Southern Soldiers: The United Confederate Veterans and History," *Louisiana History*, vol. 12 (Summer 1971): 213–42; Charles Reagan Wilson, "The Religion of the Lost Cause: Ritual and Organization of Southern Civil Religion, 1865–1920," *Journal of Southern History*, vol. 46 (May 1980): 219–38; Elna C. Green, "Protecting Confederate Soldiers and Mothers: Pensions, Gender, and the Welfare State in the U.S. South, a Case Study from Florida," *Journal of Social History*, vol. 39 (Summer 2006): 1079–1104.

African Americans added their own service during the Civil War and produced a distinct generation of veterans. See Larry M. Logue and Peter Blanck, "'Benefit of the Doubt': African American Civil War Veterans and Pensions," *Journal of Interdisciplinary History*, vol. 38 (Winter 2008): 377–99; David J. Naumec, "'Let Us Fight the Devil with Fire': People of Color and Military Service During the Civil War Era, 1861–1866" (Ph.D. dissertation, Clark University, August 2019); Tunde Adeleke, *Martin R. Delaney's Civil War and Reconstruction* (Jackson: University of Press of Mississippi, 2020); Bruce A. Glasrud, ed., *Brothers to Buffalo Soldiers: Perspectives on African American Militia and Volunteers, 1865–1917* (Columbia: University of Missouri Press, 2011).

Chapter Four
American Empire

The quote at the start of the chapter is from "The Camp at Montauk," *New York Times*, September 5, 1898, 2.

There are a number of useful examinations of early American empire that include Max Boot, *The Savage Wars of Peace: Small Wars and the Rise of American Power* (New York: Basic Books, 2002) and Jonathan M. Katz, *Gangsters of Capitalism: Smedley Butler, the Marines, and the Making of America's Empire* (New York: St. Martin's Press, 2022).

There are many applicable studies of military affairs on the frontier. Albert Winkler, "The Case for a Custer Battalion Survivor: Private Gustave Korn's Story," *Montana: The Magazine of Western History*, vol. 63 (Spring 2013): 45–55; Michelle Ann Abate, "'Bury My Heart in Recent History': Mark Twain's 'Hellfire Hotchkiss,' the Massacre at Wounded Knee, and the Dime Novel Western," *American Literary Realism*, vol. 42 (Winter 2010): 114–28.

Veterans' studies that address the late nineteenth and early twentieth centuries may be found in William Pencak, *For God & Country: The American Legion, 1919-1941* (Boston: Northeastern University Press, 1989); Barbara A. Gannon, "'They Call Themselves Veterans': Civil War and Spanish War Veterans and the Complexities of Veteranhood," *Journal of the Civil War Era*, vol. 5 (December 2015): 528–50; John Pettegrew, "'The Soldier's Faith:' Turn-of-the Century Memory of the Civil War and the Emergence of Modern American Nationalism," *Journal of Contemporary History*, vol. 31 (January 1996): 49–73; Alys D. Beverton, "'We Knew No North, No South': U.S.-Mexican Veterans and the Construction of Public Memory in the Post-Civil War United States, 1874–1897," *American Nineteenth Century History*, vol. 17 (March 2016): 1–22; Joshua A. Britton, "Remembering the War of 1812: Hiram Cronk's Funeral Procession," *New York History*, vol. 94 (Summer/Fall 2013): 300–306.

Contemporary newspaper accounts were a valuable resource for this chapter. See "The City's Great Fourth," *New York Times*, July 5, 1898, 10; "Boston's Naval Parade," *New York Times*, September 3, 1898, 2; "Returning Heroes Warmly Welcomed," *New York Times*, August 30, 1898, 1; "Soldiers Escort Body of Last 1812 Veteran," *New York Times*, May 19, 1905, 16.

For recent treatments of veterans' cemeteries see Michelle A. Krowl, "'In the Spirit of Fraternity': The United States Government and the Burial of Confederate Dead at Arlington National Cemetery," *Virginia Magazine of History and Biography*, vol. 111 (April 2003): 151–86; Michael Burns, "A Confederate Memorial the 'Equal of Gettysburg': Sectionalism and Memory in the Establishment of Manassas National Battlefield Park 1890–1940," *Virginia Magazine of History and Biography*, vol. 123 (2015): 140–70; Carol A. Grissom and Ronald S. Harvey, "The Conservation of American War Memorials Made of Zinc," *Journal of the American Institute for Conservation*, vol. 42 (Spring 2003): 21–38.

Chapter Five
The Great War

The quote at the start of the chapter is from Wilfred Owen, "The Next War," in *The Poems of Wilfred Owen*, ed. Jon Stallworthy (New York: W. W. Norton & Company, 1985), 142.

For general context of the period, see Edmund Morris, *Colonel Roosevelt* (New York: Random House, 2010) and Robert K. Murray, *Red Scare: A Study in National Hysteria, 1919-1920* (New York: McGraw-Hill, 1964).

There are many helpful general military histories of the World War I era. See David M. Kennedy, *Over Here: The First World War and American Society* (New York: Oxford University Press, 1980); Nancy Gentile Ford, *Americans All! Foreign Born Soldiers in World War I* (College Station: Texas A&M University Press, 2001); Nancy Gentile Ford, *The Great*

War and America: Civil-Military Relations During World War I (Westport, CT: Praeger Security International, 2008).

For academic treatments of World War I veterans see Jennifer D. Keene, *Doughboys, the Great War, and the Rebuilding of America* (Baltimore: Johns Hopkins University Press, 2001); Christopher C. Nehls, "'A Grand and Glorious Feeling': The American Legion and American Nationalism between the World Wars" (Ph.D. dissertation, University of Virginia, 2007); George L. Mosse, *Fallen Soldiers: Reshaping the Memory of the World War* (New York: Oxford University Press, 1990); Beth Linker, *War's Waste: Rehabilitation in World War I America* (Chicago: University of Chicago Press, 2011); Evan P. Sullivan, "The Unseen Army," in *Service Denied: Marginalized Veterans in Modern American History*, eds. John M. Kinder and Jason A. Higgins (Boston: University of Massachusetts Press, 2022); Tracey Loughran, "Shell Shock, Trauma, and the First World War: The Making of a Diagnosis and Its Histories," *Journal of the History of Medicine and Allied Sciences*, vol. 67 (January 2012): 94–119; Scott Gelber, "'A Hard-Boiled Order': The Reeducation of Disabled WWI Veterans in New York City," *Journal of Social History*, vol. 39 (Autumn 2005): 161–80; Annessa C. Stagner, "Healing the Soldier, Restoring the Nation: Representations of Shell Shock in the USA During and After the First World War," *Journal of Contemporary History*, vol. 49 (April 2014): 255–74.

Scholarship on African American veterans of World War I is taken from Jonathan S. Coit, "'Our Changed Attitude': Armed Defense and the New Negro in the 1919 Chicago Race Riot," *Journal of the Gilded Age and the Progressive Era*, vol. 11 (April 2012): 225–56; Vincent P. Mikkelsen, "Fighting for Sergeant Caldwell: The NAACP Campaign Against 'Legal' Lynching After World War I," *Journal of African American History*, vol. 94 (Fall 2009): 464–86; Chad L. Williams, "Vanguards of the New Negro: African Americans and Post-World War I Racial Militancy," *Journal of African American History*, vol. 92 (Summer 2007): 347–70; Jennifer D. Keene, "The Long Journey Home: African American World War I Veterans and Veterans' Policies," in *Veterans' Policies, Veterans' Politics: New Perspectives on Veterans in the Modern United States*, ed. Stephen R. Ortiz (Gainesville: University Press of Florida, 2012).

The quote from Dubois is from "Returning Soldiers," (May 1919). https://www.americanyawp.com/reader/21-world-war-i/w-e-b-dubois-returning-soldiers-may-1919/.

Numerous newspapers and periodicals were used for this chapter. "Opening of Campaign to Secure 2,000,000 Members," *Foreign Service*, January 1919, 2; "Roosevelt Issues Call to Veterans," *New York Times*, April 9, 1919, 7; "American Legion Chief Warns All Members Against Taking Law Into Their Own Hands," *New York Times*, December 23, 1919, 15; "Grand Army Men Become Honorary Members of V.F.W.," *Foreign Service* (November 1919): 1; "More Than 600,000 in American Legion," *New York Times*, September 22, 1919, 20; "Sees Legion as a Great Civic Force," *New York Times*, November 1919, E2; "In Defense of Law and Order," *Foreign Service* (February 1919): 1, 9; "Legion and Guard Mass in Spokane to Repel I.W.W.," *New York Times*, November 15, 1919; "16," *New York Times*, December 27, 1919; "Blames War Risk Bureau," *New York Times*, November 7, 1919, 12; "The Legion and Bonuses," *New York Times*, October 12, 1919, 37; "Legion Chiefs Plan Parley in Capital," *New York Times*, December 1919, 8.

Chapter Six
The Interwar Period

The quote at the start of the chapter is from Christopher C. Nehls, "'A Grand and Glorious Feeling': The American Legion and American Nationalism between the World Wars" (Ph.D. dissertation, University of Virginia, 2007), 234.

For histories of veterans during the twenties see Rosemary Stevens, *A Time of Scandal: Charles R. Forbes, Warren G. Harding, and the Making of the Veterans Bureau* (Baltimore: Johns Hopkins University Press, 2016); Niall A. Palmer, "The Veterans' Bonus and the Evolving Presidency of Warren G. Harding," *Presidential Studies Quarterly*, vol. 38 (March 2008): 39-60; John Sullivan, "The Unseen Army: Neuropsychiatry, Patient Agency, and World War I," in *Service Denied: Marginalized Veterans in Modern American History*, eds. John M. Kinder and Jason A. Higgins (Boston: University of Massachusetts Press, 2022), 50-67.

For accounts of the 1932 Bonus March see Robert V. Parker, "The Bonus March of 1932: A Unique Experience in North Carolina Experience and Social Life," *North Carolina Historical Review*, vol. 51 (January 1974): 64-89; Jennifer D. Keene, "1932: The Bonus March," *Washington History*, vol. 32 (Fall 2020): 30-32; Stephen R. Ortiz, "The 'New Deal' for Veterans: The Economy Act, the Veterans of Foreign Wars, and the Origins of New Deal Dissent," *Journal of Military History*, vol. 70 (April 2006): 415-38.

For newspaper and periodical sources on the interwar commemoration of veterans, see "G.A.R. On Parade, 800 Scorning Ride," *New York Times*, September 22, 1932, 16; "Want the World to See Your Post in Action? Try a Float in a Home-Town Parade," *American Legion Weekly*, vol. (January 4, 1924): 14; "Fitting in the Scheme of Things," *American Legion Weekly*, November 9, 1923, 18, 26; Victor E. Devereaux, "Junior Rifle Clubs Provide Ideal Plan for Youth Training," *Foreign Service*, August 1940, 8-9; Edwin Grant Conklin, "The Price We Pay," *American Legion Weekly*, August 3, 1923, 3. On Hoover's treatment of veterans see "Veterans Bureaus United by Hoover," *New York Times*, July 9, 1930, 11. On the 1932 Bonus March see "500 Join Bonus March," *New York Times*, June 3, 1932, 2; "500 on Way from Chicago," *New York Times*, June 1, 1932, 7; "Weary Bonus Army Reaches Capital by Truck; Police Demand Congress Care for Hundreds," *New York Times*, May 30, 1932, 1; "Says Reds Inspired Bonus Marchers," *New York Times*, June 10, 1932, 12; "Hoover Orders Eviction," *New York Times*, July 29, 1932, 1; "Report Criticizes Bonus March," *New York Times*, September 22, 1932, 14; "Bombs and Sabers Win Capitol Battle," *New York Times*, July 29, 1932, 1. For New Deal approaches to veterans see James P. Richards, "Guns for the C.C.C.: Military Training Essential to America's Future Security," *Foreign Service*, July 1940, 11. For veterans and foreign policy before World War II see Burt M. McConnell, "Plattsburg: 1940," *Foreign Service*, September 1940, 8; "Legion Yells Down a Neutrality Call," *New York Times*, September 27, 1940, 12.

Chapter Seven
World War II

The quote at the start of the chapter is from William Manchester, *Goodbye Darkness: A Memoir of the Pacific War* (Boston: Little, Brown, 1979), 380.

For useful general histories of World War II see James Bradley with Ron Powers, *Flags of Our Fathers* (New York: Bantam Books, 2000); George Q. Flynn, *The Draft, 1940-1973* (Lawrence: University Press of Kansas, 1993); John Morton Blum, *V was for Victory: Politics and American Culture During World War II* (New York: Harcourt Brace Jovanovich, 1976); Keith E. Eiler, *Mobilizing America: Robert P. Patterson and the War Effort, 1940-1945* (Ithaca: Cornell University Press, 1997).

For studies of the American propaganda effort during World War II see Mark Harris, *Five Came Back: A Story of Hollywood and the Second World War* (New York: Penguin Press, 2014); Clayton R. Koppes and Gregory D. Black, "Wartime Films as Instruments of Propaganda," in *Hollywood's America: United States History Through Its Films*, eds. Steven Mintz and Randy Roberts (St. James, NY: Brandywine Press, 1993), 157-68.

For African Americans and the civil rights movement during World War II, Jennifer E. Brooks, "From Hitler and Tojo to Talmadge and Jim Crow: World War Two Veterans and the Remaking of Southern Political Tradition" (Ph.D. dissertation, University of Tennessee, 1997) is an outstanding treatment of the immediate postwar. Lawrence P. Scott and William M. Womack, *Double V: The Civil Rights Struggle of the Tuskegee Airmen* (East Lansing: Michigan State University Press, 1994); Catherine A. Barnes, *Journey from Jim Crow: The Desegregation of Southern Transit* (New York: Columbia University Press, 1983). See also "Police Chief Bonded in Beating of Negro," *New York Times*, September 29, 1946, 20; "The GI Assault Bill," *New Republic*, vol. 112 (February 5, 1946): 166; "Birmingham War Vets March Through Streets for Vote Rights," *Chicago Defender*, February 2, 1946, 7; "Hines Pledges Aid to Negro Veteran," *New York Times*, March 14, 1945, 1.

There are many World War II veterans' histories. An excellent contemporary study is Samuel A. Stouffer, Arthur A. Lumsdaine, Marion Harper Lumsdaine, et al., *The American Soldier: Combat and Its Aftermath*, vol. 1 (Princeton, NJ: Princeton University Press, 1949). Michael D. Gambone, *The Greatest Generation Comes Home: The Veteran in American Society* (College Station: Texas A&M University Press, 2005) is used throughout this chapter.

For other scholarship on the minority veteran experience after World War II see Carl Allsup, *The American GI Forum: Origins and Evolution* (Austin: Center for Mexcan American Studies) and Jere Takahasi, *Nisei/Sansei: Shifting Japanese American Identities and Politics* (Philadelphia: Temple University Press, 1997).

There are extensive treatments of the creation of the Serviceman's Readjustment Act. See David Camelon, "I Saw the G.I. Bill Written," *American Legion Magazine*, vol. 47 (September 1949): 11-13; David Camelon, "I Saw the G.I. Bill Written, (Part Two)," *American Legion Magazine*, vol. 47 (October 1949): 18-19, 55; David Camelon, "I Saw the G.I. Bill Written, (Conclusion,)" *American Legion Magazine*, vol. 47 (November 1949): 18-19, 43.

A number of authors have addressed Bradley's impact on the Veterans Administration. Omar N. Bradley and Clay Blair, *A General's Life* (New York: Simon & Schuster, 1983) and Steven L. Ossad, *Omar Nelson Bradley: America's GI General, 1893–1981* (Columbia: University of Missouri Press, 2017).

Newspapers and periodicals covered the post-1945 veterans' transition at length. See "Claims of World War II Soldiers Increase Constantly," *Foreign Service*, vol. 30 (March 1944) 38; "Wounded Men Seek to Live Normally, Gen. Kirk Declares," *New York Times*, October 13, 1944, 1; "Charges Neglect of War Wounded," *New York Times*, December 15, 1943, 13; "Opposes High Pay on Mustering Out," *New York Times*, January 13, 1944, 11; "Roosevelt Signs 'G.I. Rights Bill,'" *New York Times*, June 23, 1944, 32; "Conferees Accept GI Bill of Rights," *New York Times*, June 11, 1944, 26; "Committee Votes 'GI Bill of Rights,' Sweeping Aid Plan," *New York Times*, March 18, 1944, 1; "5,000,000 Expected to Lose Arms Jobs," *New York Times*, August 12, 1945, 1.

Chapter Eight
The Early Cold War

The quote at the start of the chapter is from Sloan Wilson, *The Man in the Gray Flannel Suit* (Cambridge, MA: Da Capo Press, 2002); 13. Original edition published in 1955.

For veterans' studies during this era, see Andrew J. Huebner, "The Embattled Americans: A Cultural History of Soldiers and Veterans, 1941–1982" (Ph.D. dissertation, Brown University, 2004) and Peter D. Hoefer, "A David Against Goliath: The American Veterans Committee's Challenge to the American Legion in the 50s" (Ph.D. dissertation, University of Maryland, 2010).

Newspapers and periodicals covered a broad array of topics. For Cold War commentary, see William R. Kintner, "Is Your Home Town Ready for Global War?" *V.F.W. Magazine*, vol. 38 (January 1951): 10–11; John M. Devine, "Let's Train Them to Live," *American Legion Magazine*, vol. 53 (December 1952): 14–15; "One-Year Military Training for Youth Asked by Truman," *New York Times*, October 24, 1945, 1.

For articles on the Korean War see John Osbourne, "Report from the Orient: Guns are Not Enough," *Life*, August 21, 1950, 77; "Army Rotation Details Disclosed," *Pacific Stars & Stripes*, August 5, 1951, 2; George Barrett, "Portrait of the Korean War Veteran," *New York Times*, August 9, 1953, SM12; James C. Jones, "All's Quiet on the Home Front," *American Legion Magazine*, vol. 52 (February 1952): 20; Gene Gilmore, "I'm Bitter," *American Legion Magazine*, vol. 53 (November 1952): 24.

Veterans' charity work is covered in Robert B. Pitkin, "The American Legion in Louisiana," *American Legion Magazine*, June 1959, 19, 40–42, Robert B. Pitkin, "The American Legion's Youth Programs," *American Legion Magazine*, January 1960, 20; "Legion Baseball," *New York Times*, July 6, 1945, 15; Ty Cobb, "Batting Out Better Boys," *Rotarian*, July 1947, 11.

For McCarthy's pogrom against the military, see "McCarthy Sees a Plot: He Will Attack Marshall," *New York Times*, June 13, 1951, 12, "McCarthy v. Army," *New York Times*, February 21, 1954, E1; James Reston, "Officers Ordered to Defy McCarthy and Not Testify," *New York Times*, February 21, 1954, 1.

Suspicion of Korean War POWs appeared frequently in the fifties and veterans' publications were no exception. See Charles W. Mayo, "How the Commies Get 'Confessions,'" *V.F.W. Magazine*, vol. 41 (February 1954): 10, Philip Bloemsma, "The Fence Complex of a P.O.W.," *V.F.W. Magazine*, vol. 41 (March 1954): 10; "Some G.I. Captive May Seem Pro-Red," *New York Times*, April 13, 1953, 3, Edward Hunter, "Are Americans Being Brainwashed?" *American Legion Magazine*, vol. 61 (November 1956): 19.

On the Korea G.I. Bill, see "We've Been Asked: Veterans' Help—Still On?" *U.S. New & World Report*, April 30, 1954, 52; Benjamin Fine, "Educators Back Korean Veterans," *New York Times*, January 15, 1954, 2; Benjamin Fine, "Veterans of Korea Flock to Colleges under U.S. Grants," *New York Times*, September 14, 1953, 1.

On the Bradley Commission report see Omar B. Ketchum, "Washington Newsletter," *V.F.W. Magazine*, vol. 43 (May 1956): 35.

For contemporary public opinion data see George H. Gallup, *The Gallup Poll: Public Opinion, 1935-1971*, vol. 2 (New York: Random House, 1972). See also Steve Crabtree, "The Gallup Brain: Americans and the Korean War," *Gallup*, February 4, 2003. https://news.gallup.com/poll/7741/gallup-brain-americans-korean-war.aspx, Jeffrey M. Jones, "Who Had the Lowest Gallup Presidential Job Approval Rating?" *Gallup*, December 26, 2019. https://news.gallup.com/poll/272765/lowest-gallup-presidential-job-approval-rating.aspx.

Chapter Nine
Vietnam

The quote at the start of the chapter is from Philip Caputo, *A Rumor of War* (New York: Holt, Rinehart and Winston, 1981), 3.

For studies of the Vietnam War, see George C. Herring, *America's Longest War: The United States and Vietnam, 1950-1975* (New York: McGraw Hill, 1996); Denis Warner, *The Last Confucian* (New York: Macmillan, 1963); Douglas S. Blaufarb, *The Counterinsurgency Era: U.S. Doctrine and Performance, 1950 to the Present* (New York: Free Press, 1977).

On civil-military relations, see George Q. Flynn, "Conscription and Equity in Western Democracies, 1940-1975," *Journal of Contemporary History*, vol. 33 (January 1998): 5–20; Charles C. Moskos, "The American Dilemma in Uniform: Race in the Armed Forces," *Annals of the American Academy of Political and Social Science*, vol. 406 (March 1973): 94–106.

There are excellent studies of public opinion during the Cold War. See Adam J. Berinsky, *In Time of War: Understanding American Public Opinion from World War II to Iraq* (Chicago: The University of Chicago Press, 2009); Leslie H. Gelb with Richard K. Betts, *The Irony of Vietnam: The System Worked* (Washington: Brookings Institution, 1979); Frank

Newport and Joseph Carroll, "Iraq Versus Vietnam: A Comparison of Public Opinion," *Pew Research Center*, August 24, 2005, https://news.gallup.com/poll/18097/iraq-versus-vietnam-comparison-public-opinion.aspx.

An excellent examination of Vietnam veterans may be found in Paul Starr, *The Discarded Army: Veterans After Vietnam: The Nader Report on Vietnam Veterans and the Veterans Administration* (New York: Charterhouse, 1973). See also Gerald Nicosia, *Home to War: A History of the Vietnam Veterans' Movement* (New York: Crown Publishers, 2001); Melvin Small, *Antiwarriors: The Vietnam War and the Battle for America's Hearts and Minds* (Lanham, MD: SR Books, 2004).

There are both published and unpublished works on veterans' activism in the sixties. Lance Hill, *The Deacons for Defense: Armed Resistance and the Civil Rights Movement* (Chapel Hill: University of North Carolina Press, 2004); Charles E. Cobb, *This Nonviolent Stuff'll Get You Killed: How Guns Made the Civil Rights Movement Possible* (New York: Basic Books, 2014); Andrew E. Hunt, "The Turning: Vietnam Veterans Against the War, 1967 to the Present" (Ph.D. dissertation, University of Utah, 1997); Richard Stacewicz, *Winter Soldiers: An Oral History of the Vietnam Veterans Against the War* (Chicago: Haymarket Books, 1997).

For Kerry's testimony during Dewey Canyon III, see "Complete Testimony of Lt. John Kerry to Senate Foreign Relations Committee on Behalf of the Vietnam Veterans Against the War," 92nd Congress, 1st Session, April 22, 1971, 182.

On Project 100,000, see Neil Sheehan, "Military Ready to Absorb Influx of Former 'Rejects,'" *New York Times*, October 16, 1966, 9; "Rights Leaders Deplore Plan to 'Salvage' Military Rejects," *New York Times*, August 26, 1966, 3; "The Plight of Viet Nam Era Vets," *Time*, December 27, 1971, 57.

For veterans' support of the Nixon administration see Douglas E. Kneeland, "Agnew Stresses Equality to V.F.W.," *New York Times*, August 22, 1968, 27; "'Mail Call' Response," *American Legion Magazine*, vol. 87, December 1969, 4; "Nixon to Get Legion Medal," *New York Times*, June 12, 1969, 10; John Herbers, "Backers of Nixon Policy Rally in Capital," *New York Times*, November 12, 1969, 20; Hedrick Smith, "Targets at Home and Abroad for Nixon's Peace Initiative," *New York Times*, May 18, 1969, E2; "New Director of V.A.," *New York Times*, June 6, 1969, 20; "A Close Look at the Cold War GI Bill," *American Legion Magazine*, September 1966, 24–28.

For accounts of atrocities committed during the Vietnam War, see Donald Duncan, "The whole thing was a lie!" *Ramparts*, vol. 4 (February 1966): 13–24; Jack Raymond, "Veteran of Special Forces Denounces U.S. Policy in Vietnam as a 'Lie,'" *New York Times*, February 10, 1966, 2; Seymour Hersh, "The Massacre at My Lai: A Mass Killing and Its Coverup," *The New Yorker*, January 14, 1972, https://www.newyorker.com/magazine/1972/01/22/coverup; The Pulitzer Prizes, "I sent them a good boy and they made him a murderer," https://www.pulitzer.org/article/i-sent-them-good-boy-and-they-made-him-murderer; Osha Gray Davidson, "My Lai Massacre Leader Speaks," *Mother Jones*, August 23, 2009, https://www.motherjones.com/politics/2009/08/my-lai-massacre-leader-speaks/.

For relations of veterans and the antiwar movement see Ronald Sullivan, "Veterans for Peace Simulate the War," *New York Times*, September 5, 1970, 6; Jackie Robinson, "Deacons Here to Stay?" *Chicago Defender*, July 31, 1965, 10; Art Goldberg, "Vietnam Vets: The Anti-War Army," *Ramparts*, vol. 10 (July 1971): 12; Neil Sheehan, "Conversations with

Americans: Book Review," *New York Times*, December 27, 1970, 165; "Week of Protests on War to Start," *New York Times*, April 19, 1971, 5; "Veterans Discard Medals in War Protest at Capitol," *New York Times*, April 24, 1971, 1, 12; Hunter S. Thompson, "More Fear and Loathing in Miami: Nixon Bites the Bomb," *Rolling Stone*, September 28, 1972, https://www.rollingstone.com/feature/more-fear-and-loathing-in-miami-nixon-bites-the-bomb-40151/17/.

Chapter Ten
Veterans and the All-Volunteer Military

The quote at the start of the chapter is from David H. Hackworth, *About Face: The Odyssey of an American Warrior* (New York: Simon and Schuster, 1989), 831.

Secondary sources on military operations after Vietnam include William P. Head, "Gunships and 'Ding-Bats': U.S. Military operations During 'Just Cause,'" *Journal of Third World Studies*, vol. 28 (Fall 2011): 87–105; Brian McAllister Linn, *The Echo of Battle: The Army's Way of War* (Cambridge, MA: Harvard University Press, 2007); Rick Atkinson, *Crusade: Untold Story of the Gulf War* (New York: HarperCollins, 1994); Timothy M. Karcher, "The Victory Disease," *Military Review*, vol. 83 (July–August 2002): 9–17.

There is a significant body of work on peacekeeping and peace enforcement missions. Henry F. Jackson, "Egypt and the United States after Sadat: Continuity and Constraints," *Issue: A Journal of Opinions*, vol. 12 (Autumn/Winter 1982): 70–75; Larry L. Fabian, "The Middle East War: Dangers and Receding Peace Prospects," *Foreign Affairs*, vol. 62 (1983): 632–658; Jeffrey Clark, "Debacle in Somalia," *Foreign Affairs*, vol. 72 (1993/1994): 109–23; Ramesh Thakur, "From Peacekeeping to Peace Enforcement: The UN Operation in Somalia," *Journal of Modern African Studies*, vol. 32 (September 1994): 387–410; Nynke Salverda, "Blue Helmets as Targets: A Quantitative Analysis of Rebel Violence Against Peacekeepers, 1989–2003," *Journal of Peace Research*, vol. 50 (November 2013): 707–20.

There is extensive scholarship on the all-volunteer military. Beth Bailey, "Soldiering as Work: The All-Volunteer Force in the United States," in *Fighting for a Living: A Comparative History of Military Labour, 1500-2000*, ed. Erik Jan Zürcher (Amsterdam: Amsterdam University Press, 2013): 581–612; William Schneider, "Personnel Recruitment and Retention: Problems and Prospects for the United States," *Annals of the Academy of Political and Social Science*, vol. 457 (September 1981): 164–73; Tom Evans, "All We Could Be: How an Advertising Campaign Helped Remake the Army," *On Point*, vol. 12 (Summer 2006): 8–15; Timothy W. Cooke and Aline O. Quester, "What Characterizes Successful Enlistees in the All-Volunteer Force: A Study of Male Recruits in the U.S. Navy," *Social Science Quarterly*, vol. 73 (June 1992): 238–52; James E. Grefer, *Comparing Military and Civilian Compensation Packages* (Alexandria, VA: CNA, March 2008).

As National Guard and reserves deployments ramped up in the nineties, it attracted the attention of a number of professional journals. Lawrence J. Korb, "Fixing the Mix: How to Update the Army's Reserves," *Foreign Affairs*, vol. 83 (March-April 2004): 2–7; Miranda

Summers Lowe, "The Gradual Shift to an Operational Reserve: Reserve Component Mobilizations in the Nineties," *Military Review*, vol. 99 (May-June 2019): 119-27; James C. Kitfield, "Are We Wearing Out the Guard and Reserve?" *Air & Space Forces Magazine*, February 1, 2001. https://www.airandspaceforces.com/article/0201reserve.

There is a large body of secondary sources on the commemoration of Vietnam veterans. "Still Missing, Never Forgotten: POW/MIA Recognition Day," *On Point*, vol. 16 (Fall 2010): 30; Karal Ann Marling and Robert Silberman, "The Statue Near the Wall: The Vietnam Veterans Memorial and the Art of Remembering," *Smithsonian Studies in American Art*, vol. 1 (Spring 1987): 4-29; Christa Grewe-Volpp, "'Memory Attaches Itself to Sites': Bobbi Ann Mason's 'In Country' and the Significance of the Vietnam Veterans Memorial," *American Studies*, vol. 49 (2004): 173-89; Daphne Berdahl, "Voices at the Wall: Discourses on Self, History, and National Identity at the Vietnam Veterans Memorial," *History and Memory*, vol. 6 (Winter 1994): 88-124; "Stop That Monument," *National Review*, vol. 33 (September 18, 1981): 1064; D. Keith Mano, "The Vietnam Veterans' Parade," *National Review*, vol. 37 (July 26, 1985): 52-53; David Fitzgerald, "Support the Troops: Gulf War Homecomings and a New Politics of Military Celebration," *Modern American History*, vol. 2 (March 2019): 1-22; Robert J. McMahon, "Contested Memory: The Vietnam War and American Society, 1975-2001," *Diplomatic History*, vol. 26 (Spring 2002): 159-84.

Both professional journals and mainstream publications addressed Gulf War Syndrome. Gozde Ozakinci, William K. Hallman, and Howard M. Kipen, "Persistence of Symptoms in Veterans of the First Gulf War: 5-Year Follow-up," *Environmental Health Perspectives*, vol. 114 (October 2006): 1553-57; Hollie V. Thomas, Nicola J. Stimpson, Alison L. Weightman, Frank Dunstan, and Glyn Lewis, "Systematic Review of Multi-Symptom Conditions in Gulf War Veterans," *Psychological Medicine*, vol. 36 (January 26, 2006): 735-47; William K. Hallman, Howard M. Kipen, Michael Diefenbach, et al., "Symptom Patterns Among Gulf War Registry Veterans," *American Journal of Public Health*, vol. 93 (April 2003): 624-30; Fred Milano, "Gulf War Syndrome: The 'Agent Orange' of the Nineties," *International Social Science Review*, vol. 75 (2000): 16-25.

There is an extensive catalogue of research on mental health in the military. Douglas R. Bey and Walter E. Smith, "Organizational Consultation in a Combat Unit," *American Journal of Psychiatry*, vol. 128 (October 1971): 401-6; Sandra L. Huppenbauer, "A Portrait of a Problem," *American Journal of Nursing*, vol. 82 (November 1982): 1699-1703; Wilbur J. Scott, "PTSD in *DSM-III*: A Case in the Politics of Diagnosis and Disease," *Social Problems*, vol. 37 (August 1990): 294-310; Chaim F. Shatan, "The Grief of Soldiers: Vietnam Combat Veterans' Self-Help Movement," *American Journal of Orthopsychiatry*, vol. 43 (July 1973): 640-53; Sarah A. Haley, "When the Patient Reports Atrocities: Specific Treatment Considerations of the Vietnam Veteran," *Archives of General Psychiatry*, vol. 30 (February 1974): 191-96; Alair MacLean, "The Things They Carry: Combat, Disability, and Unemployment among U.S. Men," *American Sociological Review*, vol. 75 (August 2010): 563-85; Alair MacLean and Glen H. Elder, "Military Service in the Life Course," *Annual Review of Sociology*, vol. 33 (March 2007): 175-96; Janet S. Pierson and Raymond F. Pierson, "Posttraumatic Stress Disorder or Midlife Crisis in Vietnam Veterans?" *Social Work*, vol. 39 (May 1994): 328-30; Rani A. Hoff and Robert A. Rosenheck, "The Use of VA and non-VA Mental Health Services by Female Veterans," *Medical Care*, vol. 36 (November 1998): 1524-33.

As women entered the military in increasing numbers, scholarship and media interest in the issue increased. See Kristy N. Kamarck, *Women in Combat: Issues for Congress*, R42075 (Washington, DC: Congressional Research Service, December 13, 2016); Nancy Goldman, "The Changing Role of Women in the Armed Forces," *American Journal of Sociology*, vol. 78 (January 1973): 892–911; Kate A. Arbogast, "The Procurement of Women for the Armed Forces: An Analysis of Occupational Choice" (Ph.D. dissertation, George Washington University, 1974); Kara Dixon Vuic, "Our First Sister: Lynda Van Devanter and the Vietnam Veterans of America's Women's Project," in *Service Denied: Marginalized Veterans in Modern American History*, eds. John M. Kinder and Jason A. Higgins (Boston: University of Massachusetts Press, 2022); 143–59, Louis Harris Associates, *Survey of Female Veterans: A Study of the Needs, Attitudes, and Experiences of Women Veterans*, Study No. 843002 (New York: Louis Harris and Associates, Inc., 1985); Elaine Sciolino, "Military Women Report Pattern of Sexual Abuse by Servicemen," *New York Times*, July 1, 1992, A1.

Newspapers and periodicals covered a variety of topics in this chapter. "302,000 Men Face Draft During '68, A 72,000 Increase," *New York Times*, January 20, 1968, 3; Ben A. Franklin, "Lag in a Volunteer Force Spurs Talk of New Draft," *New York Times*, July 1, 1973, 1; Judy Klemesrud, "For Women in the Military, New Attractions," *New York Times*, August 2, 1971, 28; Tom Wicker, "Ghosts of Vietnam," *New York Times*, January 26, 1991, 29; Stanley W. Cloud, "Exorcising an Old Demon," *Time*, vol. 137 (March 11, 1991): 52–53; James Reston, "Carter's Ends and Means," *New York Times*, January 23, 1977, 153; "10,000 Affected Now," *New York Times*, January 22, 1977; Tom Carhart, "Insulting Vietnam Veterans," *New York Times*, October 24, 1981, 23; Philip M. Boffey, "Vietnam Veterans' Parade a Belated Welcome Home," *New York Times*, November 14, 1982, 1; "A Father's Pride, A Yellow Ribbon," *New York Times*, 9 January 9, 1991, A8; Richard Halloran, "G.I. Bill, Once a Reward, Is Now a Lure," *New York Times*, December 5, 1986, A32; Eric Schmitt, "Fighting the Iraqis: Four Scenarios, All Disputed," *New York Times*, 19 November 19, 1990, A1; "Potential War Casualties Put at 100,000" *Los Angeles Times*, September 5, 1990, https://www.latimes.com/archives/la-xpm-1990-09-05-mn-776-story.html; Alessandra Stanley, "War's Ribbons are Yellow with Meaning of Many Hues," *New York Times*, February 3, 1991, 1.

Chapter Eleven
After September 11th

The quote at the start of the chapter is from David Bellavia, *House to House* (New York: Pocket Star, 2007), 20.

Michael D. Gambone, *The New Praetorians: Modern American Veterans, Society, and Service in the Forever War* (Amherst: University of Massachusetts Press, 2021), is used throughout this chapter.

Studies of post–September 11 military operations include Jay D. Pellerin, "Tanks and 'Shock and Awe,'" *Armor*, vol. 112 (September/October 2003): 32–40; Sean Griffin, "Time to Reevaluate Rapid Decisive Operations," *U.S. Naval Institute Proceedings*, vol. 135 (January

2009): 77–79; Christopher Ankersen, "Rapid Decisive Ops are Risky Business," *U.S. Naval Institute Proceedings*, vol. 129 (October 2003): 52–55; and Max Boot, "The Struggle to Transform the Military," *Foreign Affairs*, vol. 84 (March-April 2005): 103–18.

There are numerous examinations of Operation Iraqi Freedom. Charles H. Briscoe, Kenneth Finlayson, Robert W. Jones, et al., *All Roads Lead to Baghdad: Army Special Operations Forces in Iraq* (Fort Bragg, NC: USASOC History Office, 2006); Nora Bensahel, Olga Oliker, Keith Crane, et al., *After Saddam: Prewar Planning and the Occupation of Iraq* (Santa Monica, CA: RAND Corporation, 2008).

There are useful treatments of civil-military relations. These include Sebastian Junger, *War* (New York: Twelve, 2010); Michael D. Gambone, "Iraq War Veterans: For the Troops, But Against the War," in *Encyclopedia of the Veteran in America*, ed. William Pencak (Santa Barbara, CA: ABC-CLIO, 2009); 237–46. Jeff Schlogol, "Marine Who Pissed on Taliban Wins in Court," *Marine Times*, November 9, 2017, https://www.marinecorpstimes.com/news/your-marine-corps/2017/11/09/marine-who-urinated-on-dead-taliban-wins-in-court/; Lee Ferran, "Marine Who Urinated on Taliban Dead Says He'd Do It Again," *ABC News*, June 17, 2013, https://abcnews.go.com/Blotter/marine-urinated-taliban-dead-hed/story?id=19687916.

Ruth Igielnik and Kim Parker, "Majorities of U.S. Veterans, Public Say the Wars in Iraq and Afghanistan Were Not Worth Fighting," *Pew Research Center* (July 10, 2019), https://www.pewresearch.org/fact-tank/2019/07/10/majorities-of-u-s-veterans-public-say-the-wars-in-iraq-and-afghanistan-were-not-worth-fighting/.

This chapter used the following newspapers and periodicals: Eric Schmitt, "Troops Queries Leave Rumsfeld on the Defensive: Lack of Equipment," *New York Times*, December 9, 2004, A1; Bruce Drake, "On Memorial Day, Public Pride in Veterans, But Distance," *Pew Research Center*, May 24, 2013.

For studies of reserve and National Guard service see Lawrence Kapp, *Recruiting and Retention: An Overview of FY2013 and FY2014 Results for Active and Reserve Component Enlisted Personnel*, RL32965 (Washington, DC: Congressional Research Service, June 26, 2015); John A. Nagle and Travis Sharp, "Operational for What? The Future of the Guard and Reserves," *Joint Forces Quarterly*, Issue 59 (2010): 21–29, https://ndupress.ndu.edu/portals/68/Documents/jfq/jfq-59.pdf; Lawrence Kapp, *Defense Primer: Reserve Forces*, CRS 7-5700 (Washington, DC: Congressional Research Service, December 12, 2018); Lieutenant Colonel Kevin S. Dailey, "Air National Guard Structure for the Twenty-first Century: The Multimission Framework for Total Force Integration," *Air War College* Maxwell Paper No. 43 (Maxwell Air Force Base, Alabama, May 2008); David Kieran, "'The Patriot Penalty': National Guard and Reserve Troops, Neoliberalism, and Manufactured Precarity in the Era of Perpetual Conflict," in *Service Denied: Marginalized Veterans in Modern American History*, eds. John M. Kinder and Jason A. Higgins (Boston: University of Massachusetts Press, 2022); 181–202; Alexandra Zavis, "National Guard Soldiers and Airmen Face Unemployment Crisis," *Los Angeles Times*, November 23, 2012, https://www.latimes.com/world/la-xpm-2012-nov-23-la-me-national-guard-employment-20121124-story.html.

For studies of wounds and injuries see David A. Blum and Nese F. DeBruyne, *American War and Military Operations Casualties: Lists and Statistics*, RL32492 (Washington: Congressional Research Service, July 2020); Stephanie Gaskell, "VA Might Have Denied PTSD Claims Related to Military Sexual Trauma," *Veterans of Foreign Wars Magazine*, vol. 106

(November/December 2018): 10–11; Matthew S. Goldberg, "Death and Injury Rates of U.S. Military Personnel in Iraq," *Military Medicine*, vol. 175 (April 2010): 220–26; David Vergun, "Survival Rates Improving for Soldiers Wounded in Combat, Says Army Surgeon General," *Army Times*, August 24, 2016, https://www.army.mil/article/173808/survival_rates_improving_for_soldiers_wounded_in_combat_says_army_surgeon_general; Art Levine, "How the VA Fueled the National Opioid Crisis and is Killing Thousands of Veterans," *Newsweek*, vol. 169 (October 20, 2017), https://search.proquest.com/docview/1981858768?accountid=11920; Karen H. Seal, Ying Shi, Gregory Cohen, et al., "Association of Mental Health Disorders with Prescription Opioids and High-Risk Opioid Use in US Veterans of Iraq and Afghanistan," *Journal of the American Medical Association*, vol. 307 (March 7, 2012): 940–47, Aaron Glantz, "VA's Opiate Overload Feeds Veterans' Addictions, Overdose Deaths," *Center for Investigative Reporting*, 28 September 28, 2013, https://www.revealnews.org/article/vas-opiate-overload-feeds-veterans-addictions-overdose-deaths/.

The Walter Reed scandal drew significant media attention. See Dana Priest and Anne Hull, "Soldiers Face Neglect at Army's Top Medical Facility," *Washington Post*, February 18, 2007, A1. See also Tom Bowman, "Walter Reed was the Army's Wake Up Call in 2007," *National Public Radio*, 31 August 31, 2011, https://www.npr.org/transcripts/139641856; Michael Winerip, "And This was Called Care? The Walter Reed Story," *New York Times*, September 30, 2013, https://www.nytimes.com/2013/09/30/booming/and-this-was-called-care-the-walter-reed-story.html.

On the 2014 VA scandal, see German Lopez, "The VA Scandal of 2014, Explained," *Vox*, May 13, 2015, https://www.vox.com/2014/9/26/18080592/va-scandal-explained; Bill Chappell, "VA Chief Eric Shinseki Resigns Post, Obama Announces," NPR, May 30, 2014, https://www.npr.org/sections/thetwo-way/2014/05/30/317350806/calling-va-problems-indefensible-shinseki-will-fire-phoenix-leaders; Patricia Kime, "A Decade After Scandal, VA Health Care May Be at Another Crossroads," *Military.com*, April 12, 2024, https://www.military.com/daily-news/2024/04/12/decade-after-scandal-va-health-care-may-be-another-crossroads.html.

On military recruiting and subsequent struggles see Yashaar Hafizka, "Harvard Youth Poll: Decreasing Interest in Community and Military Service," *Harvard Political Review*, April 25, 2018, https://harvardpolitics.com/united-states/harvard-youth-poll-decreasing-interest-in-community-and-military-service/; Lawrence Kapp, *Recruiting and Retention: An Overview of FY2013 and FY2014 Results for Active and Reserve Component Enlisted Personnel*, RL32965 (Washington, DC: Congressional Research Service, June 26, 2015); General David H. Berger, *Commandant's Planning Guidance: 38th Commandant of the Marine Corps* (Quantico, VA: USMC, 2019).

On women in the military after September 11, see the Department of Veterans Affairs, National Center for Veterans Analysis and Statistics, *America's Women Veterans: Military Service History and VA Benefit Utilization Statistics* (Washington, DC: Department of Veterans Affairs, November 2011); Rachel Kimerling, Kristian Gima, Mark W. Smith, et al., "The Veterans Health Administration and Military Sexual Trauma," *American Journal of Public Health*, vol. 97 (December 2007): 2160–66; Alina Suris and Lisa Lind, "Military Sexual Trauma: A Review of Prevalence and Associated Health Consequences in Veterans," *Trauma, Violence & Abuse*, vol. 9 (October 2009): 250–69.

There are many articles on veterans and marketing. See Simon Van Zuylen-Wood, "The Heavily-Armed Millennials of Instagram," *Washington Post*, March 4, 2019, https://www.washingtonpost.com/news/magazine/wp/2019/03/04/feature/the-heavily-armed-millennials-of-instagram/; Michelle Miller and Vidya Singh, "Black Rifle Coffee: Behind the Company Selling Beans with a Message," *CBS News*, February 2, 2018, https://www.cbsnews.com/news/black-rifle-coffee-company-veterans-culture-conservative-approach/.

Robert D. Putnam, *Bowling Alone: The Collapse and Revival of American Community* (New York: Simon & Schuster, 2000) is an excellent primer on period volunteerism. For more specific treatments of twenty-first-century veterans' activism, see "VFW Snaps 27 Year Membership Decline," Veterans of Foreign Wars, July 16, 2019, https://www.vfw.org/media-and-events/latest-releases/archives/2019/7/vfw-snaps-27-year-membership-decline; The Center for Media and Democracy, Operation Truth, n.d., https://www.sourcewatch.org/index.php/Operation_Truth; Laila Al-Arian, "Winter Soldiers Speak," *The Nation*, March 20, 2008, https://www.thenation.com/article/archive/winter-soldiers-speak/. See also Iraq Veterans Against the War, Winter Soldier, http://www.ivaw.org/wintersoldier; Student Veterans of America, About Us, https://studentveterans.org/aboutus; Dave Spiva, "Student Veterans Helping Student Veterans," *VFW Magazine*, vol. 106 (February 2019), https://www.vfw.org/media-and-events/latest-releases/archives/2019/3/student-veterans-helping-student-veterans; Service Women's Action Network, What We Do, https://www.servicewomen.org/#what-we-do; Service Women's Action Network, For Immediate Release: SWAN Statement on lawsuit against Department of Defense, December 19, 2017, https://www.servicewomen.org/press-releases/for-immediate-release-swan-statement-on-lawsuit-against-department-of-defense/; Women Veterans Interactive, COVID-19 Safety Net, https://connectingvets.radio.com/articles/11-women-veteran-organizations-help-you- transition-out-military; SWAN, Weekly COVID 19 Resource Notice, https://www.servicewomen.org/covid-19/.

Both contemporary media and official agencies covered post-September 11th veterans' educational programs in detail. See Cassandria Dortch, *GI Bills Enacted Prior to 2008 and Related Veterans' Educational Assistance Programs: A Primer*, R42785 (Washington, DC: Congressional Research Service, October 6, 2017); Cassandria Dortch, *The Post-9/11 GI Bill: A Primer*, R42755 (Washington, DC: Congressional Research Service, August 1, 2018); Tim Dyhouse, "167,000 GI Claims Filed in 2009," *VFW Magazine*, vol. 97 (April 2010): 13; Natalie Gross, "Senate Stalls on Bill to Help Student Vets, Even as GI Bill Processing Delays Spike," *Military Times*, October 25, 2018, https://rebootcamp.militarytimes.com/news/education/2018/10/25/senate-stalls-on-a-bill-to-help-student-vets-even-as-gi-bill-processing-delays-spike/; Douglas Herrmann, Douglas Raybeck, and Roland Wilson, "College is for Veterans, Too," *Chronicle of Higher Education*, vol. 55 (November 21, 2008): A33; Aaron Glantz, "The Soldier and the Student," *The Nation*, November 27, 2007, https://www.thenation.com/article/archive/soldier-and-student/; Young M. Kim, and James S. Cole, *Student Veterans/Service Members' Engagement in College and University Life and Education* (Washington, DC: American Council on Education, December 2013); Margaret Bellafiore, "From Combat to Campus," *Knowledge and Technology*, vol. 98 (September-October 2012): 33–36.

Conclusions

The quote at the start of the chapter is from Sam R. Watkins, *1861 vs. 1882: "Co. Aytch," Maury Grays, First Tennessee Regiment: or a Side Show of the Big Show* (Nashville: Cumberland Presbyterian Publishing House, 1882), 234–35.

Eleanor L. Hannah, *Manhood, Citizenship, and the National Guard, 1870–1917* (Columbus: Ohio State University Press, 2007) offers important insights on the culture of citizen soldiers.

For a discussion of veterans in civil society see Tom Regan, "Wars of the Future ... Today," *Christian Science Monitor* (June 24, 1999), 1 and William S. Cohen, "The Atlantic Alliance: A View from the Pentagon," *Joint Force Quarterly*, Issue 21 (Spring 1999): 31–35.

The impact of combat on the individual is covered in James Jones, *WWII* (New York: Ballantine Books, 1975); Eugene B. Sledge, *With the Old Breed at Peleliu and Okinawa* (New York: Ballantine, 2007); and Dave Grossman, *On Killing: The Psychological Cost of Learning to Kill in War and Society* (New York: Back Bay Books, 2009).

For statistics on the contemporary veteran's population see US Census Bureau, Veteran Status, Gulf War (9/2001 or later) Veterans. For the percentage of women veterans see Department of Veterans Affairs, National Center for Veterans Analysis and Statistics, *Women Veterans Report: The Past, Present, and Future of Women Veterans* (Washington, DC: Department of Veterans Affairs, February 2017). Information on post–September 11 suicide rates may be found in Rajeev Ramchand, "Suicide Among Veterans," Rand, July 15, 2021, https://www.rand.org/pubs/perspectives/PEA1363-1.html. Colby Buzzell, "The Best Years of Our Lives," *Esquire*, vol. 145 (March 2006): 206–15.

INDEX

Abrams, Creighton 187
Abu Ghraib 221, 223
Addams, John 17
Adjusted Service Certificates 109
Afghanistan 222–23
    casualties 217, 221
    contractors 212
    and Global War on Terror 207–08, 217, 229
    illnesses from service 200, 216
    invasion 209
    policies regarding 210
    reserves in 213
African American veterans 59, 108
    all-volunteer military 181, 183
    American Legion 94–97
    American Revolution 16–19
    Bonus March 113
    Civil War 46, 59–63, 97
    Deacons for Defense and Justice 164, 171–72
    Early Republic 30–31
    G.I. Bill 130
    pensions 39, 62
    Reconstruction 60–61
    Spanish-American War 70, 83
    Vietnam 167
    World War I 89
    World War II 121, 133–36, 171
Agent Orange 195, 199–201, 205
Agnew, Spiro 170
AirLand Battle Doctrine 187, 189
American Expeditionary Force 97–98
American Federation of Labor (AFL) 91
American Legion 5, 101, 154, 156–59, 162, 204, 206, 222, 230
    and African American veterans 96
    anti-communism 158, 94–97
    and Department of Veterans Affairs 226, 229
    conflicts with younger veterans 176, 179
    founding 91–92
    and G.I. Bill 127–29
    lobbying 108, 113, 116–17, 155, 160, 239–46
    nationalism 104, 107
    neutrality debate 118–19
    and the Red Scare 93
    Vietnam 163, 170–71, 192–94, 200
    World War II 141
American Legion Baseball 105, 120, 156
American Legion Weekly 107
American Red Cross 97
American Revolution 9–25, 75, 232
    benefits for veterans of 53
    influence on military service 32, 34–36, 51, 65, 82, 141, 144
    veterans 39, 43
American Veterans Committee 141, 156–58, 163, 171, 193, 209, 227
American Women's Project 203, 209
Americans with Disabilities Act (ADA) 225
amnesty 193
Anderson, Constance 185
Anderson, F. W. 12, 16
Anderson, Robert 42
André, John 23
Arears Pension Act (1879) 62, 78
Armed Forces Qualification Test (AFQT) 167, 209
Armistice Day 5, 104
Army 21, 32, 34, 40, 118, 131, 144–45, 169
    African Americans in 59, 89, 167, 185
    Bonus March 114

budget cuts 30, 183, 187, 211
conscription 32–33
Continental 20
desertions from 17, 67
on the frontier 67
Global War on Terror 207, 211–14
Korean War 147–50
peacetime 30, 37, 41, 47–48, 90, 144–45, 153–54
pensions 36, 53
Revolutionary War 14
recruiting 15, 40, 184, 197, 216–19
Spanish-American War 70–72
World War II 118, 124
Army Division of the Atlantic 67
Army Medical Department 98
Army of Northern Virginia 56, 58
Army-McCarthy Hearings 150
Associated Press 71
Atherton, Warren H. 127
Attucks Guard 60
Aztec Club 2, 77, 239

Baby Boom 6, 144–45, 163, 166, 177, 181, 218, 222
Bellows, Henry W. 51
Berstch, Friedrich 46
Bigelow, Timothy 24
Black Rifle Coffee 218
Blair, Clay 152, 162
"Blue-Gray" reunions 74
Board of Veterans' Appeals 116
Bonus March (1932) 5, 104, 112–15
Boot, Max 68
Bowker, Benjamin C. 137
Bowdoin, James 22
Boxer Rebellion (1900) 69
Bradley, James 123
Bradley, John 123
Bradley, Omar N. 138–40, 160–62, 230
Brands, H.R. 32
Bratton, James Rufus 58
Breeds Hill 14
Brown v. Board (1954) 157
Buckner, Simon Bolivar 74

Bunker Hill Memorial 35–36
Bureau for Returning Soldiers, Sailors, and Marines 100, 102
Bureau of Pensions 53, 82, 100, 112
Bureau of Refugees, Freedmen, and Abandoned Lands 59–60
Bureau of Veterans Affairs 97, 110–12, 120
Bureau of War Risk Insurance 5, 93, 99–100, 110
Burgoyne, John 15, 25
Burnside, Ambrose 51
Bush, George H.W. 189–90, 197
Bush, George W. 207
Butler, Richard 9, 15

Calley, William F. 170
Capra, Frank 123
Caputo, Philip 163, 166, 232
Carter, Jimmy 192–94
Castro, Fidel 165
casualties 188–89
    Battle of Mogadishu 190
    Battle of New Orleans 33
    Civil War 46–47
    First Gulf War 197–98
    Global War on Terror 210, 213–14, 221, 226, 229
    Korean War 148, 152
    PTSD 99, 202
    Spanish-American War 71
    Vietnam War 169, 189
    World War I 97, 109, 111
    World War II 45, 123–25, 130, 137
    women 217
Central Command (CENTCOM) 210
Chicago Defender 172
Childers, Thomas 3, 234–35
Civil War 1–2, 4–5, 28, 45–63, 85, 88, 95, 125, 235, 237–38
    African Americans in 46, 59–63, 97
    commemoration 71–74, 105
    pensions 66, 78, 81–82, 99–100, 102
    reconciliation after 77
    service in 27

INDEX 263

substitutes 11
veterans 65, 75, 83, 144, 162
and trauma 201
Civilian Conservation Corps (CCC) 51, 116, 118, 126
Clarke, Bennett Champ 128
Cleveland, Grover 78, 80
Clinton, Bill 190, 204
Cody, William Frederick "Wild Bill," 72
Coffee, John 34
Cold War 1, 6–7, 119, 151, 166, 197–98
    and Korean War 147
    legacy 189, 205
    mobilization 211, 235
    new military missions in 143, 152, 163, 165, 179, 181
    nuclear weapons 153
    service in 154
    veterans 144, 157–58, 162, 176, 178, 182, 230
Cold War G.I. Bill (1966) 176–80
Colson, William M. 95
Combat Fatigue 202
Committee on Public Information 5, 86
Condon, Richard 151
Confederate Memorial Association 56–57
Confederate Memorial Day 56
Confederate Survivors' Association 55
Confederate Veteran 57
Confederation Congress 4, 17
Congress of Racial Equality 168, 172
Congressional Research Service 219
Conklin, Edwin Grant 107–08
Continental Congress 15, 17–18, 20, 23
Continental Line 15, 17, 19, 231
Creel, George 86
Crumb, Jan 175
Cuba 3, 4, 65, 69–72, 75–76, 83, 85, 165
Custer, George Armstrong 48, 67, 72

D'Olier, Franklin 92–93
Deacons for Defense and Justice 164, 171–72
Decoration Day 71

Defense Department 145, 147–48, 188, 236
    Global War on Terror 211
    and Montgomery G.I. Bill 197
    Project 100,000 167
    programs for veterans 177
    and women 186, 204, 216, 225
Delaney, Martin R. 60
Department of Veterans Affairs 7, 201–04, 209, 217, 224, 226–28
Dependent Pension Act (1890) 79–80
Devanter, Lynda Van 203, 206
Diagnosis and Statistical Manual of Mental Disorders (DSM) 202
Dick Act (1903) 29
Disabled American Veterans (DAV) 128–29, 160–61
discharges 178, 193, 208
Dodge Report (1899) 80, 98
Donovan William T. 91
Doubek, Robert 194
Double V Campaign 133, 157
doughboy 5, 105
Douglass, Frederick 59
Dubois, W.E.B. 95.
Dudley, W.W. 79
Duncan, Donald 169
Duncan, Jeremy 227
Dust Bowl 112
Dyer, Gwynne 239

8th Army 146
8th Illinois U.S. Volunteer Regiment 70
Economy Act (1933) 115–16
Eisenhower, Dwight D. 138, 148, 153, 158, 160–61, 165
Ellis, John 87–88
"Era of Good Feelings," 40
expeditions 3–4, 10

1st U.S. Volunteer Cavalry, See "Rough Riders"
Federal Board for Vocational Education (FBVF) 100, 110
Fetterman Massacre (1866) 66

First Gulf War, See Operation Desert
    Storm
Flynn, George 6
Fonda, Jane 173
Forbes, Charles R. 110-11, 137
Ford, Gerald 192
Ford, Nancy Gentile 108
Foreign Service 115
Forever War 7, 208-10, 212-15
Forrest, Nathan Bedford 58
Fort Sumter 42, 44
French and Indian War 12, 16
Friedan, Betty 152
fuero militar 31
Fuller, J.F.C. 87
Fullerton, Maureen 186
Fussell, Paul 3, 106, 122

Gallup poll 146, 148, 183, 221
Garfield, James 52, 78
Gates Commission 183-84
Gelber, Scott 90
General Pension Act (1862) 52-54, 61, 66,
    77, 239
German Coast Slave Rebellion 31
Gettysburg 74-75, 88, 235
G.I. Assault Bill 134-35
G.I. Bill, See Serviceman's Readjustment
    Act
Gilded Age 4, 51-52, 76-80, 82, 105, 239
Gilmore, Gene 149-50
Glassford, Pelham 114
Global War on Terror (GWOT) 7, 207-09,
    211, 217, 227
Goldsborough, Robert 38
Gordon, George W. 58
Gordon, John B. 58-59
Goulden, Joseph C. 138
Government Accountability Office (GAO)
    203-04, 214
Grand Army of the Republic (GAR) 2, 4,
    56, 62, 66
  and Bonus March 114
  commemoration 71, 81, 104

    formation of 49-51
    legacy 91, 101, 120
    lobbying 77-78, 80, 83, 94, 239
    relationship with American Legion
        92
    segregation 76
    Spanish American War 70, 75
Grant, Ulysses S. 4, 40, 51, 74, 78
Great Depression 104, 112, 117, 131
"Greatest Generation," 3, 122, 141, 144,
    208-09
Gulf War Syndrome 200-201, 205

Hackworth, David 148, 154
Halberstam, David 161-62
Hamilton, Alexander 18, 28
Hannah, Eleanor 11-12, 68, 232
Harding, Warren 103, 108-09, 111, 130
Harris, G.B. 57
Harris poll 6, 169, 184
Harrison, Benjamin 52, 78, 80
Hassler, Warren W. 66
Hawley, Paul 139-40
Hayes, Rutherford B. 52, 78
Hearst, William Randolph 69-70, 156
Hemingway, Ernest 105-06, 117
Hersh, Seymour 169
Hines, Frank T. 128, 135, 138
Holman, William Steele 52-53
Holmes, Oliver Wendell 83
Homestead Act (1862) 54
Hood, John Bell 57
Hoover, Herbert 91, 104, 111-15, 120
Hoover, J. Edgar 152
House Armed Services Committee 197
House Committee on Government
    Reform 214, 216
House Un-American Affairs Committee
    117
House Veterans Committee 128-29, 164,
    202
Howell, Clark 73-74
Hurley, Patrick J. 114
Hussein, Saddam 189

INDEX

Immigrants 5, 20, 28–29, 40, 46, 67–68, 86, 107
Improvised Explosive Device (IED) 210
Inouye, Daniel 176
International Workers of the World (IWW) 93
Iraq 189–90, 197–98, 200–01, 205, 207–10, 212–13, 216–17, 219, 221–23, 229, 233
Iraq Veterans Against the War (IVAW) 223

Jackson, Andrew 31, 33–34, 128
James, William 82–83
Japanese American Citizens League 136
Jefferson, Thomas 28
Johnson, Bud 89
Johnson, Lyndon 172
Johnston, Joseph 74
Joint Chiefs of Staff 140, 183
Joint Veterans Committee 115
Jones, James 237
Junger, Sebastian 220

Keene, Jennifer 89, 112
Kenaday, Alexander M. 77
Kendrick, John F. 75
Kennan, George F. 144
Kennedy, John F. 165
Kent State 171, 179
"Kentucky Rifles," 33
Kerry, John 174–75
Ketchum, Omar B. 128, 161
King, Martin Luther 172
Knox, Henry 21, 24, 35
Korean War 6, 140, 143, 145–50, 152, 154, 158–59, 161–67, 176–77, 185, 194–97, 211, 213, 215, 236, 239
Korean War G.I. Bill 158–62, 176–77
Ku Klux Klan 58, 107

Ladies Memorial Association 56
Lafayette, Marquis de 35
Lansing, Michael J. 101

League for Democracy 96
Leed, Eric 102
Legion of the United States 30, 49
Lend-Lease 119
Lexington and Concord, Battle of 14
Lin, Maya Ying 194
Lincoln, Abraham 52–53, 107, 196
Lincoln, Benjamin 35
Linker, Beth 99, 102
Little Big Horn, Battle of 72
Long, Thomas 46
"Lost Cause," 57, 63

MacArthur, Douglas 113–14, 146
Madison, James 32
Mahan, Alfred Thayer 67
Manchester, William 237
Manhattan Project 124
Marine Corps 48, 68–69, 96, 110, 145, 163, 183, 185, 203–04, 211, 219
Marne, Second Battle of (1918) 88
Marshall, George C. 150
Marshall, John 35
Martí, José 69
Masaoka, Mike 136
Massachusetts Bay Colony 10
Massive Retaliation 153, 165
Mauldin, Bill 147, 156, 158
May, Andrew Jackson 128
Mazey, Emil 132
McCarran-Walter Immigration Act (1952) 136
McCarthy, Eugene 172
McCarthy, Joseph 148, 150–51, 158
McConnell, Stuart 50
McDougall, Alexander 20
McGovern, George 173, 176
McKinley, William 52, 70, 73–74, 78
McKissick, Floyd 168
McNamara, Robert S. 167
Meade, George 42
Meadlo, Myrtle 169
Mellon, Andrew 109
Mexican War 65–84

milicias de color 30–31
Military Operations Other Than War (MOOTW) 212
Military Order of the Loyal Legion of the United States 49
Military Order of the Purple Heart 128
Military Sexual Trauma (MST) 7, 204, 217, 225, 227, 240
Military Training Camp Association 118
militia 4, 28–30, 33, 35, 65–68, 211, 235
   African Americans 16–17
   American Revolution 10–15
   Antebellum 40–41
   Battle of New Orleans 34
   Civil War 47
   commemorating 23, 25, 36
   Early Republic 22
   Mexican War 42
   pensions 19–20, 23, 38, 43, 57
   Reconstruction 60–61
   War of 1812, 32–33
Militia Test Oath 41
Millis, Walter 9–10
Monroe, James 37–38, 40, 43–44, 47
Montgomery G.I. Bill (1984) 197, 223
Moore, Charles 105
Morgan, Daniel 36
Morris, Gouveneur 34
Morton, Oliver P. 51
Moskos, Charles 167
Murray, Robert 89
My Lai Massacre (1968) 169–70

Nat Turner Revolt (1831) 41
National Association for the Advancement of Colored People (NAACP) 96, 133–36, 156–57, 162, 171
National Association of Veterans of the Mexican War 77
National Commission of Fine Arts 105
National Guard 7, 65, 67–68, 81, 166, 182, 187, 191–92, 205
   Desert Storm 201

Global War on Terror 208, 211–16, 219, 223
Korean War 147–49
and Reconstruction 61
Spanish American War 70
World War I 93
World War II 118
National Home for Disabled Volunteer Soldiers 112
National Peace Jubilee 73
National POW/MIA Recognition Day 194
National Youth Administration 126
Naval Home 42
Navy 32, 40–42, 47, 96, 144, 163, 174–75, 178, 184–85, 187–88, 211, 234
New Look 152–54
New Orleans, Battle of 33–34, 38
New York Times 91, 113, 114, 131, 138, 149, 173, 174, 193, 195, 196
Nisbet, Charles 29
Nisei 130
Nisei Veterans Club 136
Nisei Veterans Committee 136
Nixon, Richard 169–72, 174–75, 178, 181, 183–89, 192, 216
Northern Alliance 209
Nye-Lea Act (1935) 108

Office of Price Administration 131
Office of War Information 123
Operation Bright Star 187
Operation Continue Hope (1993) 190
Operation Desert Shield (1990) 189, 191, 201, 211
Operation Desert Storm (1991) 182, 189–91, 197–98, 200–01, 204–05, 209, 211–12, 221
Operation Dewey Canyon III (1971) 174–75
Operation El Dorado Canyon (1986) 186
Operation Iraqi Freedom 209, 229
Operation Joint Endeavor (1993) 191
Operation Just Cause (1989) 189
Operation Northern Wedding 187

Operation Outreach 177
Operation Provide Comfort (1992) 190
Operation Ranch Hand 199
Operation Rapid American Withdrawal (Operation RAW) 172–73
Operation Restore Hope (1992–1993) 190
Operation Roll Up (1950) 146
Operation Rolling Thunder (1965–1967) 165, 168
Operation Urgent Fury (1983) 188–89
opioids 227
Osbourn, John 146
Owen, Wilfred 117
Owsley, Alvin M. 107, 119

Packenham, Edward 33
Paine, Thomas 17
Panetta, Leon 221
Panic of 1873, 67
Patterson, Robert 132
peace enforcement 182, 190–91, 205, 208, 212, 221
peacekeeping 182, 188, 190–91, 205, 212
Pearl Harbor 110, 117
Pentagon 210
    Global War on Terror 211, 233
    Gulf War Syndrome 201
    Korean War 147
    mobilization 153, 181, 208, 211, 219
    Project 100,000 167
    PTSD 202
    recruiting policy 182–83, 186
    returning POW 151
    and veterans 178
Perot, H. Ross 194
Petraeus, David H. 210
Pettus, Edmund 58
Philadelphia Committee of Privates 13
Philippines 65, 72, 75–76
Philippine Insurrection (1899–1901) 69
Pierce, Franklin 42
"Plattsburgh Idea," 118
Plessy v. Ferguson (1896) 76
Post-9/11 G.I. Bill (2008) 223–24

Post-Traumatic Stress Disorder (PTSD) 99, 199, 201–02, 205, 217, 223, 225, 227, 229
President's Commission on an All-Volunteer Armed Force, See Gates Commission
prisoners of war 150–51, 194, 221
Private Military Company (PMC) 212
Private Soldiers and Sailors' Legion 91
Project 100,000 167
Project Transition 177
Promise to Address Comprehensive Toxins (PACT) Act 228
Putnam, Robert D. 222
Pyle, Ernie 138, 147

Quantrill, William 55

race riots 41, 89
Randolph, A. Philip 95
Rankin, John 128–29
Reagan, Ronald 7, 182, 189, 195–97, 218
Reconstruction Act (1867) 60
recruitment 153, 185
Red Scare 89, 150
Remarque, Erich Maria 106, 117, 237
Retreads 147
Return of Forces to Germany (REFORGER) 187
Robinson, Jackie 172
Rockwell, Norman 1
Rogers, Edith Nourse 128
Roosevelt, Franklin Delano 91, 104, 115–17, 119–20, 126, 129, 133
Roosevelt, Theodore 3, 65, 67, 71, 73, 75, 82, 85, 102, 235
Roosevelt, Theodore, Jr. 91–92
Roper poll 134, 159, 183
Rules of Engagement (ROE) 166, 188, 191, 209
Rumsfeld, Donald 211

7th Kansas Cavalry 72
71st New York Volunteer Infantry 72

Sampson, William T. 72
Sassoon, Siegfried 117
Saxton, Thomas 20
Scott, Robert K. 60
Scott, Winfield 43
Scruggs, Jan 194
Selective Service 118, 145, 166, 175, 183, 185, 193, 221, 235
Selective Service College Qualification Test (SSCQT) 167
September 11th 96, 207, 232, 240
   civil-military relations 218–22
   military missions 186–92
   nature of 209–12
   new veterans' organizations 222–25
   PTSD 99
   public policy 226–30, 239
   reservists 212–16
   women serving in 216–17
Service Women's Action Network (SWAN) 225–26
Serviceman's Link to the Peace Movement (LINK) 172
Serviceman's Readjustment Act (1944) 6, 125–30, 141, 158, 239
Shays, Daniel 22, 43
Shays Rebellion 22
Sheehan, Neil 174
Shell Shock 89, 98–99, 111, 199, 202
Sheridan, Phil 74
Sherman, William Tecumseh 55, 67, 74
Shiloh, Battle of 52, 74–75, 235
Singletary, Otis A. 60
Shinseki, Eric 228
Skeen, Edward 14
Sledge, Eugene 237
Sloan, William M. 81–82
Social Darwinism 61, 66, 77, 81, 108
Society of the Army of Northern Virginia 56
Society of Cincinnati 21, 37, 239
Soldiers' Home 42–43
Sons of Confederate Veterans 2, 56
Spanish American War 69–71, 75, 80–81, 235

Spanish Flu 90, 101
Stephens, Benjamin 51
Stephenson, Michael 236
Stevens, Henry L. 113
Stevens, Raymond T. 150
Stevenson, Adlai 160
Stimson, Henry 91
strikes,
   Great Railroad Strike (1877) 68
   Pullman Strike (1890) 68
   and American Legion strikebreaking 93
   after World War I 89, 125
   after World War II 131
Student Veterans of America (SVA) 7, 225

370th Illinois Infantry Regiment 89, 95
Tanner, James 79
Tanner, John M. 70
Task Force Eagle 191
Taylor, Maxwell 153
Teague, Olin 164, 176–77, 202
Tet Offensive (1968) 169, 189
Thames, Battle of (1813) 32
Thomas-Black Company 111
Thompson, Hunter S. 175
Timberg, Robert 6, 163, 180
Tomb of the Unknown Soldier 94
Total Force 187, 192, 211
Trainbands, See Militia.
Training and Doctrine Command (TRADOC) 187
Traumatic Brain Injury (TBI) 210, 225–26
Truman, Harry 134, 138, 145, 148, 154

Uniform Militia Act (1792) 29
Uniformed Services Employment and Reemployment Rights Act (USERRA) 215
United Auto Workers (UAW) 132
United Confederate Veterans 56, 58
United Daughters of the Confederacy 56
United Nations Relief and Rehabilitation Administration (UNRRA) 128

INDEX

United Spanish War Veterans 4, 76
United States Colored Troops 59
United States Soldiers and Sailors
    Protective Society 49
Universal Military Training 118, 137, 145
Upton, Emory 67
U.S. Public Health Service 97, 99, 111
U.S. Sanitary Commission 51, 62
U.S.S. *Maine* 70

Veterans of Foreign Wars (VFW) 4, 84, 93,
    101, 115, 141, 163, 222, 235
  commemoration 94, 104
  community service 155, 162
  conflicts with younger veterans 156,
    158, 163
  expansion 91, 222
  founding 76
  and G.I. Bill 128, 179
  lobbying 107, 116, 120, 127–28, 161,
    230
  neutrality 117–19
  segregation 157
  Vietnam 160, 170–71, 173, 179
Veterans Administration 13, 128, 130
  African Americans 135
  Agent Orange 200
  budget cuts 239
  creation 111–12
  reform 137–41, 161, 177
  scandals 127, 156
Veterans Bureau 97, 110–12, 120
Veterans Employment and Training
    Service 159, 215
Veterans Readjustment Assistance Act
    (1952), See Korea G.I. Bill
Veterans Readjustment Benefits Act
    (1966), See Cold War G.I. Bill
Viet Cong (VC) 166, 174, 199
Vietnam Veterans Against the War
    (VVAW) 164, 172–75, 179, 209,
    222
Vietnam Veterans Memorial 195–97
Vietnam Veterans Memorial Fund 194

Vietnam War 163, 165, 189, 222, 224
  activism 168–75, 207
  combat 166
  illnesses 199–202, 228
  legacy 181, 183–87, 196, 198, 205, 208,
    211, 221
  service 3, 148
  mobilization 235–36
  veterans 164, 169–70, 192–97, 232
  veterans' policy 176–80
  women's service 203

Waller, Willard 2, 234
Walter Reed Army Hospital 98, 214
War of 1812 31–34, 36, 42–43, 77, 81, 84
War Department 24, 39, 42–43, 61–62, 90,
    100, 123–24, 127, 130–32, 155–56
War Risk Insurance Act (1918) 5, 93,
    99–100, 110
War Risk Insurance Bureau 100
Washington, George 2, 16–17, 21, 32,
    35–36
Waul, Thomas Neville 57
Wayne, Anthony 13, 30, 35
Wayne, John 232
Wells, H.G. 106
West Point 23, 74, 138
Westmoreland, William 183–84, 195
Wheeler, Dorothy 139
Wheeler, John 194
Whitman, Walt 48, 66
Williams, Jim 61
Wilson, Woodrow 86
Winter Soldier Investigation 174
Woman's Armed Forces Integration Act
    (1948) 185
Women's Army Corps 134
Woodard, Isaac 134
Works Progress Administration 126
World War Adjusted Compensation Act
    (1924) 109, 113
World War I 103, 110, 117–18, 122, 125,
    187, 107–09
  African Americans in 94–97, 134–35

Bonus March 114
commemoration 71, 75
memoirs 106
nature 90
veterans 119–20
veterans' lobby 91–94
veterans' policies 81, 97–102, 104
World War II 1–6, 27, 45, 121, 143, 162, 170, 181, 192, 218, 220, 226–27, 232, 234, 238–39
   African Americans 97
   combat 123–25
   creation of G.I. Bill 125–30
   demobilization after 130–37
   impact on Cold War 144, 147–48, 153
   and Korean War 149, 152
   neutrality debate 117–20
   service in 122–23
   women's service 186
   wounded 139–40, 202
   veterans 141, 154–59, 164, 171, 173, 176–77, 179, 196, 230
Wounded Knee, Battle of (1890) 66, 72
Wyler, William 123

Yarborough, Ralph W. 176–77
York, Alvin 91
Yorktown, Battle of 19

Zwicker, Ralph 150

ABOUT THE AUTHOR

Dr. Michael D. Gambone is the author of eight books, including *The New Praetorians: Modern American Veterans, Society, and Service in the Forever War* (2021), *Long Journeys Home: American Veterans of World War II, Korea, and Vietnam* (2017), and *The Greatest Generation Comes Home: The Veteran in American Society* (2005). He is currently a professor of history at Kutztown University of Pennsylvania and a veteran of the 82nd Airborne Division. In 2006, he deployed to Iraq as a Department of the Army contractor and served in the city of Mosul.